Primary Curriculum

Teaching the Foundation Subjects

Also available from Continuum

Primary Curriculum – Teaching the Core Subjects, Rosemary Boys and Elaine Spink
Observing Children and Young People, Carol Sharman, Wendy Cross and Diane Vennis
Psychology and the Teacher, Dennis Child
Reflective Teaching 3rd Edition, Andrew Pollard
Teaching 3–8 3rd Edition, Mark O'Hara

Primary Curriculum

Teaching the Foundation Subjects

Edited by
Rosemary Boys and Elaine Spink

continuum

Continuum International Publishing Group

The Tower Building   80 Maiden Lane
11 York Road   Suite 704
London   New York
SE1 7NX   NY 10038

www.continuumbooks.com

British Library Cataloguing-in-Publication Data
A catalogue record for this book is available from the British Library.

ISBN: 9780826488408 (paperback)

Typeset by Free Range Book Design & Production Limited
Printed and bound in Great Britain by Cromwell Press Ltd.

Contents

Notes on Contributors

Paul Bowen is a senior lecturer in education at Manchester Metropolitan University. He teaches on undergraduate and postgraduate education programmes and is coordinator of foundation subjects for the PGCE course. He has experience of teaching in the primary and secondary sectors. Paul has particular interest and expertise in the history of education, an area in which he has published. He is a recognized authority in traveller education from an historical perspective.

Kate Buchanan is Director of Professional Studies at the Royal Northern College of Music, Manchester, where she manages a wide-ranging programme of vocational and specialist training including educational and community work. Kate trained in music and musical performance at the Guildhall School of Music and Drama and Goldsmiths College, University of London. She taught for ten years (music services, adult education, local education authority) before becoming senior lecturer at Trinity College of Music (1995–2005). Since 1997, she has acted as music education consultant on a range of projects and training initiatives for Channel 4 Learning, the London Philharmonic Orchestra and the National Foundation for Youth Music. She maintains links with classroom practice through project work and mentoring in schools.

David Coulbeck has worked in primary education since 1971, as a teacher and advisory teacher for the county, and then as a head teacher since 1981. He has substantial experience in curriculum leadership and innovation and is an active member of the art education community.

Alison Heap is a lecturer in primary physical education. She was previously a primary school teacher and local authority advisory teacher. Alison works with undergraduate and postgraduate student teachers and is actively involved in community sports and sports promotion initiatives. Her research interest is in motor development in early years education.

Dr Elaine McCreery is a senior lecturer in the Institute of Education at Manchester Metropolitan University. She teaches religious education and professional teaching studies on undergraduate and postgraduate teacher training courses and works with students on their school placements. She has taught in primary and secondary schools, specializing in religious education. Her PhD studies explored the role of the teacher in children's spiritual development and her current research interests include teacher biography and its impact on professional practice and the place of faith schools in a state education system.

Dr Gee Macrory is a former teacher of languages (French, German and Spanish) in primary, secondary and further education. After teaching modern languages, she spent two years as an advisory teacher for teaching English as an additional language for Manchester Local Authority prior to taking up a post at Manchester Metropolitan University, where she has been involved in teacher education for 17 years. She is currently responsible for teacher education in both English and modern languages in the Institute of Education. Her research interests include early bilingualism, language learning and teacher education in primary and secondary modern languages education, the global dimension in language teaching and the impact of school links abroad.

Ivy Roberts is a senior lecturer in art education at the Institute of Education, Manchester Metropolitan University. Previously, she was a primary school head teacher. Her particular interest is in creativity in relation to art education, an area in which she has also published.

Su Sayers is a senior lecturer in design and technology education at Manchester Metropolitan University. She specializes in food and textiles. Su was previously Coordinator for design and technology education at Middlesex University. She has extensive experience of teaching in schools, in secondary, primary and early childhood sectors and has been involved in national examining. Su was chief advanced level examiner in fashion and textiles for ten years. She has published in design and technology education and worked for many years in community art and design projects.

Introduction

'The curriculum is so much necessary raw material, but warmth is the vital element for the growing plant and for the soul of the child.' Carl Jung (Jung and Sabini, 2002)

This book is about the teaching of art and design, design and technology, history, modern foreign languages, music, physical education and religious education in primary schools. More specifically, it deals in *how* to teach those subjects, drawing on conceptions of pedagogy which are firmly grounded in research and practice. It is not about subject content per se, nor about the delivery of one particular curriculum.

The content of education within a national or state system always extends beyond the boundaries of a prescribed curriculum and is not confined exclusively to subject demarcations. Our understanding of the word 'curriculum' needs to be broader than that suggested by the term 'national curriculum'. Nevertheless, the education system, certainly in England and arguably in many other parts of the world, has become more focused on formal curricula, with an emphasis on what teachers must teach and what children must be taught. The curriculum is 'content heavy' and this content is organized into separate subject 'boxes', for pragmatic as well as for educationally justified reasons. Thus, this book also offers sections immediately recognizable as the foundation subjects of the English National Curriculum (DfEE, 1999), plus modern foreign languages and religious education. In this way, it will best be able to support its intended audience in developing teaching of a diverse range of subject areas.

There have undoubtedly been advantages to having a National Curriculum in England: learning objectives have focused teachers' attention on what they want children to *learn*, rather than simply 'do'; assessment has been placed at the centre of teaching and learning; the National Curriculum legislates for equality of access. But times are changing – when do they ever not? – and as we move further into the twenty-first century, new conceptions of what effective education looks like are forming. These are unlikely to be so content-driven. In the last decade, the rapid obsolescence of taught knowledge has become ever more apparent. It has been suggested that for five-year-old children today, over 60 per cent of the jobs they will do as adults have yet to be invented (Barrett, 2006). How do we educate for such rapid change? Certainly not by transmitting facts and taking a 'jugs and mugs' approach to teaching, where the teacher fills the pupils with knowledge. There will of necessity be increased focus on skills development, on understanding how to access information and on lifelong learning. We are also seeing a movement away from the subject boxes to more integrated approaches. But the need for teachers to understand the principles of good practice in the individual subject components will remain. For example, as part of an integrated project on 'communication' the children are making a musical instrument. It is design and technology for the elements of design, production and evaluation; it is music in producing and controlling sounds, in composing and in listening and performing. It is also science and history and potentially RE…! As the teacher, I will draw on my awareness of the development of skills in music, my understanding of how and why design and technology came to be recognized as an essential part of primary education, my knowledge of effective practice in both subjects. My practice will be informed and enriched by my depth and breadth of knowledge of the component parts of my teaching, not just in relation to subject content knowledge but in its established pedagogy.

Not only has there been an emphasis on knowledge content but also on certain subject areas at the expense of others. We know from the insistent voices of teachers, student teachers, parents and children (and from a growing body of research evidence) that teaching time and effort in England has been too narrowly focused on English and mathematics, limiting attention to the rest of the areas of learning. And yet the Foundation subjects plus modern foreign languages and religious education have the potential to be the most powerful, most meaningful and most relevant areas of learning for all learners (and their teachers). Reviews of the curricula in Scotland, Wales and Northern Ireland reflect a commitment to re-focus on over-arching themes and perspectives.

Teaching the formal curriculum 'effectively' (and this notion will be explored in the chapters) is but a part of the broader education we seek to provide in schools. For this reason, each subject considers, in a second chapter, elements which lie beyond the formal curriculum, identifying and analysing the contribution of the subject to wider development and the contribution of wider experiences to engagement with subject content and issues.

The book will inevitably emphasize the English curriculum, since England is where its contributors are based and where they have garnered their expertise, but it draws on practice elsewhere in the UK and on international perspectives and examples.

At the heart of government drives to raise standards of attainment in primary education lies a curriculum much greater than one nationally imposed. This diverse curriculum entitles all children to the knowledge, understanding, skills, values and principles of their communities, societies, countries and world.

Intended audience

This book is primarily intended for newly qualified teachers and for trainee teachers following undergraduate and postgraduate routes into the profession. However, by virtue of the fact that its purpose is for the reader to understand the principles underlying recommendations of practice, as well as to know what those teaching principles are and how to apply them, it will support all those who wish to improve their teaching of art and design, design and technology, history, modern foreign languages, music, physical education and religious education in primary schools.

Structure

Each subject area is addressed in two chapters. The first chapter for each subject, 'Teaching the Curriculum', asks you to consider the role of that subject in the primary curriculum, principles of good practice related to a theoretical framework (or frameworks), essential knowledge for effective teaching and the components for teaching a lesson or session – planning, teaching strategies and assessing and monitoring progress. The second chapter for each subject, 'Beyond the Curriculum', asks you to consider the richness of teaching and learning beyond that which is specified in a national or prescribed curriculum. This chapter encourages reflection on enriching teaching of the subject in a variety of ways, such as cross-curricular projects, out-of-school learning and partnerships with external agencies.

The chapters will address **you**, rather than 'the reader', and will seek to engage you in the issues and debates.

'**Pauses to think**' will encourage you to reflect on practice in relation to your own views and experiences. It is important not to underestimate the importance or power of reflection. As we move towards teaching becoming a profession in which practitioners continue to develop and to upgrade their qualifications to the point where most teachers will have a Masters degree, independent and self-directed analysis will become ever more significant. Those to excel will be teachers who successfully blend theory and practice, informed and constantly modified by reflection, asking, for example, why am I doing this? What is the most appropriate theoretical framework? How does this relate to my professional context? What do I need to do to improve the outcomes for the pupils?

Case studies and other examples from learning environments will enable you to contextualize the information, visualize applications and will challenge you to evaluate your own practice.

Different voices are represented – teachers', students', children's – to offer a broad perspective and to enable you to view situations from different angles.

Each chapter stands alone so that you may choose to focus on a specific subject but reading across the chapters reveals the inter-relatedness of methodologies. Non-sequential reading is possible – and encouraged. No hierarchy of subjects is implied in the order of presentation.

Contributors

The contributors are all subject specialists with extensive experience of primary teaching and/or teacher education.

A shared philosophy is the foundation for the book. Building on that, each subject section will reflect the particular nature of that subject and the individuality of the author.

To conclude, we recognize that you will already be a reflective practitioner, with a well-formed understanding of the basics of all of the subjects contained herein. We hope, through your engagement with this text, to enable you to articulate your understanding, for each one of the primary curriculum subjects considered here, of what to teach, how to teach, why to teach it and what the outcomes are for the children. This book seeks to support you in your further development. We wish you well in your future professional life.

Rosemary Boys & Elaine Spink

References

Barrett, N. (2006), 'Creative Partnerships: Manchester and Salford', www.ioe.mmu.ac.uk/cue/seminars/BARRETT%20Urban%20seminar1.doc (accessed 21 July 2007).

DfEE (1999), 'English National Curriculum'. London: DfEE.

Jung, C. G. and Sabini, M. (2002), *The Earth Has a Soul*: *the nature writings of C.G. Jung.* Berkeley, California: North Atlantic Books.

Art and Design: Teaching the Curriculum

Ivy Roberts

Chapter Outline

'Art and Design provide children with an expression of self. Children can observe their environment and the visual impact it has on them. It provides children with a vehicle to respond to their world in a safe way. Most of all it's a relaxing and creative activity for children to enjoy.' Year 2 trainee teacher

Introduction

The above response to the question 'Why is teaching art and design important in primary schools?' is fairly typical of trainee and beginning teachers. Most will mention creativity; the development of interesting and useful skills; a way of making sense of the world; expressing feelings and providing a way for children to communicate. In this, they are acknowledging a human need to have access to a visual means of responding to stimuli. Blenkin and Kelly (1996) would argue that the subject is significant in terms of the way in which it interacts with the learner's development and promotes their intellectual and emotional development.

Art and design is an important and integral part of the rich curriculum children need to become effective adults.

The place of art and design in the curriculum

According to the Plowden Report (Department of Education and Science, 1967), 'Art is both a form of communication and a means of expression of feelings which ought to permeate the whole curriculum and the whole life of the school. A society which neglects or despises it is dangerously sick' (paragraph 676). These are strong words from the body commissioned by the government of the day to examine the quality of education in England and Wales. The Plowden Report can perhaps be seen as a watershed in the course of all primary school education.

The Forster Act of 1870 provided free education for children between the ages of five and 12. The curriculum consisted of an emphasis on three core subjects – reading, writing and arithmetic – with additional facts-based instruction in other subjects. This was considered appropriate to keep the masses just educated enough to become useful, law-abiding citizens suited to the growing industrial needs of the country. Creative art work in any form had little status.

Initially, art consisted of careful copying of twigs, flowers and geometric shapes; copying from pictures, or copying from the blackboard, usually with a hard pencil on thin paper and an emphasis on accuracy. Colour was rarely used.

Any design or craftwork consisted of woodwork for the boys and needlework for the girls. In both of these, pupils worked on teacher-designated projects, and emphasis was placed on accuracy and neatness.

A more child-centred approach began to emerge in the 1920s under the influence of Marion Richardson. She and other like-minded, influential educationists encouraged teachers to give guidance and act as facilitators rather than imposing instruction. At this time it became more common for schools to place emphasis on a simple, descriptive kind of imaginative work and free use of media.

Herbert Read (1959) endorsed Richardson's philosophy and advocated a pedagogy which focused on the importance of child art and sought to place art at the centre of the primary curriculum as a vehicle through which all other subjects should be taught. Read has devoted followers to this day for his commitment to art education, but his ideas about the structure of the curriculum were largely disregarded.

Lowenfeld's work in the 1940s categorized children's stages of development in art and identified a sequence of stages through which children evolve as they mature and develop creatively. His findings were first published in 1946 and have been reprinted regularly since. For many years they provided a useful framework to enable teachers to structure pupils' experience so that a process of learning in art can evolve, based on children's needs and abilities at a given time, rather than placing undue emphasis on delivering an accurate product.

It is clear that the Plowden Report was in favour of a child-centred approach to art education, and praised schools performing accordingly. In the wake of Plowden, a great deal of excellent work was done in the name of child art and progressive education. It must also be said that the opposite was also often the case. Some commentators now look back and cite Plowden as the beginning of a decline in standards and the 'progressive movement' as a charter for teachers to do nothing.

During the post-Plowden years of the 1970s and 1980s, schools in England and Wales enjoyed a great deal of freedom to devise their own schemes of work and determine the way in which the curriculum was to be conducted. This worked well in schools that valued the contribution art made to children's education and development with good leadership and teams of teachers committed to agreed aims and standards. Where there was balance and depth of study in all subjects across a broad curriculum, art flourished. Equally, in schools where this was not the case there was rightly a cause for concern.

By the end of the 1980s there was a growing demand for a mandatory national curriculum which would provide basic requirements and standards in all subjects, including art and design.

In 1989 the first draft orders of what was to become the National Curriculum were published. This curriculum was significant as it made art and design a mandatory subject for all primary schools, and gave all primary school children an entitlement to participate in art and design as a legitimate subject, rather than as a recreational activity.

The more formalized pedagogy supporting this document was not, however, received positively by those who supported a developmental and child-centred approach to education. Even in the art and design curriculum, prescriptive programmes of study were set and attainment targets against which children were to be measured were introduced.

In the revised National Curriculum (1999) the implementation of the art and design curriculum was less rigorous and content-based, and attainment targets were removed for all but the core subjects. The tentative moves towards the recognition of enjoyment and creativity have been confirmed with the publication of documents such as *Excellence and Enjoyment* (DfES, 2003).

> **Pause to think**
>
> As we move to a curriculum that espouses more inclusive practices and personalized learning it could be argued that the children's voice is still not always heard when we teach art and design. The work of Matthews (1999) was concerned with identifying children's priorities and issues when they engaged in painting, drawing, constructing and other creative work.
>
> If we implement contemporary practices into our teaching of art and design, how will we recognize and address children's priorities and issues?

Process versus product?

It is clear from the brief synopsis above that the emphasis has swung between product and process since 1870. Pupils were initially expected to follow instructions and copy accurately, the result being an acceptable **product**.

Then came the long period of allowing children to evolve and develop 'naturally' as artists. This could be interpreted as demanding little more of the teacher than to be a provider of resources and uncritical encouragement. However, if art is to be acknowledged as a subject that involves intellectual activity and critical thought, teachers have to know when and how to intervene in the learning **process**, and perhaps also to recognize when to allow children the time and space to reflect on their own work, and the work of others.

Planning

Long-term planning should be used to identify the content and skills to be taught across all year groups, and ensure continuity and progression. It is the subject-leader's role to coordinate planning and ensure that this scheme of work is inclusive of the ideas and input of all practitioners responsible for teaching art and design. This is necessary to ensure that all teachers feel comfortable with the curriculum content and secure in their understanding of what is involved. Clement, Piotrowski and Roberts (1998) focus on the role of the subject-leader in art and offer guidance about curriculum content and planning at this level.

Medium-term planning will focus on an aspect of the art and design curriculum identified in the scheme of work used by the school. Such units of work are usually planned to last for half a term and will include detail about the sensibilities, skills and visual elements on which the unit will be based. The Qualifications and Curriculum Authority (QCA) units of planning offer an example of what such medium-term planning might look like. These can be amended to address the specific needs of individual schools (www.standards.dfes.gov.uk/schemes2/art).

Short-term plans provide the documentation for specific lessons which are carefully sequenced to take steps towards achieving the medium-term objectives. It is important that planning at this level is detailed enough to be of genuine use in the teaching situation but not over-burdened with superfluous detail that has no relevance. As teachers gain experience, school policy usually permits a streamlined approach to planning where several sessions of activities can be included in one lesson plan. Lesson plans are working documents and need to be flexible in order to suit the ongoing needs of all pupils.

In some lessons risk assessments may be necessary. These are often seen as an irritating aspect of the subject, but their role is not only to ensure the safety of the children in your care, but also to protect you from litigation should an accident occur.

Teaching strategies

Understanding of the ways in which children learn and develop in art is important if the teacher is to plan effectively and to adopt appropriate and effective teaching strategies.

Even the youngest of children's mark-making soon comes to have meaning for the child as they begin to make sense of their surroundings. As part of a natural creative progression, children will proceed to use increasingly complex symbols to convey meaning as their mark-making evolves into more sophisticated representations as they progress through the primary school.

We are all familiar with the circles, squares and triangles which make up a young child's depiction of a house. These shapes and symbols are used to convey many different meanings. The triangular roof becomes the triangle of a woman's skirt; the circular sun shining down on the roof will mean someone's face in a different drawing or painting, and the adult can now understand the images without the child needing to explain. This ability to communicate through art is generally achieved with enjoyment and purpose. Children, even very young children, can recognize the power of drawing to represent, and that they themselves can be in control of this (Cox, 2005). It is therefore very rare for children to be reluctant to engage in art.

It is important that as teachers we are seen to value art and design, and that we understand how to encourage, facilitate and support children's skills in art so that they can make effective use of this form of communication.

Using discussion and encouragement

For children of all ages in the primary school, discussion and encouragement are the most essential teaching strategies at a teacher's disposal in the development of children's learning in art. If children are aware that their work is valued, they are willing to engage in discussion and to respond to questions that encourage their thinking and their efforts. The use of questions such as those used in the case study below allow children to maintain ownership of their work and to make their own decisions about how their work will develop.

Case study

In her self-portrait (Figure 1.1), four-year-old Ellen has made effective use of circular and triangular shapes. She has distributed the features with some accuracy across the face and has made effective choices of colour to match her hair and eyes.

Figure 1.1 Ellen's self-portrait

The lines are drawn boldly and with confidence. This child will be encouraged to talk about how she made her drawing, what she likes about it and what she might change.

Discussion between teacher and child will focus on drawing attention to details such as eyelashes and eyebrows as the child examines her own face in a mirror.

Three key terms

The National Curriculum Orders; The Foundation Stage Document; QCA Guidance; and individual school and commercial schemes of work all offer support to teachers in planning the art and design curriculum. The support chosen will be of more use in meeting the needs of the individual child if three key terms are fully understood. These terms are 'sensibilities', 'skills' and 'visual elements' and they are central to the development of structured, coherent planning. They are addressed in more detail below.

Sensibilities

The sensibilities of memory, imagination and observation are what we all bring to the art-making process. Children, like Ellen in Figure 1.1, who are in the early developmental stages of using mark-making and simple symbols, will be using mainly the sensibilities of memory and imagination to inform their drawings and depictions of the world around them. It is important to encourage young children to look closely, to observe and talk about what they see, but it is natural for them to rely less on observation than on memory and imagination. Watch a young child at work, and you will find that their drawings will reflect what they remember after a quick glance at the object, rather than the sustained, continual looking and observing which a child at a later stage can be encouraged to engage in. This is a natural part of the development process, and one that we need to be aware of so that we can plan appropriate experiences and stimuli. It is not something we should feel the need to 'correct'. In fact, it is important to guard against too early an emphasis on observation at the expense of the other two sensibilities. We will always need memory and imagination and at every stage need to ensure that children are offered experiences which will demand that they use all three sensibilities. For a useful summary of how children progress in making images see Clement *et al.* (1998: 59).

Skills

Drawing is a central skill which pupils need every opportunity to experience. From these earliest moments we can see, through children's drawings, how much they are noticing. We can identify the point at which scribble begins to make meaning. We can see the shapes and symbols as they begin to appear to 'stand for' objects and ideas. We can plan activities and experiences which will enable pupils to make increasingly sophisticated use of these symbols to express the stories of their imagination and their thoughts and feelings from memory. Constant discussion about these drawings will encourage children's powers of observation as they seek to create more and more detailed images, and will support the development of their speaking and listening skills.

Rhoda Kellog's (1972) seminal work on analysing children's art makes fascinating reading for teachers and trainees interested in the detail of the stages through which children progress in making art.

Although the stages through which children develop are age-related, they are not age-determined. In seeking to meet the needs of pupils in art, whatever their overall ability, the teacher's awareness of the level at which children are drawing will elicit information about the experiences they need. Some children will observe and draw analytically at a very early age, while others may still be using symbols towards the end of their time in primary education. This may be appropriate for that individual. However, a child whose pre-school experience was lacking in opportunities to practise drawing and who then attends a school similarly lacking in opportunities, may underachieve. Drawing, like all skills, needs constant practice if it is to develop.

Drawing clearly involves a range of media and is not confined to pencil and paper.

The other skills which need to be taught and which will arise from children's drawings are painting, printmaking, collage, textiles, digital media and work in 3D. Trainees and teachers need experience in all of these skills and need to acquire control of the necessary tools and materials and media involved if they are to teach children to use them.

Visual Elements

The visual elements – line, tone, shape, colour, pattern, texture, form and space – provide us with a vocabulary with which to talk and think about art. Pupils need to be introduced to and understand this basic vocabulary. It helps them to think and talk about the work of other artists. It helps to give structure to their thinking when they are evaluating and discussing their own work, enabling them to say what they might improve, change and develop.

For example, a child might be encouraged to stop and compare her painting with the object she is painting, such as a piece of seaweed. Questions which would encourage self-evaluation might include:

- Are the lines that you have painted thicker or thinner than the strands you can see?
- Is the colour you are using the same as the seaweed's colour? Is it lighter or darker?
- Can you see more than one tone of that colour?
- Which part of your painting looks most like the seaweed?
- Can you see different textures in your painting that show where the seaweed is knobbly and where it is smooth?
- Which part of the painting do you like best and why?
- Are there any parts that you would like to change and do differently?

More questions and discussion will arise from the answers.

Sketchbooks

For the reasons given below it is useful for all children to keep a sketchbook/notebook, as do all artists. Sketchbooks should be well-used, even battered in appearance, from accompanying pupils on excursions beyond the school walls, including visits to museums or galleries, and from being constantly used as part of the art-making process. Sketchbooks should contain drawings of various types, from rough drafts and plans to detailed sketches. There should also be experiments in tonal variation. This will include experiments with different drawing materials including all grades of pencil, graphite, charcoal, crayon and paint. The sketchbook should not be kept as a 'best book' for frigid little drawings with the eraser in too much evidence. Show the pupils examples of Turner's paintings, with corrected lines clearly visible, or Leonardo's drawings, where the **process** of achieving the final **product** is also clearly identifiable.

In addition to drawings, the sketchbook should include notes, photographs, plans for 3D work, collections of textures, small found objects, stitched fabric, dyed fabric, anything that may, or may not, be used to develop into an idea for a future piece of work. Insist that pupils get into the habit of dating their sketchbooks each time they use them. The sketchbook is a place for ideas to be collected as a basis for future creativity, or as a record of ideas that are – as yet – going nowhere.

There is also an added value to the teacher in being able to monitor the development and progression of what is contained in the sketchbook.

The learning environment

Tanner (1985), a former Her Majesty's Inspector (HMI), believed that children are greatly influenced by their surroundings. He held that classrooms should be places of order and beauty so that children will absorb high standards of presentation and respect. Tanner's central message was that children and their work should be respected, and that we should have high expectations of them at all times. Strategies to be avoided at all costs are those which diminish the status of the child's work, and ignore the stage at which the child is operating. It is very important that a teacher's intervention is sensitive and takes the form of discussion, constructive criticism, example and modelling of the use and care of tools and materials. It is never appropriate to interfere directly with the child's work by adding a line or otherwise 'improving' an outcome.

Neither is it acceptable to draw outlines for children to fill in or offer them a template to draw round. We need always to reflect upon what the children are learning. Asking them to draw round a template or fill in something that the teacher has drawn tells them only that their drawing will be no good. They will develop neither confidence nor skill from such activities and they will learn nothing.

Assessment

As in all subjects, assessment is important in providing information which will help the pupil to progress, and enable the teacher to plan coherent sequences of work which will facilitate this process.

Formative assessment should form an integral part of the process of making art. Pupils should be encouraged to review, evaluate and criticize their own work as it develops, focusing for example on texture. How have they used lines, tones and shapes to create a part of their image depicting fur or feathers as distinct from a smooth surface? Can they improve the effect or have they reached the result they want?

This evaluation procedure should be encouraged throughout the pupil's school experience, beginning with the bold lines, shapes and colours used by very young children beginning to make art. This will develop to embrace discussion and self-evaluation in all the skills outlined earlier to which all children should have access. Pupils' sketchbooks are an excellent source of information about their development in skills and ideas, use of tools and materials, responses to stimuli and ability to develop a selected starting point through to finished product. In addition, for monitoring and recording purposes, the teacher needs to select examples of pupils' work across the range of skills. These should be dated, discussed with the pupil and the discussion noted, usually on the back of the work or as a photograph of 3D work. This process needs to be selective in building up a portfolio of annotated examples which illustrate the pupils' progress across the different aspects of art and design covered during the year. There is no need to include every piece of work. In fact it would be counter-productive to do so. One or two pieces on average each half term should suffice. However, children develop at varying rates and there may be 'fallow' periods when there is little to say about progress, followed by periods when progress is very rapid. The teacher needs to judge which pieces of work will best chart this process and provide feedback, firstly for the pupil and to inform the teacher's planning and then for parents, head teacher, governors, future teachers of the pupil and in some cases the special educational needs coordinator (SENCO).

Assessment is important in deciding where the pupil is on the spectrum of development so that appropriate and differentiated activities can be planned. These activities will be geared towards helping children to acquire the skills of drawing, painting, printmaking, collage, textiles, digital media and 3D. Pupils need to be able to discuss and evaluate their work using the visual elements, line, shape, tone, colour, pattern, texture, form and space.

Pupils also need access to the work of other artists who provide examples of excellence in the various skills, together with the opportunity to develop their speaking and listening skills in talking about the work of other artists.

A teacher who works alongside the child can provide much encouragement through discussion about and evaluation of their own drawings, prints, collages and other forms of work. This is not to recommend giving demonstrations on how to produce a good drawing or painting, but to foster in the child the discipline of drawing, evaluating, commenting and making appropriate changes.

Teachers vary in attitudes to art as in other subjects. Some feel a great enthusiasm for the subject and enjoy every opportunity to explore and develop their own skills alongside the child. The classroom environment is likely to reflect this, with displays of work charting the processes and outcomes of the pupils' learning. Other teachers may lack confidence and will need to be helped to recognize their own potential and the importance of the subject to pupils' creative and mental development. The subject-leader for art has an important role to play here.

Case study

A Year 6 teacher, also deputy head teacher of a large urban primary school, has outstanding qualities as a teacher but expresses concerns about art. She has great respect for art and values it as a subject but when asked, 'Do you enjoy teaching art?' her response was 'Not hugely! I find it very frustrating and this really upsets me, that I can't give a better example to the children.'

When asked why, she went on to explain that she felt that she was no good at it personally and did not like the fact that she did not know how to move pupils forward.

So far I deduce from this that the teacher, whom I will call Alison, has been deprived of opportunities herself, whether at school or during her training, to master or at least acquire some proficiency in the various skills.

Alison was then asked. 'Do you feel competent to **teach** art?' – not the same question as 'Do you enjoy teaching art?' but the response was similar. 'I have developed a themed approach whereby pupils have the opportunity to use a range of media – pencil, pastel, batik, modroc. I'm happy doing these things but don't know how to move the pupils forward. I can do certain things, but lack ideas.'

The range of media Alison mentions actually covers most of the skills necessary such as drawing, painting, printmaking, collage, textiles, digital media and 3D. Alison enjoys doing these but worries that she is not moving the pupils on. Alison is being hard on herself. She has a good resource base and provides appropriate opportunities for pupils to practise skills. These opportunities involve all of the visual elements – line, tone, shape, colour, pattern, texture, form and space.

Alison needs to encourage the pupils to evaluate their work and consider through discussion with her and with each other how to extend and develop their use of the visual elements

Case study (continued)

they have employed. If Alison keeps recording this process in a portfolio for each pupil she will be able to chart the fact that they are indeed 'moving on'.

Alison is a very open and reflective teacher who does not flinch from self-appraisal. Asked what would make her feel better and more confident about teaching art, she had this to say: 'Probably if I was better at it myself and had a clearer understanding of the skills and competencies and the idea behind it. I'm a very logical, scientific person and find art airy-fairy and lacking right- and wrongness – I don't like that creativeness!'

This is a really interesting response, and is the response of a very conscientious teacher working in today's climate where quantification and target-setting are demanded from 'on high'. As Crace (2002) stated, 'Creativity is difficult to measure and quantify yet there is pressure in school to do just that with all areas of the curriculum'.

It is indeed difficult to quantify creativity, but Alison does not actually need to. She is doing a good job and needs to know that it is not necessary to control outcomes in art, only to facilitate pupils' development by continuing to give them plenty of opportunities to practise and evaluate.

Below are examples of work from a project with Year 1 children. This involved drawing with pencil, pen and pastels. The children were five years old and had previous experience of selecting and matching colours and engaging with the work of other artists. The school curriculum was organized so that all subjects were taught using a central theme. At this time, the beginning of the school year, the topic was 'Ourselves'.

It was decided to ask the children to produce self-portraits. The session began with children looking at and talking about examples of work by other artists who painted portraits before creating their own self-images. Three of the results are presented in Figures 1.2, 1.3 and 1.4.

Figure 1.2 Barbara

Figure 1.3 Jodie

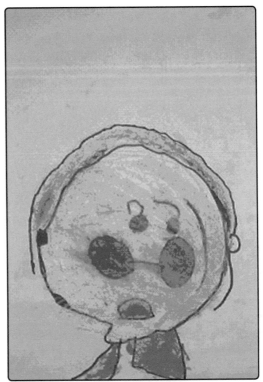

Figure 1.4 Tania

Barbara worked very meticulously and carefully and so had to hurry to finish. The lines are very confidently drawn and she has noticed small details like the Cupid's bow on the top lip. There is no nose and the neck is not coloured, which would be items to discuss with her, but the concept of the background being all around her is very mature. She is not afraid to make use of all the space available on the paper.

Her comments were that she would have liked time to make the blue background more complete.

Jodie had good pen control and blended the colours well on the dress. She noticed a lot of detail about her face and the lines and shapes show confidence. Fairly typical of her stage/age is that she has not worked out the horizon yet and the symbolic sun is important to her. She said that she liked the portrait, but would have preferred to have drawn a bigger sun.

Tania used plenty of round shapes and chose good colours to match her skin and hair. Her pen control is developing quite well although she filled in her eyes and then chose to make the spectacles blue to match her eyes. Tania has special needs and is generally at a development stage two years younger than her actual age. She found it difficult to articulate what she might like to change, but did enjoy the activity and was pleased with her portrait.

Resources

Resources, materials and tools all need to be accessible; individual schools will have their own systems for both storing and allocating these to individual teachers. Children need to be taught to take care of tools and equipment. They need to respect the materials and the needs of those who will be using them later.

For art and design lessons to be effective they must be properly equipped and should contain all the resources necessary for children to develop knowledge of all of the skills and visual elements discussed at length in this chapter.

It is the subject-leader's responsibility to make sure that adequate supplies are available and that teachers are able to use, rather than hoard, them.

The use of recycled materials should also be encouraged, though these should be collected only as required.

Conclusion

In this chapter an attempt has been made to summarize the development of art into the subject as it should be taught today and to address issues relating to the development of good practice.

It is essential that all teachers, through thought and reflection, know and understand what counts in art and design, and that they value effective models of practice (Newton and Newton, 2005).

The following chapter examines approaches to the teaching of art and design which exemplify good practice beyond the confines of a specified curriculum.

References

Blenkin, G. and Kelly, A. (eds) (1996), *Early Childhood Education: A Developmental Curriculum*, 2nd edn. London: Paul Chapman.

Clement, R., Piotrowski, J. and Roberts, I. (1998), *Coordinating Art Across the Primary School*. London: Falmer Press.

Crace. J. (2002), 'Creative Spaces'. *Education Guardian*, 18 June.

Department for Education and Skills (DfES) (2003), *Excellence and Enjoyment: A Strategy for Primary Schools*. Nottingham: DfES Publications.

Department for Education and Employment (DfEE) (1999), *The National Curriculum: Handbook for Primary Teachers in England*. London: DfEE.

Department of Education and Science (DES) (1967), *Children and their Primary Schools (Plowden Report)*. London: HMSO.

British Journal of Aesthetics, see Tanner, R. (1985).

Kellog, R. (1972), *Analysing Children's Art*. Palo Alto: National Press Books.

Lowenfeld, V. and Brittain, W. (1987), *Creative and Mental Growth*. London: Collier Macmillan.

Matthews, J. (1999), *The Art of Childhood and Adolescence: The Construction of Meaning*. London: Falmer Press.

Newton, L. and Newton, D. (2005), 'Thinking about art: Could elementary textbooks serve as models in practice to help new teachers and non-specialists support reasoning in art?' *International Journal of Art and Design Education,* 24 (3), 315–24.

Read, H. (1959), *Education Through Art*. London: Faber and Faber.

Tanner, R. (1985), 'In search of child art'. *British Journal of Aesthetics.* 25 (4), Autumn.

Useful Websites

www.standards.dfes.gov.uk/schemes2/art
Department for Children, Schools and Families

Art and Design: Beyond the Curriculum

David Coulbeck

'Every child is an artist. The problem is how to remain an artist once he grows up.' Pablo Picasso

Introduction

It is fundamental to primary school philosophy that a child should be nurtured in confidence and the development of a positive self-image. The children come with natural interests, enthusiasms and talents which the school needs to foster by planning a curriculum which refines and develops these innate abilities. The curriculum, so devised to take account of the natural learning of children, one which does not recognize subject barriers, has a powerful contribution to make to a more profound level of understanding. Art and design, as a representative of the visual arts, are a central and valued part of such a curriculum.

Cross-curricular themes

For many primary teachers who entered the profession in the early 1970s the extremes of curriculum planning have been experienced during their careers. The all-embracing web diagrams of the child-centred integrated day and the initial years of the subject-driven National Curriculum (DfEE, 1999) both produced primary curricula so broad as to dilute the learning experiences of children rather than strengthen them. 'A mile wide and an inch deep' was a comment often heard.

However, the careful planning across *appropriate* subject areas to establish *relevant* themes, endorsed and supported in current documentation such as *Excellence and Enjoyment* (DfES, 2003), supports children's learning and allows the careful development of art and design skills and visual awareness throughout their primary schooling. This should also lead to positive achievement and happy, highly motivated children who engage with enthusiasm in the art and design programme.

Such well-considered cross-curricular planning can benefit the learning and teaching of the art and design curriculum through:

- improving and strengthening the relevance and coherence of the learning experiences for the children
- ensuring that children can apply their knowledge and skills across subjects, reinforcing understanding and confidence
- engaging learners in meaningful and relevant art and design tasks that have a purposeful context
- supporting independent research and encouraging children's curiosity
- developing an awareness in children of the universality of art and design
- promoting home/community/school activities
- encouraging practitioners to take ownership of the art and design curriculum
- encouraging practitioners to develop their own skills, knowledge and personal interests to share with their pupils
- combining several subjects which can also reduce the pressure on planning time, an issue of serious concern to teachers.

Traditionally art and design has been used to support and enhance other subjects in the primary school, and consequently the idiosyncratic understandings, skills and techniques of this creative subject have not always been recognized. Care must be taken when adopting a cross-curricular approach to learning and teaching to ensure that the rigour and breadth of the art and design curriculum is not compromised, and that children's entitlement to engage with the visual arts is recognized.

All children entering school come with artistic abilities, and many have experiences which will include mark-making and construction. Although this is a unique area which cannot be imitated, it can be combined with other subjects to complete and deepen the learning experience. What is essential is that the appropriate framework of art and design teaching is recognized so that it provides a logical and well-sequenced structure to activities. These must grow in complexity as they build on previous experiences and skill acquisition. Through the development of skills and the handling and manipulation of materials and media children gain understanding in the language of line, space, shape, form, texture and colour.

Consider the medium-term plan for teaching art and design to a Year 4 class in Figure 2.1.

Learning Objectives	Teacher Input	AT1 Investigating and Making	AT2 Knowledge and Understanding	Assessment Opportunities	Resources	Skills
To understand the terms 3D and 2D and that we live in a 3-dimensional world	Appropriate language related to 2D and 3D paper and sculpture	To understand the notion of using materials and techniques in relation to 3D	To understand the qualities and possibilities of paper and clay and enable pupil discussion	Notion of 3D Use of appropriate vocabulary, confidence in handling materials	Tissue paper PVA glue and water mixture	Manipulation and moulding Painting Etching
To learn about properties of mouldable materials and how they change when wet	Demonstrate how to use, manipulate and handle tissue paper when wet to make a book cover. Discuss joining one to another	Investigation of materials and their properties e.g. what happens when you use water, when you change the shape, when you squeeze, when you press and make marks	To look at examples of Eygyptian canoptic jars and shabtis and use some of these ideas where appropriate	Fine motor skills involved in handling materials	Bowls Clay Poster paint including gold, silver, etc.	Researching and designing Imagination
To help design a canoptic jar and gain confidence in using clay to build up shape	Demonstrate a successful method of construction			Transfer of design from sketch book to shabti		
To design a shape and decoration for an Egyptian shabti following research	Draw children's attention to designs commonly used in Ancient Egypt including colour	To build up a realistic canoptic jar shape	Consider how the Egyptians made 3D shapes such as canoptic jars and how 3D shapes are made today		Rolling boards Modelling tools Sketch-books	
To develop work from drawings into 3D using appropriate tools to make shapes and patterns in clay	Use appropriate tools and demonstrate how to cut into wet clay to achieve a paintable surface	To build up a realistic shabti Cut shapes into shabti and canoptic jar, paint and glaze				

Figure 2.1 A medium-term plan for Year 4

Within this plan it is evident that the links with the history curriculum are being used to provide a context and a purpose for the children's learning (and the learning objectives). However, the plan has its main emphasis clearly focused on the children's engagement with those skills and knowledge that are unique to the art and design curriculum. It also needs to be noted that although this planning appears to be brief, through the use of subject specific terminology, specific objectives and appropriately labelled column headings, it is a very detailed plan.

The case study below is a discussion between the author and the teacher who planned the Year 4 medium-term plan above. It is evident that she has a strong commitment to cross-curricular teaching based on sound pedagogical principles, but, from her planning above, that she also values each subject in its own right.

Case study

What do you see as the advantages of doing cross-curricular work?

It gives children an overall perspective, a context in which to set the work in their minds. It makes the learning more meaningful. It gives the opportunity for creative practitioners to make lessons accessible to all pupils by using a range of learning and teaching styles.

Could you describe what you would consider an example of good practice?

For example, with Year 4 we did a cross-curricular plan for Ancient Egyptians. In art and design we designed, made and decorated canoptic jars, and decorated the shabti dolls that were made as part of design and technology. We even managed to link mathematics, looking at ancient number systems. We also studied contemporary Egypt in the context of geography and linked this to our work. During our literacy sessions, we used Egypt as the topic for compiling information texts and writing reports. Prior to that, we covered India in geography. So we also researched and replicated Rangoli patterns during art, looking at shape, colour and form. I included some traditional stories which encompassed both history and literacy. We studied Indian dance in PE, and the children were also given the opportunity within music lessons to compose Indian music to accompany their dances. We also studied the religions of India during RE lessons and linked all of this to personal, social, health and citizenship education (PSHCE) using the medium of ICT.

Pause to think

During your teacher training you will have had many opportunities to both observe art and design being taught and teach it yourself. How do your own experiences reflect the way in which this teacher plans for and teaches art and design? How does your practice teaching art and design compare with those of this practitioner?

Cross-curricular themes and inclusive practice

Addressing racial, cultural and religious diversity in art and design

Recognition of other races, cultures and religions is not something that happens just in schools with a diverse population. It is now an integral part of the curriculum in all primary schools. While it is important to avoid adopting a tokenistic attitude to this diversity, it can provide opportunities that can broaden the art and design curriculum. For example, the strength and beauty of Islamic art can provide a powerful stimulus for hand-made tiles, display friezes and decorations on ceramic pots. Children can be made aware of the history and origins of batik fabric printing, and explore the traditional designs used in such places as Indonesia and Malaysia. Reference to the work of art educators such as Nigel Meager (2006) will provide support for teachers in a very practical way linking myths, legends, beliefs and aspects of people's lives into ideas for painting, printing, textiles, graphic design, photography and drawing.

Children with special needs

In art and design children are represented by the same range of interests and ability as in any other subject. If we consider art and design within the context of Gardner's (1983) theory of multiple intelligences, it is the children with strong spatial intelligence who would exhibit most effectively 'the ability to create visual-spatial representations of the world'. (Nicholson-Nelson, 1998: 11). However, differentiation by ability would not be an appropriate way to address individual needs. Art and design is a subject in which all children can work on the same project, be involved in discussions about their work (as discussed in the previous chapter), and celebrate their achievement.

The needs of children with physical disabilities will be dependent on the nature of the disability. A child in a wheelchair may only require a low table to work on, but other disabilities may require consultation with the special educational needs coordinator (SENCO) and subject-leader for art and design.

Developing children's creativity in art and design

For the effective promotion and acquisition of art and design skills it is essential to establish a classroom environment with rich visual displays of all children's work; a workplace which values all children's participation, engagement and products. Thinking skills and discernment are encouraged by the provision of exciting learning opportunities and exposure to a range of papers, media and tools; all of which must be available and accessible.

The sequential development of skills and the use of tools and equipment are recognized in all effective schemes of work for art and design. These need to be planned at the whole-school level to ensure continuity and progression in children's learning. However, cross-curricular planning and the implementation of the scheme of work into a class-based programme should be the responsibility of the class teacher.

As in all subjects, art and design has its own terminology, and it is crucial that this area of learning develops naturally alongside the more practical aspects of the subject. Children will also use their language skills to plan, discuss and reflect on their learning.

Most primary school teachers feel quite confident providing positive learning experiences and developing skills and aesthetic awareness in drawing, printing, painting and collage. These are the areas of art and design with which they have had most personal experience through their own artistic undertakings, and are the artistic media surrounding them in everyday life. However, three-dimensional work and textiles are areas with which some teachers feel less comfortable. So let us consider some of the activities that teachers can engage with in these areas. The suggestions will have some developmental aspects, and include cross-curricular elements.

Three-dimensional work

'…choose a block of marble and chop off whatever I don't need.' Auguste Rodin

Sounds easy, doesn't it? The thought of 30 children chopping away with sharp instruments in their classroom is the health and safety nightmare of all teachers. The response of the cleaners to the mess is also rather daunting. While safety and mess are intrinsic aspects of three-dimensional (3D) work they should not put you off.

Engaging in 3D work is an important and exciting element within the art and design curriculum. As well as enhancing the child's development handling and manipulating materials and tools, it also develops the fine motor skills necessary for other work in the visual arts and encourages a 'what happens if I...?' approach in a world of discovery and exploration. It is essential that the appropriate vocabulary is developed alongside these activities:

- Having opportunities for sensory exploration of and play with construction kits, clay, sand, playdough and other appropriate materials. This enables children to explore the characteristics of the materials by squeezing, twisting, rolling, pulling and bending them. When the play is with others, accurate vocabulary can be used to describe these features, and discuss their uses. Some of these materials, particularly playdough and plasticine, must be replaced regularly for health reasons.
- From a limited range of materials children can construct responses to literature. These might include the *Hungry Caterpillar* (Carle, 1970), the houses of the Three Little Pigs or a gingerbread man. Such responses can be used throughout the primary school. Iron children would be interesting additions to the Iron Man and the Iron Woman.
- Children can investigate fastening techniques which include simple and more complex forms of joining in their constructions, and examine a range of different glues and fasteners such as staples, paper fasteners, slip and safety pins.
- They can make a simple 3D construction in basic materials from a given starting point, for example a Roman lamp or jar.
- As well as providing children with specific techniques and an understanding of the characteristics of the materials, making casts of animals and different leaves using plasticine and plaster can encourage children to develop their observational skills.
- While being rather messy, and taking time to dry, papier-mâché, modroc and clay can all provide children with opportunities to mould, layer and shape constructions. These could vary from a fragile bowl built around another bowl, to large forms of constructed elements, such as the different forms of human figures inspired by the works of Antony Gormley.
- As has already been recognized, children carving into materials with sharp tools in the pursuit of creativity requires thought and planning. Children need to be taught to handle carving tools carefully and with respect. It is the responsibility of a competent adult to model and supervise children as they develop and use their new skills. The materials carved should be hard enough to need pressure when cut, but not so hard that children need to use force when guiding their tools. Children should also be taught to respect and care for the tools. The tools themselves should be stored safely.
- During all of these activities children should be encouraged to use their sketchbooks to record, evaluate, explore and plan further work.

Textiles

> Philomela was kidnapped by her brother-in-law Tereus, the King of Thrace. He cut out her tongue so that she could not accuse him, and imprisoned her. She had no way to tell her story until, during the year of her incarceration, she began to weave her story into the fabric she wove on her loom, perhaps a tapestry, perhaps a garment. She had the fabric sent to her sister, Procne, who came to her rescue, and the sisters plotted a terrible revenge.
>
> A story taken from Greek mythology

'Textiles' in schools has come a long way from the neat and beautifully stitched samplers made by even very young girls in the early days of mass education. Today, textiles is concerned with the manipulation of fabric and related materials and the range of skills used is of interest to girls and boys alike. As many of the different forms of textiles have strong links with earlier times in our history and with other cultures and places, there is a rich vocabulary associated with each form. This all provides wonderful opportunities for cross-curricular work.

- There are few better ways to develop an awareness of colour, texture and shape than through this area of art and design.
- By their nature textiles are made to be felt, and children, especially young children, will respond in a sensory way to different textiles and their textures such as velvet, silk, cotton, wool, string, felt and hessian.
- Children can quickly develop some of the simpler textile techniques such as plaiting, felting, off-loom weaving, rag-rug making and stitching.
- Mark-making and dyeing fabrics and material can enable children to link drawing and painting to their exploration of textiles. Through experience they will learn which materials are best for batik and fabric painting, what happens if you continue to use a pot of dark green dye with wool, and how you can screen print two colours.
- The range of artefacts that can be made using textiles is vast, and can include the creation of practical items, such as a rag-rug, a printed or tie-dyed T-shirt, or a plaited bracelet, or items that are purely for decoration, such as woven and printed wall hangings.
- Because so many of these forms of textiles have quite specific tools, techniques and materials, it is an advantage to have access to craftspeople. In this way children can see finished examples of work, watch an expert using the techniques and tools and then work alongside this person to develop their own skills.

Developing your own subject knowledge and skills

You can see just from the two examples above that some aspects of art and design require quite specific knowledge, skills and techniques. You cannot be expected to be expert in each of these, and using the internet will not help you learn and develop a specialized skill. There are, however, several strategies you can adopt so that your own lack of expertise will not deny the children opportunities to experience a rich art experience.

Learning from experts

In the previous section the use of visiting craft workers was highlighted and it is also discussed further on. However, it needs to be mentioned here as these visitors can help teachers, as well as children, to develop previously unknown skills.

Case study

Several winters ago long, brightly coloured scarves were extremely fashionable for both females and males. Several well-known celebrities had also been seen knitting in public. Everyone in the class agreed that they would love such a scarf. As a male, and a child of the 1980s, Mr Evans had no idea how to knit, but he knew some people who could.

It is quite a surreal experience to enter a classroom full of children and adults all sitting quietly wrapping brightly coloured wool around long, straight needles. The children (and their teacher) were all being taught to knit by a band of mothers, aunts and grandmothers. Terms such as cast on, row, knit, purl and cast off were all being used freely – the terminology having been modelled for them by the experienced knitters. Experiments were being carried out. One child had discovered that if you use a knit one, purl one stitch sequence for a scarf it all rolls up. Others had found that if you drop a stitch it leaves a hole. Experiments were also being undertaken with different-sized needles and different ply wool.

This teacher was not afraid to learn beside his pupils, and although his 'experts' were from the local community rather than the Arts Council, they were able to contribute positively to the art and design curriculum.

If you do use members of the community surrounding the school, do remember that they must be police-checked before they may work with your class. As this may take some time you will need to plan accordingly.

You may also find 'experts' among your fellow staff members. If this is the case you can often arrange class exchanges and timetable swaps.

Some local authorities still have advisory teachers who will work in the classroom alongside the class teacher. As well as being skilled in their subject area, art advisory teachers will help you to develop your ideas, suggest books and websites that will provide you with ideas, and have up-to-date information on the latest resources and materials available.

Attending in-service courses

If these courses are available, art and design advisory teachers will provide opportunities for teachers to attend in-service courses. These are an entitlement for all teachers, especially newly qualified teachers (NQTs). The courses are usually held in teachers' centres, and will address just one aspect of the art and design curriculum. Your school will have to pay for your attendance, but the specific tools and materials are generally provided (and you are able to take your creations home).

Beyond the classroom

The school as a gallery

When walking into many schools the first thing to impress the visitor is the range of children's art and design work on display. These exhibitions say a great deal about the school and its ethos.

While most of the art and design work experienced by children themselves will be in their own classroom, the wider school environment is a valuable resource in the learning and teaching of art and design. The foyer, corridors and other spaces should provide a constantly changing exhibition of children's work. This exhibition should be hung with as much thought and care as possible to indicate its worth to the children who created it.

As well as children's work, the school environment should also contain reproductions of the work of artists that children will be studying. These could include paintings, drawings and prints. Other forms of art, including ceramics, sculptures and textiles, should also be on view. These could perhaps include artefacts from other cultures and be used in displays of children's work in other subject areas, such as religious education or geography.

The school as a working environment

As some art and design work is both messy and time-consuming to complete, areas outside the classroom should be made available for small groups of children to work in. Children also need a place to store their work which is both accessible and secure.

As with all messy work, it is the one who makes the mess that is responsible for cleaning up. This is not an aspect of life that appeals to most children, but one that must be consistently reinforced.

Access to, and the storage of, resources and materials is also a whole-school issue. As well as bought resources and materials, all schools collect and use vast quantities of recycled items. Many of these are kindly donated by parents but rules need to be made to ensure that schools are not swamped with vermin-attracting refuse.

Visiting craft workers and artists

When we were discussing the learning and teaching of textiles, the role of visiting specialist craftspeople was briefly introduced. For many professionals in all of the artistic disciplines, work in schools is a way of disseminating information about their own work and the techniques of their discipline. Visits by such people can add a breadth and depth of knowledge that children (and teachers) would otherwise not receive. These visitors can also inspire both teachers and children, and by modelling, suggestion and encouragement support the production of excellent work.

Many such craftspeople work in conjunction with local and regional arts councils, and can be contacted through these groups. As funding is difficult to find for these visits schools will often seek funding or support from local businesses. It is also increasingly common for groups of schools to share the cost of employing such visitors.

Beyond the school

Beyond the school the world is waiting with many opportunities for the children to enjoy quality experiences engaging with art and design situations.

Whether the school is in an urban or rural location, the opportunities are all around. Children can so easily take, for example, the same short walk to a park, or a nature reserve, on a monthly basis, recording their own 'Diary of an Edwardian...' style of nature notes and pencil sketches of trees, flowers, birds and mini-beasts. As Henry Moore argued, 'When you draw you look much more intensely at something'. Fewer and fewer children now know the names of native trees, wild flowers and birds. Half an hour, even an hour every month visiting a familiar landscape is time well spent, providing children with opportunities to observe, compare and contrast the annual changes. A more detailed study of a rookery or pond is also well worthwhile, and can become the inspiration for individual or collective paintings and textiles.

Children in more urban schools can enjoy and use the urban environment as a source of inspiration. Armed only with their sketchbooks children will find many places which present rich opportunities on their doorstep. Such opportunities and experiences can inform children's own creative efforts and broaden their perception of what constitutes art and design, in architecture, grafitti, advertising and street furniture.

The role of art galleries and museums cannot be underestimated, and both have a valid place in the teaching of art and design. All children have the right to experience the awe and wonder of such facilities, most of which have education departments and education officers who willingly liaise with schools, organizing visits, and providing information. While schools now have access to fine illustrations of examples of contemporary and historical art and design through books and the internet, these, however, compare sadly with the detail and magic of the real thing, so opportunities should be made for such visits.

Conclusion

In looking 'beyond the curriculum' we have identified many opportunities for providing children with new perceptions of art and design and with artistic challenges, often in unfamiliar surroundings. In many instances, taking children out of the classroom leads to a more creative approach where they are able to work in many different ways and styles. It is also important to allow for reflection along the way and not just at the end of an activity, trip or project. This is seen as *sharing* what has been learned and experienced. Through this shared talk children will become more comfortable discussing their own work and the work of others. Children of all ages will reflect on their artistic endeavours through discussions with peers and supportive adults and sketchbooks. These reflections help them to recount and summarize, capturing and reinforcing their experiences.

Although such discussion and sharing of opinions and ideas typically occurs during whole-class share time at the end of a lesson where learning is made explicit and key strategies are articulated, there are intervals during the work in hand where these strands of reflection can aid a deeper awareness. As in all lessons, talk is an integral part of each child's learning, and these opportunities for peer reflection should always be valued and encouraged.

References

Carle, E. (1970), *The Very Hungry Caterpillar*. London: Penguin.

Department for Education and Employment (DfEE) (1999), *The National Curriculum: Handbook for Primary Teachers in England Key Stages 1 and 2*. London: DfEE/QCA.

Department for Education and Skills (DfES) (2003), *Excellence and Enjoyment: A Strategy for Primary Schools*. London: DfES Publications.

Gardner, H. (1993), *Multiple Intelligences: The Theory in Practice*. New York: BasicBooks, HarperCollins.

Golomb, C. (1992), *Children's Creation of a Pictorial World*. Oxford: The University of California Press.

Meager, N. (2006), *Creativity and Culture – Art Projects for Primary Schools*. London: NSEAD Publications.

Nicholson-Nelson, K. (1998), *Developing Students' Multiple Intelligences*. New York: Scholastic.

3 Design and Technology: Teaching the Curriculum

Su Sayers

Chapter Outline

'Enjoyment is the birthright of every child... Children learn better when they are excited and engaged – but what excites and engages them best is truly excellent teaching, which challenges them and shows them what they can do. When there is joy in what they are doing, they learn to love learning.' Clarke (2003: 3)

Introduction

Design and technology is a subject that gives children opportunities to use materials to create, model, make things happen; opportunities to 'play' with stuff. WOW! – that is how many children spend their free-choice time: inventing playground games from whatever equipment is available; at lunchtime choosing foods to make a meal; selecting what to wear and which role to adopt in the role-play corner. During these elective experiences children are making choices and exercising judgment. We should be surprised therefore, if they did not enjoy design and technology at school, for it consists of very much these things. Children may be using the equipment and materials in a creative way, as they cut and stick materials to collage a greeting card, or build a model in Lego. They are using technological devices as they play games on the computer or play with remote-control toys, games consoles or a CD player at home. Learning about designing and making with materials and using technology are central to the activity of design and technology as a subject in the school curriculum.

The launch in England in 2003 of a primary strategy (DfES, 2003) updated teachers' expectations of how subject teaching can and should bring enjoyment and engagement into the classroom. It has been the case, however, over the past few years that expectations of teachers' technical skills and resourcefulness have been stretched. Teachers have been vulnerable to criticism, and hesitant about a perceived lack of expertise.

The place of design and technology in the curriculum

Design and technology is a relatively new subject in the curriculum. Prior to any formal recognition, many schools had included art and craft activities as part of the regular experience of children, but had not differentiated among them. Art activities allowed the creative use of materials, with associated development of skills and concepts (Taylor and Andrews, 1993). Craft activities were often associated with cross-curricular topic work, in science or the humanities; for example children studying medieval castles made a model of one, or when learning about sound in science, they made musical instruments (Mason and Houghton, 2002). National Curriculum Orders for Technology (DES, 1990) formalized the processes involved in the designing and making of such products, helping teachers to become more aware that 'making' was only one of many aspects involved in the process.

Over the years there has been some consensus on ways to describe and model the activity of design and technology (Kimbell *et al.*, 1991; Cross, 1998; Hope, 2004). A 'loop' model (Figure 3.1) shows the process as a logical set of activities through to evaluation of a finished product, and it has gained universal recognition across the international community as a framework within which teachers provide opportunities for children to design and make.

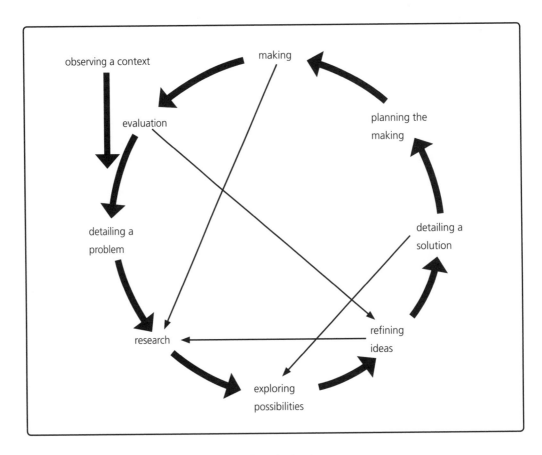

Figure 3.1 Model of processes involved in designing

It is the centrality of process that makes design and technology unique. A simplified version of the model, used to represent the main starting points and activities (context, designing, making, evaluating) does not do justice to the rich interactive nature of the design process.

Key messages for teachers about the importance of design and technology are that children, working as individuals and members of a team:

- learn to think
- learn to become creative problem solvers
- learn to make products
- learn to evaluate present and past design and technology. (DfEE, 1999)

It is a futuristic and ambitious reflection on design and technology's involvement in, and contribution to, the generic competences necessary for citizens of the future.

Principles of good practice

The discussion that follows considers 'designing' and 'making', the two essential aspects involved in teaching and learning in design and technology. The issues relating to teaching and learning this exciting subject centre round how to provide appropriate and essential opportunities for children to engage with materials and manipulate them ('play' with them) constructively.

Designing and making are the processes at the heart of the subject, but neither of these is complete without evaluation. Children's skills at deciding what worked well with their model, or how they could design it differently to improve it next time, are fundamentally important. Is this what makes design and technology unique, that practical involvement is brought together with iterative reflection? There is, however, at the same time, a significant amount of subject knowledge that teachers need to be aware of, and incorporate into their planning, to enable children to develop the resourcefulness to grasp opportunities and exploit potential. This chapter will also consider subject knowledge and the importance of 'knowing', to enable creative thinking. Knowledge and understanding of materials, tools and the specific working knowledge needed to enable children to make quality products are significant here. Choosing materials, selecting equipment, solving problems, trying out ideas, all involve the key skill of thinking, and will create opportunities for substantial reflection on process and progress, as children move towards taking increasing responsibility for their choices.

Designing and making are inevitably interlinked; however, for the purposes of this chapter they will be looked at separately so that you, as a teacher, can identify the key concerns within each aspect. It is clear that to make progress in both aspects involves children in evaluating and thinking: the teacher's challenge is to create exciting opportunities for all of this to take place.

What is involved in designing?

Children love to draw pictures, but designing is not just drawing (Fasciato, 2002). Young children will draw and can provide a commentary on their mark-making for their teacher, but are usually not ready conceptually to make use of this in their planning and making. Research into young children's designing has established that they are likely to make more sense of modelling directly, using materials, rather than the conventional order of draw–model–make, therefore allowing more scope for developing confidence and creativity. It can be useful to encourage them to draw what they have made after the product is completed (Egan, 1995). In this way the activity can lead naturally to a discussion about the merits of the construction/product they have made and how they might alter aspects or develop it further. Evaluation is clearly a key skill, involving reflection on learning and skills and target setting for improvement in a future activity.

When children are designing, they need a clear focus on a context meaningful to them. Identifying a need is, for many children, less of a problem when the need or opportunity naturally derives from something familiar: the needs of a teddy to cross a lake (Bradshaw, 1997), or the events of a familiar story. Story books, including *The Lighthouse Keeper's Lunch* (Armitage and Armitage, 1994) and *Humpty's Big Day* (Bee, Boyle *et al.*, 1991), have been used successfully to create opportunities for various projects, and problem-solving. For example: 'What might Humpty Dumpty need to transport the guests to his party?' And for food technology projects: 'How can we save Mr Grinling's lunch from being eaten by seagulls?' 'What kinds of food might be suitable for Humpty's birthday tea?'

The starting point chosen may usefully be explored further as a physical education (PE) or drama activity, either prior to or during the run-up to the making stage. Drama gives children a chance to stretch imagination and creativity using others in the class to inspire ideas. Prior to designing a tiger puppet, for example, role-playing animal movement and animal noises can provide a stimulus for ideas about how the animal uses its head, mouth and jaws (Barlex, 2001). Drama also helps all the children, not just those who have visited a zoo or seen animals in the wild, to contextualize the activity and identify with the topic.

Creativity in designing

Good practice in designing allows children scope to be imaginative and produce something original, that is of value and has a purpose. Children's product outcomes reflect their confidence in the use of materials and tools but rarely result in stereotyped and mundane outcomes. The NACCCE report (1999) puts creativity into context:

> 'Our starting point is to recognise four characteristics of creative processes. First, they always involve thinking or behaving imaginatively. Second, overall this imaginative activity is purposeful: that is, it is directed to achieving an objective. Third, these processes must generate something original. Fourth, the outcome must be of value in relation to the objective. We therefore define creativity as: Imaginative activity fashioned so as to produce outcomes that are both original and of value.' (NACCCE, 1999: 30)

Use the case study to reflect on your views on providing open-ended situations where children have freedom to explore materials.

> **Case study**
>
> To develop the pupils' imagination, I encouraged them to learn about the properties of plastics in their own way before introducing formal skills through focused practical tasks. I'd never used this approach before but it proved very successful. It gave pupils an opportunity to respond intuitively and to explore, experiment and play with ideas. Many responses were spontaneous and unpredictable… Similarly, giving the pupils the freedom to choose what product they made encouraged creativity in their responses. Robert's design started the other pupils off and they then adapted and modified his idea. It was vital to set up an open environment for practical work, where the pupils could try out for themselves different ways of cutting, shaping and joining different materials (DfES, 2007).
>
> To what extent does the situation described above accord with your philosophy and/or your experiences? Why do you think the teacher gave the pupils the freedom to explore and experiment?

Planning

Design and technology is a very broad area of the curriculum, often with restrictions on time due to priorities elsewhere. It is important, therefore, to have a very clear curriculum plan in place for specific design and technology activities (Design and Technology Association [DATA] 2005). This will be organized by a subject-leader, who will have tried to ensure that there is breadth, balance and progression in design and technology learning over different year groups. There are considerable advantages though, of the class teacher trying to introduce design and make into other core subjects to capitalize on time and develop experience and skills.

DATA's help sheets (DATA, 1999) provide structured guidance for a variety of projects, with prompts for ideas and techniques for products children could make. Teachers have found them useful and they can be easily adapted for different time allocations or resources. In addition, useful exemplar lesson plans can be found to guide planning, managing, and differentiating lessons (DATA, 2005).

Planning needs to take account of resources and safety, and the teacher will be guided by expectations and experience to support children with individual needs. Often when making, children experience manipulative difficulties (e.g. threading a needle) and teachers' resourcefulness will help children develop independent ways to overcome the problems (e.g. have large-eye needles, pre-cut sewing threads in appropriate lengths, thread-up needles before the lesson, and secure them to a felt-covered wallboard).

Class management: grouping children

The management of resources and equipment for designing and making often pose a problem. Therefore many teachers choose to organize making activities with one table group at a time. Whole-class activities are very useful, however, and might be used:

- for introducing and discussing the project or when evaluating ideas or products
- for research into the context and for generating ideas, using ICT as well as the IWB for internet-based research
- when using focused practical tasks where all children are learning a skill, e.g. using a card and lever system to make a moving picture
- where additional adults are available.

It is often inappropriate (unless there are enough resources and teaching assistants) to have all children working on practical making at once, so planning needs to be strategic in balancing the opportunities for paper-based/ICT-based design, and for materials work so that groups have a rota. This can help to manage assessment for learning in an effective way too.

Teaching strategies

Teachers can provide many opportunities for designing, from using construction kits prior to making playground equipment, mechanical toys or vehicles, to modelling with playdough prior to learning cutting skills with real food. A 'Hungry Caterpillar' (Carle, 1998) made with card disks and joined using a variety of fastenings provides an excellent preliminary activity to a variety of 3D constructions such as making card boxes into homes and making puppets and moving toys.

Specific food knowledge and understanding is the key to being able to design in food technology, using functional properties of ingredients to modify recipes: adding flavour, adding texture, binding together, sweetening and decorating can be discussed and taught as focused inputs in lessons. Rarely are recipes used as they stand: rather the focus is on children designing by modifying the standard recipe to create an individual product. The working characteristics of foods, melting, cooking, whisking, grating, peeling, can be explored in small investigations prior to this knowledge being used in designs.

Using a drawing to plan from, when producing a 3D product, children between the ages of seven and 11 are able to use conventional schema for drawing (such as plan, side view, back-front, exploded diagram) and are able to apply annotations and draw diagrams to include measurements, with an increasing level of precision and complexity (SCAA, 1997). The teacher who models techniques using a demonstration, perhaps using large-scale visual aids, often finds that children are more confident and inventive in developing their own design ideas. Perhaps running contrary to popular opinion, demonstration *can* be an effective teaching strategy.

Observational drawing using a range of materials appropriate to the object being studied can be used in conjunction with product analysis. Providing children with a pen will allow them to draw the lines and shapes of a mechanical toy, whereas pastels or pencil crayons will depict the form and texture of a garment or fabric more easily.

Help in drawing for designing can be provided in the form of templates to draw round, scaffolding the learning by moving children past their main area of difficulty: drawing an accurate outline shape in proportion. This framework gives an outline structure to the drawing (like a writing frame in literacy). The basic shape of a glove puppet, for instance, can be elaborated with different eyes, hair, and a hat or ears added to give it a personality, to enable children to develop their creative ideas with some of the difficulties removed. They will then have more freedom to consider the sort of materials that will be suitable. Isometric grids under thin paper allow 3D drawing to take shape more easily.

Designing in food is often helped by using playdough to try out shapes and by examining existing products carefully, for example to find out what is in a salad, a sandwich or muesli, prior to trying out ideas and designing their own product.

What is involved in making products?

Design and technology differs from, but has a symbiotic relationship with, both art and with science. A key difference as identified in Sayers (2002) is the requirement in design and technology to make quality products. Children will use skills, knowledge and understanding from a range of subjects, but only in design and technology is the emphasis on making products central to the subject. In England teachers are encouraged to give children opportunity to design 'quality' products and to make products, which they, rather than someone else, have designed (Barlex, 2001). The teacher plays a crucial role here in guiding and supporting the child whose ambitious design may be unrealistic in terms of skill level, time and materials.

Resistant materials

There is a gendered history to teachers' experiences with materials: woodwork for boys and sewing for girls (Sayers, 2002). The majority of primary teachers have had less experience with cutting, shaping and joining rigid materials, to the detriment of curriculum possibilities. Resistant materials (for example construction materials such as wood, card, plastics and kits) therefore often provide the greatest challenge for primary teachers. However, pupils tend to be better at making than designing (Ofsted, 1999) and teachers better at teaching making (Wilson, 2005). Indeed children can be so enthusiastic that, without guidance, they might waste and squander scarce resources. So the job of the teacher is to steer this enthusiasm into productive activity where 'the teacher's role, beyond encouragement, involves intervening, actively teaching creative techniques and strategies' (Davies and Howe, 2005: 183).

The skills involved in making with resistant materials such as wood and plastic include safe and accurate use of tools and equipment to measure, cut, shape, assemble, modify, construct, decorate and so forth. With resistant materials this usually involves using:

- a saw to cut
- glass paper to shape and smooth
- possibly a drill to help in the assembly.

Construction and decoration use components such as staples and glue. The popular Jinks frame technology (Williams and Jinks, 1985; Jinks, 2000) allows for a great deal of versatility in making products. Children use strips of timber, which can be cut safely even by young children with a junior hacksaw, to then join sections with wood glue and card triangles to strengthen the corners. The techniques are easily taught and learned, require little space to work in and are efficient in terms of use of materials.

Teaching making skills requires teachers to plan for and model working with a variety of materials and structures, but more importantly, allow children time to practise. Initially children will be intrigued: encouraging them to play with new materials shows them some of the characteristics and creative potential. Demonstration by the teacher of particular skills and techniques, combined with learning through focused tasks and experimentation, will extend children's repertoire of skills with the materials. Teachers need a level of confidence to allow them to become more inventive with the materials, and set appropriately engaging challenges for children. Unfortunately the lack of time for Foundation subjects in Initial Teacher Education courses can restrict the overall level acquired in training, and so teachers feel the need for professional development, to become more adventurous in their design and technology teaching.

Other materials such as yarns and fabrics give children opportunities to exploit the textiles area of design and technology. However, a review of design and technology in English primary schools (Ofsted, 1999) commented that too much was still collage without understanding of the true 3D potential of yarns and fabrics and their technology. Weaving, spinning and embroidery as well as sewing take time and only cursory attention is paid to the technology and knowledge content. Making slippers, Joseph's coat, puppets, 'Jitter Bug' projects, and the use of smart materials (photochromic crayons, or thermal transfer paper for instance) can bring textiles to life in primary school. A focus on puppets from other cultures can link with wide-ranging curricular activities.

Producing a torch to fit with a topic or theme provides a popular product focus for children to develop using ICT and bulbs, batteries and switches. A classroom with access to an electronic interactive whiteboard (IWB) is superb for running simulation software, allowing the teacher to involve children in demonstrations of models, circuits and mechanical systems. The use of a classroom IWB to search the internet allows children access to the work of professional designers and their ideas and worldwide contexts.

Sustainability is a topic closely associated with resource and material use in design and technology. Children's awareness of renewable and non-renewable energy sources may have come from humanities lessons, and in design and technology for instance they can make promotional posters, wind-powered machines, use natural dyes for textile fabrics, and study organic or Fair Trade foods. Websites which have interactive games can be a good focus for bringing an awareness of ecological issues to the fore. The 'Winners and Losers' target diagram (Martin, 2001: 214) can be used with seven- to 11-year-old children, as Martin has suggested, to widen discussion of the impact of products on the environment. You can ask children to consider their personal views and also the views of other consumers (users), and to think about the impact on the public, the manufacturer or designer (Howe *et al.*, 2001). This is, as Davies argues, an ideal opportunity to value and understand products from different cultures: 'They learn to value, respect and celebrate diversity. Products and technologies are considered in their context rather than seen as exotic or unusual. Products are presented with the story of precisely where they come from, who made them and why so that its value can be understood.' (Davies, 2004: 2)

Because of increasing public awareness of issues of sustainability, creative teachers can draw on many more resources to plan inventive design and technology projects that touch on global issues around the world and look at design and technology from a multicultural perspective (Brand, 2000).

Case study: a multicultural cross-curricular week with design and technology activities

Read the case study and reflect on the questions below.

- What sort of design and technology activities may have resulted from this event?
- Which other subjects and areas of the curriculum are covered?

A useful follow-up activity may be to research the designs and artefacts from one of the countries listed.

The context: an inner city school, 48% minority ethnic children. The aim was to foster cultural awareness and also celebrate the diverse culture of the school. A multicultural week was started in the Foundation stage and soon became a whole-school event with many vibrant activities across the school.

Case study (continued)

Multicultural Week workshops involved:

- whole-school assembly, including an introduction to the week, with each class representative talking about their chosen multicultural theme.
- Indian dance workshop: performance to the whole school
- African storyteller workshop: involving parents and children
- African experience: Adorn Africa – bean-making workshop
- evening band, with food from around the world.

Classes were provided with the resources needed and chose countries which represented children and staff in the school.

Activities included:

- Foundation stage: Looking at art/artefacts, food, music, religion, story-telling and dance
- Year 1: The African Continent
- Year 2: The Caribbean Countries
- Year 3: Ireland and Scotland
- Year 4: Italy
- Year 5: North and South America
- Year 6: Egypt.

Key factors to making this a success:

1. Involve parents in the activities to provide positive role models.
2. Advertise the event to a wider audience and get the local press involved.
3. Plan well ahead.
4. Seek suggestions and ideas from all stakeholders.
5. Always complete an evaluation for the next year's activity.
6. Involve a wide variety of specialists.

Food

Food as a material for designing and making has many exciting possibilities for using a very familiar material. Grouping foods and examining their sources leads to the introduction of the concepts of healthy eating and balanced diets. Recent national and international concerns in relation to health in the population and dietary guidelines have led to a variety of high-profile initiatives. Interventions, such as pressure for amendments to policy on school meals, the UK government green paper 'Every Child Matters' (DfES, 2003), and the Healthy Schools Initiative, have implications for teachers of design and technology, and for the subject in the curriculum. Design and technology has significant contributions to make to *being healthy* and *staying safe* (two of the five outcomes specified in 'Every Child Matters').

Which food-making activities are suitable for primary classrooms?
Children love to taste and evaluate the sensory qualities of foods. Product analysis should be part of design and technology at all key stages, so teachers can legitimately bring food tasting into lessons. It is essential, however, to inform parents prior to such activities taking place, so that problems with allergies, or preferences for cultural or religious reasons, are avoided. Food tasting is sometimes used as a precursor to designing and making: for instance a tasting of commercial yogurts prior to the children designing and making their own yogurt. Such activities help develop design ideas and subject-specific vocabulary, especially adjectives and sensory vocabulary.

Involvement in sorting and classifying tools, selecting equipment and considering safety measures also has rich potential for learning. A great deal of subject-specific and technical terminology can be taught; for example, sieve, spatula, chopping tools, squeezing, mixing. There are opportunities for links with mathematics in weighing and measuring. Teachers should avoid using non-food equipment (i.e. maths weighing scales) for food, as there is a danger of cross-contamination. Rather, the specialist equipment for food should be stored in separate containers. If resources are to be shared among classes, a trolley may be useful for storage.

Health and safety

Teachers need to help children learn safe use of tools and equipment such as saws and pliers, wire strippers and drills, and to become self-sufficient in assessing their own risks. However, teachers' subject knowledge and expertise may need supplementing to enable them to develop greater confidence and assurance. There are useful videos to support skill development, and many equipment suppliers have developed their own guides. The outcome should be that children learn to assess the risks themselves and take appropriate precautions.

Few of the tools and equipment used by pupils offer more risk to them than food preparation. There are not only the sharp tools, but also the serious problem of contamination by bacteria, since the food they handle and prepare is going to be eaten. Clearly common sense dictates that appropriate precautions are in place prior to food designing and preparation to make sure that the hazard of bacterial contamination is minimized. Guidance should be sought. It is important also that children are involved in personal and work space preparation, and can learn to take responsibility for their own safety. Good practice involves having tools available that are suitable: sharp knives for cutting up fruit and vegetables are safer than blunt ones as they require less effort and are less liable to slip. However, the teacher identifies the hazard and has to control the risk by teaching the children how to hold food using a fork or 'fingers like little claws', or with older children, the hand as a bridge.

It is common sense to avoid metal graters and instead use plastic flat graters for small children. Identification of the hazard of heat in ovens and hotplates often makes teachers take the safest route to avoid risk altogether by putting food into and removing it from ovens for children, sometimes even taking food away to cook it elsewhere. Not only is it disappointing for children to miss the excitement of seeing their food cooking and just cooked, but it can remove ownership of the making process.

Evaluating products

Any kind of product from a design and make activity can provide a relevant focus for critical judgements. Children will often be able to say what they like about the model they have made: this is the beginning of evaluating, as they can then go on to consider what they would like to change or add to their product, i.e. put a 'value' on certain features that could be improved. The critical thinking skills involved need to be encouraged and developed from a young age. Even at secondary school level, children find it difficult to formulate critical ideas.

Children will need much practice at evaluating against specific criteria: the objectives for the task or the design brief for the project should contain sufficient specific criteria, or you could even use the specifications that they have devised for their product. To use such criteria widens the scope of objective evaluation, focuses on rational judgements, and prevents the evaluation becoming personal criticism.

They can be given opportunities to practise the skills of evaluation by looking at existing products. Familiar objects such as clothing, trainers, pencil cases or yogurts can be used as a product analysis exercise. They might look at how it is made, identify the materials and component colours chosen and consider why these are appropriate. Children may be able to consider the form the product takes and its function, including its aesthetic aspects, and perhaps also its sustainability.

Inclusive practices

Inclusive practices are a key consideration in design and technology. Your design and technology activities may have to be modified: tools, materials, design activities, choice of foods and so on demand prior research into children's needs. The following strategies have been identified (DfEE, 1999) to overcome any potential barriers to learning in design and technology:

- alternative tasks to overcome any difficulties arising from specific religious beliefs held in relation to the ideas or experiences they are expected to represent
- alternative or adapted activities to overcome difficulties with manipulating tools, equipment or materials – for example, the use of computer-aided design and manufacture (CAD/CAM) to produce quality products or the assistance of others to carry out activities according to the instructions of the pupil
- specific support so pupils can engage in practical activities – for example, technological aids such as talking scales, jigs for cutting, kettle tipping devices, or specialist ICT software to help with sequencing and following instructions
- opportunities to communicate through means other than writing or drawing and help to record or translate design ideas into drawings
- opportunities to work in ways that avoid contact with materials to which pupils may be allergic
- time and opportunity to use non-visual means to gain understanding about, and to evaluate, different products and to use this information to generate ideas
- sufficient time to complete the range of work – for example, by doing shorter assignments, by combining experience in more than one material in an assignment (based on DfEE, 1999: 36).

However, you will still need to ensure that all children have as broad an experience in designing and making as possible.

Assessment

How and *when* to assess the children's progress are crucial decisions that all teachers need to build into their planning. In a busy classroom, teachers are constantly assessing progress in an ongoing way, providing targeted support for any children struggling with the activity. In design and technology the centrality of process (Figure 3.1), including evaluation, a skill that is crucial to success in the subject, means that design and technology provides an ideal context for self-assessment.

The assessment of pupils' working processes and their product outcomes is undertaken to provide information for both teachers and pupils. It is best used to give immediate feedback to the pupils and other colleagues and to help plan and modify the teaching and learning in subsequent activities. Children show their involvement in assessment of their own progress in knowledge and skills by adapting and modifying their ideas. Self-assessment followed by target setting can be incorporated into lessons, perhaps in a discussion in the plenary; with older children it could be an individual activity, with time allowed for reflection and notes in their coursework folder. Research (Black and Wiliam, 1998; Black, 2003) has highlighted the value to children of 'metacognition', including setting targets for their own progress. In design and technology, this means that teachers' and children's ongoing assessment of progress is crucial. Effective assessments for learning would include: effective use of questioning; observations of children during teaching and while they are working; holding discussions with children; analysing work and reporting to children; conducting tests and giving quick feedback and engaging children in the assessment process.

Conclusion

The enjoyment children experience when doing design and technology should allow them to enhance their designing skills, allow them to make quality products, and ensure that they are allowed to choose materials and equipment safely. In this way the learning process will progress them towards achievable and worthwhile goals. The teacher will need to inspire and motivate, setting appropriate challenges to include all children in the wonders of discovery and solving problems. It is often a mutual learning exercise for teachers and children: this subject of design and technology is a creative part of the teaching and learning in primary school.

Note

1. The National Curriculum for England, in the programmes of study, section 5 (Breadth of study), identifies three key sorts of learning activity: (a) product analysis; (b) focused tasks; and (c) design and make assignments. These provide children with a variety of challenges to enhance their learning, and the versatile teacher will be able to build each of these into units of work..

References

Armitage, R. and Armitage, D. (1994), *The Lighthouse Keeper's Lunch*. London: Scholastic.

Barlex, D. (2001), *Primary Solutions in Design and Technology*. Wellesbourne: Design and Technology Association.

Bee, G., Boyle, D. *et al.* (1991), *Humpty's Big Day*. Cambridge: Cambridge University Press.

Black, P. and Wiliam, D. (1998), *Inside the Black Box: raising standards through classroom assessment*. London: King's College London School of Education.

Black, P. J. (2003), *Assessment for Learning: putting it into practice*. Buckingham: Open University Press.

Bradshaw, J. (1997), 'Using water play to support designing and making in the early years.' *Journal of Design and Technology Education*, 2 (2). Wellesbourne, DATA.

Brand (2000), *Toying with Technology [Multimedia]: A Resource for Design and Technology with a Global*

Perspective. Edinburgh: Scotdec.

Carle, E. (1970), *The Very Hungry Caterpillar*. London: Penguin.

Clarke, C. (2003), Foreword, in DfES, *Excellence and Enjoyment: A Strategy for Primary Schools*. London: DfES Publications.

Cross, A. (1998), *Coordinating Design and Technology Across the Primary School*. London: Falmer Press.

Design And Technology Association (DATA) (1999), *DATA Helpsheets for Year 2000 and Beyond*. Wellesbourne: DATA.

DATA (2002), *Design and Technology Primary Lesson Plans: Based on the QCA Schemes of Work*. Wellesbourne: DATA.

DATA (2005), *Primary Subject-leader's File*. Wellesbourne: DATA

Davies, D. and Howe, A. (2005), 'Creativity in Primary Design and Technology', in A. Wilson, *Creativity in Primary Education*. London: Learning Matters.

Davies, L. T. (2004). 'Developing responsible citizenship', www.foodinschools.org/curriculum/pdfs/developing_responsible_citizenship.pdf (accessed 7 April 2006).

DES (1990), *Technology in the National Curriculum*. London: HMSO.

DfEE (1999), *The National Curriculum: Handbook for Primary Teachers in England*. London: HMSO.

DfES (2003), *Every Child Matters*. London: TSO.

DfES (2007), *National Curriculum in Action*. www.ncaction.org.uk (accessed 17 July 2007).

Egan, B. A. (1995), *How do children perceive the activity of drawing?* IDATER 95 Loughborough University of Technology.

Fasciato, M. (2002), 'Designing – what does it mean at Key Stage 1 and 2?' in S. Sayers, B. Barnes and J. Morley (eds), *Issues in Design and Technology Teaching*. London: RoutledgeFalmer.

Hope, G. (2004), *Teaching Design and Technology 3–11: The Essential Guide for Teachers*. London: Continuum.

Howe, A., Davies, D. and Ritchie, R. (2001), *Primary Design and Technology for the Future: Creativity, Culture and Citizenship*. London: David Fulton.

Jinks, D. (2000), *Structures*. Huddersfield: EduVision.

Kimbell, R., Stables, K., Wheeler, T., Wosniak, A. and Kelly, V. (1991), *The Assessment of Performance in Design and Technology: The Final Report of the APU Design and Technology Project 1985–1991*. London: SEAC.

Martin, M. (2001), 'Values and attitudes in design and technology', in S. Sayers, B. Barnes and J. Morley (eds), *Issues in Design and Technology Teaching*. London: RoutledgeFalmer.

Mason, R. and Houghton, N. (2002), 'The educational value of making', in S. Sayers, B. Barnes and J. Morley (eds), *Issues in Design and Technology Teaching*. London: RoutledgeFalmer.

NACCCE (1999), *All Our Futures: Creativity, Culture and Education*. London: DfEE Publications.

Office for Standards in Education (Ofsted) (1999), *A Review of Primary Schools in England, 1994 –1998*. London: Ofsted Publications.

Sayers, S. (2002), 'Issues in planning design and technology at Key Stages 1 and 2', in S. Sayers, B. Barnes and J. Morley (eds), *Issues in Design and Technology Teaching*. London: RoutledgeFalmer.

Sayers, S., Barnes, B. and Morley, J. (eds) (2002), *Issues in Design and Technology Teaching*. London,

RoutledgeFalmer.

SCAA (1997), *Expectations in Design and Technology at Key Stages 1 and 2.* London: SCAA.

Taylor, R. and Andrews, G. (1993), *The Arts in the Primary School*. London: Falmer Press.

Williams, P. and Jinks, D. (1985), *Design and Technology 5 –12*. London: Falmer Press.

Wilson, A. (ed.) (2005), *Creativity in Primary Education*. Exeter: Learning Matters.

Design and Technology: Beyond the Curriculum

4

Su Sayers

Chapter Outline

'Design is directed toward human beings. To design is to solve human problems by identifying them and executing the best solution.' Ivan Chermayeff, 1997

Introduction

This chapter considers the ways in which design and technology teaching can go beyond the areas touched on in the previous chapter, by exploring in more depth and using more examples of the kinds of project work children can engage in, both during times which are designated as design and technology, but also where an activity will offer opportunities for delivery as a cross-curricular topic. This chapter will help you select appropriate and creative ways to use resources in the classroom, including ICT, and see opportunities for using time in literacy lessons to introduce design and technology skills, concepts and vocabulary. The issues of embedding citizenship and sustainable design and technology into the experience of children are developed, as well as the benefits and constraints that come from working outside the normal school setting. By reading this chapter and reflecting on the research, you should have more ideas for ways to lead the subject effectively in your school, perhaps in partnerships with outside agencies. Since a leadership role often involves managing the transition between age phases and schools, where differences in expectations and subject delivery can sometimes impede the progress of children's development, ways to smooth this process are looked at. By studying the chapter, and engaging with the case studies, you will develop your ability to argue a stronger case for the subject as an essential component of the school curriculum.

Designing and making activities: project work in different materials

The essential purposes of project work in designing and making are to provide opportunities for children to design, make and evaluate quality products, while learning to become capable and creative as innovators. The flourishing of capability has been a focus of debate in the subject (Morley, 2002; Sayers *et al.*, 2002). Design and technology 'capability' implies skilled designing and making, but also essential is the synthesis of knowledge of the best way to shape and form materials accurately, independently and with confidence. Children naturally use the interaction of hand and mind (Kimbell *et al.*, 1991) in a dynamic and progressive way. While the product is important as an indicator of prowess and capability to both the teacher and the child, engendering self-esteem and confidence, the journey (the child's to-ing and fro-ing through the model) (Hope, 2004) is equally as important as evidence of the children's level of capability in solving problems and generating ideas, and planning. These are sometimes considered to be the key transferable skills children acquire through the subject: as life skills they can help the child approach any decision-making situation in a logical way.

Design and technology project ideas and examples

Teachers have successfully tried out a wealth of project ideas in primary schools using a full range of compliant and resistant materials: from crazy hats to jewellery, and from motorized models to aerodynamic kites. Exemplar lesson plans are available to support units of work (Design And Technology Association [DATA], 2002). You too need to look for ideas and inspiration for projects, in books, shops and museums: keep notes and ideas, and your list of possible projects will grow as you become more experienced with your class, and as you realize what motivates the children and what is feasible with the resources you can acquire. Funding rarely allows teachers to purchase as freely as they would like, so investigate your local resources (including donations from parents, local shops and businesses) and where you can obtain recycled materials.

- **Textiles**. Excitement is a key part of using textiles. The variety of texture or surface quality (fluffy, shiny, smooth, crisp) will appeal to children's senses. Soft materials that will respond to stretching and shaping will make covers for boxes. Colour and pattern can make a box look like a cuddly animal, or a fantastic sea monster. Projects such as slippers, puppets, money containers, all allow this excitement to be channelled into the design and construction of a functional item, for themselves, or as a gift for someone else, where the technology of the fabric can be discussed. Is the fabric closely or loosely constructed? Is it going to tear/fray/wear out too quickly? Fabric with pre-formed holes (Binca weave) is often used for learning to sew and practising stitches: it is useful but is a singularly unappealing base material. Non-woven fabrics, such as colourful felts, are more appealing and easy for younger children because they do not fray, and their greater rigidity means they lie flat rather than curling at the edges. Puppet design leads to performance ideas, linking with drama lessons and language development.
- **Resistant materials**. Wood, wire and plastic in all shapes and sizes can be used creatively in designing and making. Teachers will need to demonstrate safe use of tools such as junior hacksaws, pliers and hand drills, and be sure that children know the importance of holding the materials firmly in a bench hook or vice before cutting or drilling (NAAIDT, 1992). Older children are surprised that triangles are more stable structures than rectangles, and that frameworks, when reinforced with triangles, will withstand stress and strain: a group challenge of making a bridge to cross a 50cm ravine, to support a toy car, limited to ten art straws and one metre of sticky tape allows nine- or ten-year-old children to be guided to find this out for themselves. Construction kits can be used to help children invent structures that are stable and balanced, and to incorporate mechanisms to make their models work (such as gears, pulleys, wheels and axles). The teaching can draw out the link with scientific principles, for instance mass/force/strength relationships, and go on to produce 3D products.
- **Graphic materials**. Colours and textures of paper and card, including tissue paper, cellophane, doyleys, corrugated card and cardboard rolls offer variety which can itself be inspirational and enchanting. Many children would respond to the richness of a careful collection of A5 pieces of paper or card, to make and then decorate a fairy-tale castle, or a monster's lair. Moving pictures, which use card levers and sliders to make something happen, focused on a theme such as 'under the sea', or a message such as 'healthy lifestyles', might be used to design and make a class book, or posters, or greetings cards for celebrations. The study of buildings (perhaps linking with a history topic) leads to ideas for structures that provide shelter for people, or animals, where children's construction is based on re-designing an existing cardboard box. An extension of this idea led one teacher to focus a unit of work on 'robots that help us': children used hinges and levers in their robots and some incorporated circuits for lights or buzzers.
- **Systems and control**. Systems, mechanical, electrical and organizational, may inspire a design and make project. Technology fascinates and intrigues many children. They respond well to the challenge

of making a system with input (battery), process (circuit and switch) and output (bulb or buzzer, or electric motor), using wire-strippers and other tools safely, to design and build their own torch or a picture with lights. Mechanical systems using levers and linkages may involve construction kits, or wood or graphic materials. Older children can add lights, or a motor with pulley, to their fairground ride (perhaps a carousel, made from dowel and card disks). Links with science lessons need to be planned and made explicit, of course: design and technology often gives children the opportunity to apply science learning in a different context. Construction kits provide a way to link with ICT to make models work by controlling them via the computer. The school needs hardware in the form of computer control boxes and software: a financial investment to benefit designing and making which is linked to the real world of children's everyday experience of computer-controlled toys and appliances. Teachers comment that new ideas for computer control tend to become more user-friendly with each technological development.

- **Food technology**. Where children are designing and making with food, hygiene precautions need to be the first consideration, focusing on the ingredients, personal hygiene, equipment and the work surfaces (Farrell, 2007). Storage and purchase issues mean that the organization of a food session involves careful planning ahead of time, including sending letters home to get permission, in case there are religious or personal constraints on using certain foods or any children have allergies. You can exploit the potential of seasonal fruit and vegetables, to give opportunities for children to design their own variants on a basic fruit smoothie or pasta salad recipe. Product analysis where children taste breads eaten by different cultural groups leads neatly into the making of dough products. Watching the physical and chemical changes as the foods are combined and cooked links with science and health knowledge. Learning about where in the world the foods come from can provoke discussion of food miles, and why it may be better to source foods locally and in season.

Organizing design and technology resources

The resources for project work need to be organized effectively so that their potential is not overlooked: sorting shapes, sizes and colours for example. Children can help with this by sorting collections of resources such as card wheels, felt squares and clothes pegs into separate, labelled plastic drawers or crates that will stack or slot into a cupboard or trolley.

All hold potential for skills development and creativity but children will also learn that resources may be subject to squandering by inappropriate use. It is important to emphasize the three Rs of sustainability in materials: 'Reduce, Re-use, Recycle' (Harper, Rowland *et al.*, 1997). Children do not appreciate the cost, unless this is part of the lesson: projects for older children may include costing as an element of the specification.

Resources can be rich in potential, and can come from recycled packaging or other materials. For instance, 'Joseph's Technicolour Dream-Coat' (National-Curriculum-in-Action, 2007), made from a template pattern to fit a soft toy, can use assorted fabric scraps decorated with remnants of ribbon and braid. The ribbon and appliqué panels are stitched in place, or glued if necessary, before the coat is sewn together. The children learn in the process the skill of planning ahead and the need to allow extra width for seams.

Design and technology in a wider context

Project work allows children to appreciate and know more about the design of garments, toys, tools, foods and so on from different cultures, times and places, and therefore has clear potential for widening children's horizons, learning to respect diversity and cultivating cross-cultural understanding (NACCCE, 1999). The sensitivity to, and participation in, community events is an aspect of responsibility as a member of the community, and teachers might foster this in design and technology by planning activities where younger children make gifts to send to a charity or plan a family assembly with song, dance and masks/costumes, or produce a puppet show. Invitations, made in advance, are a good link with literacy teaching, which might also involve the children in designing and making the posters or invitation cards, perhaps also using ICT. Teachers of older children might have reservations about reinforcing racial stereotypes through a token focus on one culture or region and its artefacts and/or foods and should not overlook debates about anti-racism and prejudice.

Global awareness

An increasing worldwide concern about global issues requires teachers to set contexts and provide resources to deal effectively with global citizenship in the classroom. The (draft) design and technology National Curriculum for Wales emphasizes sustainability issues:

> 'Learners should be made aware of human achievements and the big ideas that have shaped the world. They should be encouraged to be creative and innovative in their designing and making while being made aware of issues relating to sustainability and environmental issues in the twenty-first century.' Department for Education, Lifelong Learning and Skills (2006: 11)

Published resources and lesson plan ideas in the literature (Young and Commins, 2002; Oxfam, 2006) are mainly concerned with developing children's awareness of the plight of children like themselves, with a link to literacy and science. Others have practical ideas for things children can do, which can arguably make a long-term difference. Food is a popular focus: it is relatively easy to obtain examples of food from around the world for children to see, smell and taste. They can evaluate products such as breads from different cultures, and then begin to use this to devise their own innovative bread products (Farrell, 2007; Oxfam, 2007). The 'Every Child Matters' agenda in the UK (DfES, 2003) has prompted agencies to look at the way they are able to contribute to health and well-being. British children with notoriously poor diets have particularly high rates of obesity, and this pattern is also prevalent in the USA. Studies have found around 25 per cent of UK school children are significantly overweight or obese (British Medical Association, 2005), and that more than two-thirds of Americans are overweight or obese (Department of Health and Human Services, 2007).

In general, children and adolescents are eating more salt, sugar and saturated fats than is recommended and not enough fruit and vegetables. Attention has also focused on adolescents' high consumption of fast food and soft drinks (EPPI-centre, 2003). The problem is most acute for those who are born into low-income families, with inadequate income and inadequate access to healthy food making it much more difficult to improve the diet. There is increasing evidence that adult susceptibility to disease is associated with nutrition in early childhood and adolescence, and therefore early intervention is vital (British Medical Association, 2005).

Some would argue (Steuer and Marks, 2006) that improving the quality of food in schools is an opportunity for a sustainability 'double dividend': there would be health benefits for children who had access to good quality, locally-sourced, seasonal food, and this would also reduce the 'food miles' and therefore the environmental impact of food production.

It might be possible to arrange visits to a spice importer, a restaurant or supermarket to enrich children's knowledge and understanding of foods (QCA, 1997). In Howe *et al.* (2001) the dangers of a tokenistic approach to some design and technology work associated with food and festivals is acknowledged: 'the spiritual significance of light to Divali needs to be an important focus of such work, rather than an excuse for some designing and making' (p. 54). All such festivals (including Christmas, Hanukkah, Eid, New Year) can give a focus for the designing and making of cards and gifts but the teacher needs to be careful not to overlook the real cultural meaning behind the event.

Cross-curricular themes

Embedding language, literacy and mathematics in design and technology lessons is now becoming accepted as good practice, with teachers feeling that learning in all subjects is enhanced. Citizenship education, while a relatively new area of learning with a cross-curricular focus in England, has had a long tradition in France. Other countries (for example, Australia) devolve curriculum policy to states. Within design and technology children can research, using knowledge of materials and properties, and in the process raise levels of awareness about community responsibilities. For instance polar fleece fabrics, made from recycled plastic drinks bottles (polyethylene terephthalate [PET]), are an alternative to expensive landfill sites for disposing of waste. Some schools have successfully linked projects with local community issues, designing systems for recycling school waste paper, or devising innovative litter bins with lids (Department for Education, Lifelong Learning and Skills [DELLS], Wales, 2006): a useful focus for a debate on social, economic and political issues when designing products (Howe *et al.*, 2001).

Case study: designing for the local community

Read the case study and reflect on the questions below.

- Which lessons have the most potential for designing and creativity?
- What skills and knowledge are being learned, beyond technology?
- Think of materials (other than textiles), which could be used for a communal creation. Where could it be situated: indoors/outdoors/on a wall/on the floor?
- Consider the evaluation of the finished project work, and the process: how would you plan for it?

Making a community banner

This project took place in a small village school, with a mixed age range of children. The nursery children (aged three to five) did the printing; older children were involved in quilting and decorating the printed squares. Parents helped with sewing it together.

Planned links were made with creativity, art, science and community.

Previous experience: Prior to the lessons children were able to look at and handle cotton fabrics with decorative flower and leaf motifs including Indian and African designs, and William Morris art nouveau fabrics. The bold colours and strong shapes gave them ideas for putting shapes together and for regular repeats. Patterns on wrapping paper were looked at too.

Lesson 1: Drawing round the outline of a petal or a leaf; enlarging if necessary on a photocopier to approximately 8cm diameter; using this as a template pattern to make printing blocks using wood blocks and foam.

Lesson 2: Practising with printing blocks on paper; trying out repeating patterns and creating symmetrical designs.

Lesson 3: Printing on a length of white or pastel-coloured fabric using paints or fabric colours, a communal activity. The printed fabric was cut into manageable sections (20cm squares).

Lessons 4–6: Children decorated fabric squares further, using quilting and appliqué, with additions such as sequins and beads sewn or glued in place, or using fabric crayons or fabric sublimation dyes.

Lesson 7: Referring to Indian and African prints which often have a border and a central panel, designs were produced for the central panel based on greetings (welcome, willkommen, akwaba) and on a maypole as an emblem of community festivities.

Case study (continued)

Finally: Teachers and parents helped with pinning, tacking and machine-sewing the pieces together, completing a banner for the school hall. The completed banner is shown in Figure 4.1 a–c.

Figure 4.1a: Fabric printed by 3–4-year-olds; the embroidery and appliqué by 7–10-year-olds; then the quilting by 11-year-olds and above

Figure 4.1b: Beginning to assemble the banner with adult help

Case study (continued)

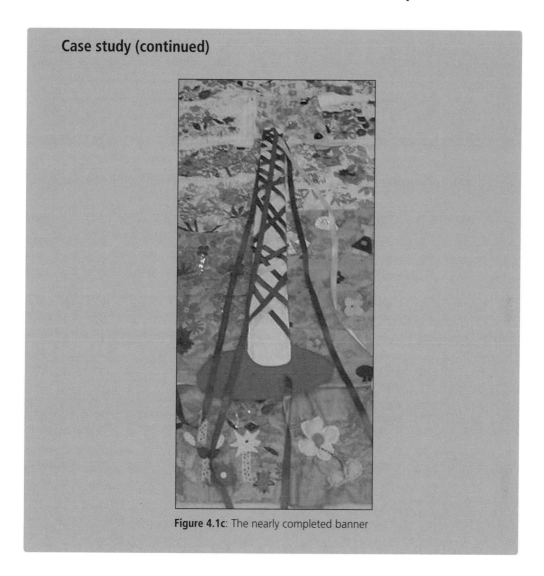

Figure 4.1c: The nearly completed banner

English and design and technology

The emphasis placed on the core subjects means that opportunities to link the teaching of English with design and technology activities need to be utilized wherever possible. Communication is a purposeful activity, central to the process of making meaning, and many teachers now recognize that it needs to be supported and encouraged across the curriculum. The practical nature of designing and making involves children in communicating with one another, as well as with teachers and other adult helpers: hence oracy, in terms of speaking and listening, is fundamental. Compensation for reduced time for foundation subjects has come from teachers using design and technology contexts more effectively in literacy lessons to introduce and develop vocabulary.

While the UK government's focus on literacy has formulated the principles and the practice, the design and technology association has produced materials to support teachers in their role as teachers of literacy (DATA, 1999). This is not to diminish the effectiveness of pre- and non-verbal forms of communication, however, where teachers demonstrate and model. The nature of the subject matter in design and technology demands that these are also vital strategies, across all age ranges, to help establish skilful use of materials, tools and equipment.

Bearne (2002) has criticized the narrow focus of government guidelines with their emphasis on correct speech, and on written grammar, spelling and punctuation.

'The reservation about such a requirement is that its scope is narrow, threatening to restrict any shared understanding about language to *language as effective communication*, more valued for accuracy than for conviction, critical awareness or opinion. It also lays much more emphasis on teaching than on learning, suggesting a straightforward delivery model of curriculum content.' (Bearne, 2002: 24)

Vocabulary of ideas

The language of designing involves children in using and understanding the names of components and equipment. A project with seven-year-old children on making a vehicle necessitates correct use of words such as axle, chassis and wheel but, as Bearne (*op. cit.*) points out, it should not hamper children's discussion of processes that defy precise terminology. Extracts from children's conversations as they work demonstrate a more 'flexible' use of vocabulary:

'Does this thingy stop the wheel falling off?' (referring to a rubber tap washer); 'What if we use one of those card bits to put the rod things through?' (referring to an axle support).

The children's language may be criticized for lack of precision but is evidence of progressive teamwork and problem-solving. They are clearly formulating ideas: and that is a key point in design and technology.

There are so many opportunities for language and expressive skills in analysing the world around them: this can be products, places, and environments linked to the design and technology within them. A 'handling collection' in the classroom can provide a useful set of products to analyse in this way. You could easily collect some of your own objects together, with the help of children bringing things from home: plastic bottles, packaging, onion or fruit nets, left-over knitting wool and fabrics, that would have good potential for language development and making.

Direct experience through a focused walk around the school or neighbourhood to look at details of house designs, roofs, doors and windows, and to describe the street signs, the street furniture or the playground equipment, is useful research for their designs.

Writing, communication and ICT

Project design work has potential for a range of language and literacy development opportunities, annotating diagrams and design ideas for instance to explain the thinking process. In a puppet project, children will learn a great deal about designing and making quality creative products, and teachers can also draw out the language in evaluating the project outcome. A project evaluation sheet in the form of a writing frame would prompt for descriptive words about appearance, taste and texture, and justification of suitability for the purpose (I think…would like it because…). A rich field of value terms can be explored: children may need a word bank. Older children might need to be encouraged to extend reflection on learning and improvements.

There are many links with ICT, from using word-processing to enhance the look of a designed product, creating advertising copy or a logo for a product, using a digital camera, to using ICT to control a toy made from a construction kit. The key thing to be aware of is ensuring that ICT is used appropriately, and only where it will enhance the design and technology objectives. The internet is a resource often under-used in design projects, but now with the whole-class use of an interactive whiteboard (IWB) it can provide an excellent research source for projects. Children, using individual PCs, can document their design progress using flow-chart software, and using simulation software with short animations. Free-to-download resources are available (e.g. Crocodile-clips-elementary, 2007). This brings the world of machines and mechanisms to life to help children understand how they work.

Planning for transitions across phases of education

Some children experience a setback in their development in design and technology when they start a new school, especially secondary school. It is widely recognized (Kimbell, Stables *et al.*, 1996; DfES, 2005) that the experience of design and technology at ages 11 to 16 is often radically different from that in the primary age range of five to 11. There is often wide variation in design and technology at primary schools, so some children have vastly different levels of capability when they move schools. Galton, Gray *et al.* (1999) highlighted the need for schools (and therefore teachers) to have a sustained focus on the needs of pupils as they transfer from primary to secondary schooling, and even from one phase to another in primary, especially where the change of schools or teachers is greatly different. The research by Goldsmiths University (Kimbell, Stables *et al.*, 1996) showed that some of the key differences are in:

- teaching and learning styles
- classroom organization and size
- language and conventions used
- assessment and recording systems
- resources, tools, equipment and materials
- time available and the way it is structured
- use of non-specialist teachers.

Linked schools should pay particular attention to their similarities and differences in relation to the above and their teaching of design and technology.

In the UK and beyond, to prevent the 'glitch' at transition, initiatives have been set up to support children (New South Wales, 2007; Nicholls and Gardner, 1999). As a teacher in a feeder primary school, your class could visit their new secondary schools to meet staff and sample a design and technology lesson. Sometimes a specialist design and technology teacher runs a project in the primary school so children become familiar with specialist equipment and ways of working.

Beyond the classroom, beyond the school

Where teachers, in conjunction with senior staff and the subject-leader in their school, have arranged out-of-school events, it serves to broaden horizons of the children, and give them a wider creative focus for their designing. Visits need to be planned carefully and venues visited first to complete a risk assessment. Although this is time-consuming and there is a financial cost involved, most would agree about the enormous benefits: children will look forward to the visit, as well as discuss it for ages afterwards. Useful places to consider are:

- a museum, for example to handle toys from Victorian times and to dress up in the clothes of the era
- a science and technology museum to see machines from the past
- a museum shop to see typical souvenirs and promotional items
- a theatre to see front of house and backstage
- a zoo or wildfowl centre to see direction signs and/or safety of facilities for different client groups
- a local children's nursery to examine toys and play equipment
- homes and buildings in the neighbourhood, looking at architectural details
- the local supermarket, builders' yard or garden centre

- the school kitchen
- another school to work together on a focused project
- behind the scenes at a tourist attraction.

Design and technology partnerships

Despite children's everyday contact with technological devices, design and technology in the real world is taken for granted and it is often difficult to help them really think about the social impact of technology on society and the designed environment. They are the future decision makers: are these children going to become the 'discriminating consumers' the UK National Curriculum intends? Industrial giants use technology to make profits for their shareholders: this is their *raison d'être*. Mass production, with economies of scale in production lines, increasingly takes place in the Far East, influenced by factors such as labour costs. There are no easy answers to the dilemmas: new technology may benefit one interest group over another, and it is usually under-privileged members of the population who lose out. Hope (2004) discusses the conflicting positions, suggesting ways in which older pupils can be encouraged to debate moral and ethical issues associated with technological 'progress'.

Another way of helping children to become more knowledgeable is to make links with people whose jobs involve science, technology and materials in different ways. Jobs as varied as hairdressing, catering, being a postal worker or an Olympic athlete, when used as a focus for a role-play corner for younger children, or a discussion or drama topic with older children, can provide opportunities for the design and technology teacher to help counter gendered stereotypes. For instance, the public perception of an engineer as a male, in oily overalls, is far from the truth: engineering involves designing, solving problems with machinery and materials, and can be a creative science, requiring multidisciplinary skills and teamwork. Hairdressers are artists and have to be creative designers who are also technically expert with dyes and techniques for cutting and shaping materials.

The stereotypes need to be challenged: these are future vocational sectors for both girls and boys, which design and technology may help them with. 'The rapid progress of technology means it's estimated that 60 per cent of the jobs that today's primary children will do have not yet been invented, so the capacity to be flexible and free-thinking will be increasingly important to their job prospects.' (Barrett, 2007: 3)

'Creative Partnerships' has provided a further new opportunity for partnerships with people and places. Manchester Metropolitan University's Creative Partnerships scheme (Barrett, 2007) builds on a network of artists and designers, to provide creative and energetic workshops for local primary school teachers and trainees, which are followed up by a week of activities in schools.

Case study: creative partnerships

Cornwall Local Authority's Edible Playgrounds project offered schools and communities the opportunity to design and create a garden in their school grounds. The idea was to reflect the place, the needs and wishes of the children involved, and connect with other inspirations, such as from school visits to other, great gardens. The children worked with creative people on their designs and they and school staff gained complete ownership and a sense of community and real engagement with their outside spaces.

Their stated objectives included the following:

- to raise awareness of the value of play and the need for environments conducive to play
- to improve the use of school playgrounds
- to encourage sensory and inclusive grounds and practice
- to develop the grounds as a resource for teaching AND as a teaching tool – this includes looking at curricular modules that can be effectively taught outside and what is needed in the grounds to facilitate this
- to encourage community and intergenerational involvement
- to raise awareness of produce/local sourcing and use
- to encourage environmental awareness and action as part of school ethos and community (and intergenerational) involvement.

The whole design process was child-led, focusing on sensory and inclusive elements, along with the potential for teaching the curriculum outdoors.

Pause to think

Having read the case study from Cornwall, give some thought to developing your own creative partnerships through carrying out the following activities (preferably in groups of four).

> **Example**
>
> - Find a local building or park
> - Draw it/photograph it
> - Think of ways to make it:
>   o in card/construction materials (scale, colour, use of ICT?)
>   o in food (cake, a salad, a pizza?)
>   o in fabrics (batik, embroidery, patchwork appliqué?)
> - Work in groups to design and make your own version of the place
> - Show others and gather their opinions.

Competitions

A further opportunity exists for out-of-school extra-curricular events in design and technology, associated with ICT and computer control technology: local and national competitions. There are national competitions based on, for example, robot design and construction and designing healthy contents for lunchboxes. This sort of focus may be motivational and inspire good designing, especially from gifted and talented children, but teachers will be aware of the dangers of too many competitive events: winning is not everything, and emphasis needs to be on 'taking part'.

Various multi-agency provider partnerships, such as English initiatives associated with food and health (Farrell, 2007; DfES, 2007), rely on outside funding where specialist food teachers, usually from local high schools, either train primary class teachers, or run practical food technology classes with the children. Following the training, the confidence, skills and knowledge they have gained then cascades back through each primary teacher's school.

Conclusion

This chapter has focused on suggesting ways to maximize your opportunities to plan design and technology experiences that challenge and excite children, and take them in a meaningful way on a journey of learning in a wider context.

> '...although we teach in a specialised field called design and technology, we continuously contribute within that field to the general education of all pupils – their literacy, thinking capacities, socialisation, communication skills and so on. Thus we...contribute to our pupils' education in design and technology per se, to their education for life in society, even beyond

their school years; and between these two, to their education as future users and creators of designed and technological products.' (Keirl, 2002: 191)

Keirl defines a vital purpose for design and technology, supporting its value to children's development. He believes that the credibility of the subject, and its place in the school curriculum, depends on having an ethical rationale. The work you do with your class in design and technology has implications for children far beyond the products they design and make. Planning your teaching and resources in an ethical way, to incorporate different and readily available materials, opportunities for cross-curricular work, and sustainability and citizenship, will consolidate and extend the design and technology curriculum.

References

Barrett, N. (2007), 'Creative Partnerships: Manchester and Salford', www.ioe.mmu.ac.uk/cue/seminars/BARRETT%20Urban%20seminar1.doc (accessed 21 July 2007).

Bearne, E. (2002), *Making Progress in Writing*. London: RoutledgeFalmer.

British Medical Association. (2005), 'Preventing Childhood Obesity'. A report from the BMA Board of Science. web.bma.org.uk/ap.nsf/Content/ChildObesity?OpenDocument&Highlight=2,obesity#refs.

Chermayeff, I. (1997), in P. Meggs, *Six Chapters in Design*. San Francisco: Chronicle Books.

CreativePartnerships (2004), www.creative-partnerships.com/projects.

Crocodile-clips-elementary (2007), www.crocodile-clips.com/s3_4.htm (accessed 21 July 2007).

Design And Technology Association (DATA) (1999), *DATA Helpsheets for Year 2000 and Beyond. Wellesbourne:* DATA

DATA (2002), *Design and Technology Primary Lesson Plans: based on the QCA schemes of work* Wellesbourne: DATA

Department for Education, Lifelong Learning and Skills (DELLS) (2006), *Education for Sustainable Development and Global Citizenship: A Strategy for Action.* Cardiff: Welsh Assembly Government.

DfES (2003), *Every Child Matters*. London: TSO.

DfES (2005), Foundation Subjects Design and Technology: Framework and Training Materials DVD. *Curriculum and Standards. Guidance: DfES 1973–2004 DVD.* London: TSO.

DfES (2007), *Food in Schools*. London: TSO.

Department of Health and Human Services (2007), 'US Obesity Trends 1985–2006'. www.cdc.gov/nccdphp/dnpa/obesity/trend/maps/ (accessed 3 July 2007).

EPPI-centre (2003), *Children and Healthy Eating – Final report*. London: Institute of Education.

Farrell, A. (2007), 'Principles of Primary Food Technology', www.foodforum.org.uk (accessed 21 May 2007).

Galton, M., Gray, J. *et al.* (1999), *The Impact of School Transitions and Transfers on Pupil Progress and Attainment*. London: DfEE.

Harper, P., Rowland, A. *et al.* (1997), *The Centre for Alternative Technology Guide Book*. Machynlleth: CAT Publications.

Hope, G. (2004), *Teaching Design and Technology 3–11: The Essential Guide for Teachers*. London: Continuum.

Howe, A., Davies, D. and Ritchie, R. (2001), *Primary Design and Technology for the Future: Creativity, Culture and Citizenship*. London: David Fulton.

Keirl, S. (2002), 'What has ethics to do with design and technology education?' in S. Sayers, B. Barnes and J. Morley, (eds), *Issues in Design and Technology Teaching*. London: RoutledgeFalmer.

Kimbell, R., Stables, K., Wheeler, T., Wosniak, A. and Kelly, V. (1991), *The Assessment of Performance in Design and Technology: The Final Report of the APU Design and Technology Project 1985–1991*. London: SEAC.

Kimbell, R., Stables, K. *et al.* (1996), *Understanding Practice in Design and Technology*. Buckingham: Open University Press.

Morley, J. (2002), 'How can we meet the challenges posed by a new model of practical scholarship?' in S. Sayers, B. Barnes and J. Morley, (eds), *Issues in Design and Technology Teaching*. London: RoutledgeFalmer.

NAAIDT (1992), *Make it Safe!: Safety Guidance for the Teaching of Design and Technology at Key Stages 1 and 2*. Chandlers Ford: National Association of Advisors and Inspectors of Design and Technology.

NACCCE (1999), *All our Futures: Creativity, Culture and Education*. London: DfEE Publications.

National-Curriculum-in-Action (2007), 'Joseph's coat project.' www.ncaction.org.uk/search/item.htm?id=1123.

New South Wales (2007), 'Primary-Secondary Transition Support Materials'. www.schools.nsw.edu.au/gotoschool/highschool/transitions/index.php (accessed 21 July 2007).

Nicholls, G., Gardner, J. (1999), *Pupils in Transition: Moving Between Key Stages*. London: Routledge.

Oxfam (2006), *Education for Global Citizenship: A Guide for Schools*. Oxford: Oxfam GB.

Oxfam (2007), 'Cool Planet', www.oxfam.org.uk/coolplanet/index.htm (accessed 21 July 2007).

QCA (1997), *Food in Schools: Ideas*. London: Qualifications and Curriculum Authority.

Sayers, S., Barnes, B. and Morley, J. (eds) (2002), *Issues in Design and Technology Teaching*. London, RoutledgeFalmer.

Steuer, N. T. and Marks, N. (2006), 'Review of the environmental dimension of children and young people's well-being', *A Report for the Sustainable Development Commission*. London: New Economics Foundation.

Young, M. and Commins, E. (2002), *Global Citizenship: The Handbook for Primary Teaching*. Cambridge: Chris Kington.

History: Teaching the Curriculum

Paul Bowen

'I've brought my granddad to be evidence in our history lesson. He knows all about the olden days.' (A Year 3 child introducing her grandfather to the class: part of an oral history project about children in World War Two)

Introduction

Currently, interest in history appears to be flourishing, at least at an adult level, with the growing popularity of historical sites, television documentaries and research into family histories. History in primary schools has also made exciting progress over the last two decades in terms of changing pedagogy. Emphasis has now shifted from traditional teaching passive children, to teaching the processes of history and encouraging children to develop historical skills as well as knowledge with greater opportunities for interactive work and independent learning. Ironically, despite these positive developments the status of history in primary schools has been under pressure. In the last 30 years in England there has been persistent discussion of history being 'in danger' in relation to the curriculum. It has become even more important, therefore, for primary teachers to have a clear understanding of history's value in the school curriculum and be able to convey this to interested parties such as children, parents and governors.

The place of history in the primary curriculum

What then can historical study contribute to a child's education? Learning about past events, communities and significant people can help children to make sense of and understand the world around them at the present time. It can help provide them with valuable insights into themselves and others. History is also important for making children aware of other countries and cultures both old and new. Given the current world political situation, there is an obvious need to promote an understanding of cultural diversity, and history is an ideal vehicle for this. By investigating past civilizations such as those of Ancient Egypt or the Romans children can recognize how these groups of people had very different lives from their own in terms of religion, economy, food, style of building and dress.

A key benefit of historical study is that it also promotes a valuable range of skills. Wood and Holden (1999) have neatly summarized these into the following seven categories: enquiry, communication, thinking, visual evidence, concepts, analysis, and recording. While some of these are distinctly historical, many are transferable, key skills of use across the curriculum and relevant to the world of work.

Historical enquiry is one of the most important and distinctive processes of the historian. Whether a five-year-old finding out about Edwardian seaside holidays from old photographs, or a postgraduate student analysing census data, searching for information from a range of sources, it is clearly an important skill. Children need to not only 'ask and answer questions about the past' (DfEE/QCA, 1999: 104) but also to think about the reliability of the evidence. Encouraging children to adopt a cautious and critical approach towards evidence will help them in their future lives when faced by a variety of media such as newspapers, television and the internet which may contain biased viewpoints.

Communication is another core activity within primary history and this can encompass a variety of activities, as a topic on Ancient Greece involving Year 5 children exemplifies. Outcomes included word-processed guides to aspects of Greek life. Role-play was used to show aspects of daily life and to help children explain some of the Greek myths. Model-making and art work allowed the class to show the creative aspects of Greek life such as their decorative vases and fresco work. Any history topic must provide a variety of opportunities for children to communicate their findings. Good history lessons should provide children with opportunities to discuss and explain issues, and present their ideas orally and visually as well as in written form.

Empathetic understanding is another valuable dimension of history. Exploring historical topics such as the Victorians introduces children to different ideas, viewpoints and ways of life. A common activity is for children to gain insight into schooling and the Victorians' beliefs in hard work, strictness and religion which permeated classroom life in the nineteenth century. Sands (2004) effectively shows how children can be introduced to an authentic Victorian school day and realize how the life of the Victorian schoolchild was very different from their own. In today's primary curriculum, there is increasing emphasis on the importance of thinking skills, and history can play a key role here. By using historical evidence such as some old kitchen artefacts, children may be involved in classifying, comparing, hypothesizing, remembering and deducting, all valuable thinking skills with transferable applications.

Planning

Long-term planning involves producing a history programme for the whole school, and the outcome of this process will usually be a scheme of work. This should outline the history content and skills to be covered across all year groups. It will also take into account the requirements of the prescribed curriculum for National Curriculum history (DfES/QCA, 1999). Responsibility for long-term planning will generally lie with the history subject-leader, but there clearly needs to be a teamwork approach so that other staff members can contribute their ideas and have ownership of the history programme. A history scheme of work, however, should be more than a list of units to be covered. It provides an opportunity to set out the policy and philosophy within history on issues such as differentiation, assessment, teaching strategies, out-of-school learning, citizenship or links with literacy, and should reflect the context and needs of the school. The local history of the area or proximity to significant heritage sites or museums will often influence a school's planning for history.

Medium-term planning involves taking individual units of work and developing teaching and learning activities for a period of half a term or a semester. Medium-term plans need to be well detailed, showing how the content is broken down into individual lessons and the key activities in each session. Another important feature of medium-term planning is to identify resources. History is a subject abundant in resources but identifying and locating these can be time-consuming and this stage of planning is the opportunity to do this. Medium-term planning will usually be undertaken by a group of teachers under the guidance of the history subject-leader. This has been much facilitated by the publication of many sample history units of work by QCA to support the National Curriculum (www.standards.dfes.gov.uk/schemes2/history).

Short-term planning involves the production of practical working documents for the teaching of individual lessons. Underpinning an effective history lesson plan is clarity over what the children will learn. Learning objectives need to be few in number, specific, achievable and with a clear focus on historical knowledge, skills and understanding. A good starting point for identifying objectives are the National Curriculum history programmes of study where the following five categories are clearly set out:

- chronological understanding
- knowledge and understanding of events, people and changes in the past
- historical interpretation
- historical enquiry
- organization and communication. (DfES/QCA, 1999: 104)

Examples of history lesson plans and learning objectives can be found in numerous publications such as Bowen and Hoodless (2006) and Hoodless (2006).

One of the dilemmas with planning is the level of detail in terms of documentation. Since the introduction of the National Curriculum and the influence of Ofsted, there has been great emphasis on written documentation, but a careful balance must be maintained. Planning should not be a bureaucratic chore.

Planning in history is fundamentally about devising stimulating lessons with imaginative approaches and resources. It is an opportunity for the teacher to be creative and original, producing learning activities in which they have some ownership. Over-planning can certainly be a real danger, as can planning too far in advance (Turner-Bisset, 2005). However, regular reviewing of teaching, adaptability and flexibility are all key components of good planning.

Teaching strategies

The selection of teaching strategies in history needs to be related to our own understanding of how children learn. Vygotsky, for example, stressed the importance of social interaction and the use of language to promote learning. The growing emphasis in history teaching on creating opportunities for speaking and listening, such as using small groups to discuss an artefact, links effectively to Vygotskian ideology. Gardner (1993) has emphasized the importance of recognizing pupils' multiple intelligences and the need for teachers to adopt approaches which accommodate these. Gardner initially identified seven categories of intelligence, namely intrapersonal, interpersonal, linguistic, musical-auditory, visual-spatial, logical-mathematical and bodily-kinaesthetic. Clearly some have more affinity with history, such as linguistic-verbal intelligence which covers activities such as writing, reading, speaking and listening, but even the logical-mathematical category is relevant in activities such as using timelines. Gardner's work has been influential in encouraging greater emphasis on problem solving and thinking skills in teaching. Wallace (2003) highlighted some practical suggestions for history teachers when trialling TASC (Thinking Actively in a Social Context): a problem-solving model for a range of history topics. A useful strategy to promote the use of multiple intelligences used by Wallace is to devise a menu of activities for each project broken down into Gardner's seven categories. In a topic on Ancient Egypt, for example, inventing a counting game is suggested as a logical-mathematical activity, while creating the sounds of a typical Egyptian street market is a musical-auditory possibility.

A distinctive feature of history is the activity of research and investigation, which in the History National Curriculum is included in the section 'Historical enquiry'. At Key Stage 2 level this is defined as how to find out about 'events, people and changes studied from an appropriate range of sources'; 'to ask and answer questions and to select and record information' (DfES/QCA, 1999: 105). Historical enquiry activities can take various forms. Perhaps the most common is allowing children to investigate an historical topic or question using sources such as books, photographs and the internet. An example of this approach can be found in the QCA Key Stage 2 History Unit 13, which focuses on 'How has life in Britain changed since 1948?' A key feature of this unit is organizing pupils into groups who, over several lessons, undertake their own enquiry into a variety of topics including work, home life, popular culture, population and technology.

Another useful teaching approach in history is using story. There has been a very welcome focus on this in recent years with texts such as *Narrative Matters* (Bage, 1999). The benefits of using story in history teaching have long been recognized. As Cooper (2002: 66) comments, 'In listening to stories about other times, children are required to react, to confirm, to modify or to reject their existing ideas. Listening to different versions of stories, then, helps children not only to learn about times and places and people outside their own experience, but also to understand that there is no single "correct" version of the past.' Using stories in history presents children with an approach which is familiar to them and can effectively communicate historical information in a manner easily understood. Story helps children to become involved with events, encouraging them to think about people's actions and empathize with them.

There are many different, creative ways of using story, of which whole-class shared reading is the most obvious. The widespread availability of well-illustrated big books on a variety of historical topics has been a great support for story, particularly for younger children. For older pupils there is no shortage of excellent non-fiction texts such as *Goodnight Mr Tom*, a graphic account of the life of an evacuee in wartime Britain (Magorian, 1986). Another valuable approach is for the teacher to act as a storyteller. Although this requires a strong performance element from the teacher, confidence will soon develop with practice. Any historical topic is amenable to this style of presentation. Careful planning is needed so that the story content is suitably divided into sections; producing a storyboard facilitates this. Artefacts, maps, pictures, mime and costume can be used to help make the story come alive and to encourage interaction with the children.

Storytelling inputs by the teacher are also effective, but need to be short for effectiveness; stopping at key points to allow contributions from the children is a good idea. Turner-Bisset (2005) emphasizes the importance of this interaction with storytelling. Examples given include stopping the story at a key point for children to discuss in pairs what might happen next and telling the story and asking the children to prepare freeze-frames of significant points.

A key feature of history is the emphasis on time and chronology, but these concepts are not easy to grasp. An effective strategy for promoting children's understanding of time is the use of timelines. These can come in many different shapes and sizes and can be made by the teacher or children, while many excellent examples can be purchased from publishers. A very effective timeline can be made simply with a piece of string and pegs, allowing cards with simple text, dates and pictures to be suspended. With any history topic a timeline is a useful reference point, allowing dates, people and events to be seen in a clear chronological context.

A topic on 'The Great Fire of London' shows the value of a timeline. Different stages of the story such as the start of the fire, Pepys giving advice to the King and the blowing-up of buildings can be presented as a large class timeline. It is important that such a resource is used interactively with children. For example, children might create their personal timeline of the Great Fire using pictures of the key events which they can sequence and caption.

With the younger age group another interesting approach is for them to develop a timeline of their own life. Hoodless (1996: 37) recommends children making 'growing up' booklets showing different stages in their life such as when they were born or went to school. Timelines are also essential to help older children cope with the more challenging chronology of topics such as Ancient Egypt, the Tudors and Britain since 1930. Ancient Egypt, for example, is remote chronologically and covers a vast period of three thousand years with complex subdivisions such as the Old, Middle and New Kingdoms. A good-quality Egyptian timeline is essential for children to grasp the sequencing of events, and to recognize key issues such as the association of pyramid building with the Old Kingdom, while mummification was largely a New Kingdom fashion.

Case study

A Year 2 class studying the Great Fire of London of 1666 had been introduced to the main events of the topic. The children were then given a blank timeline covering the period from Sunday 2 September 1666 until Friday 7 September 1666, together with pictures showing the key stages of the fire. Working in pairs the children were asked to discuss each picture, decide what it showed and to think of a title for it. Then they were asked to sequence the pictures chronologically to show the story of the fire. The class was brought together and children were invited to suggest an order for the pictures and to explain which part of the story they showed. The teacher was able to model the children's suggestions for the Great Fire timeline using the interactive whiteboard. Following this discussion the children assembled their own timelines using the pictures and timeline sheet. To facilitate differentiation additional pictures and printed labels with captions and dates were also available.

Inclusive practices

A vital consideration for the primary history teacher is recognizing that effective teaching is closely linked to an awareness of children's individual needs and responding to this through differentiated planning and teaching. This is a theme of *Excellence and Enjoyment*, which emphasizes that 'every teacher knows that truly effective learning and teaching focuses on individual children, their strengths, their needs and the approaches which engage, motivate and inspire them'(DfES, 2003: 39).

How might primary history cater for children's differing needs and be fully inclusive? Underpinning effective differentiation is an understanding of children as individuals, their knowledge, skills and interests, their experiences so far and preferred learning styles, which is gained from effective monitoring and assessment. It is important to recognize that pupils differ in a variety of ways and that intellectual ability is only one such criterion.

Promoting successful differentiation in history depends on the skilful deployment of teaching strategies so that the content is made accessible to all children. History can be a difficult subject for pupils to grasp given complex content and concepts such as chronology, but careful selection of teaching approaches can help overcome these challenges. With any historical topic differentiation can be promoted through the ways in which content is conveyed and the depth in which it is covered. Breaking the content into discrete, manageable sections, and the use of key questions can provide a focus for individual lessons. Frequent repetition of key facts, dates and vocabulary is often effective in allowing less able children to grasp the historical context. It is important, however, that the approach is not teacher-dominated and that children are given plenty of opportunity to speak as well as listen. Skilful questioning and prompting can encourage the children to verbalize the information. An effective way of reinforcing content is to have some visual display. While studying the life of the Victorian engineer Brunel, a teacher produced a large-scale timeline of his life, and word cards. Through these resources children were continuously made aware of important events such as the building of the Great Western Railway and key words such as steamship, bridge and engineer.

Another option is to differentiate by task. If history tasks are open-ended and resource-rich, children can all make a response, and gain a measure of success. A sensible compromise highlighted by O'Hara and O'Hara (2001) is to use a common core task, but with extra activities allowing some children to progress further in their learning. This approach can be made more successful by providing adult support for some individual children. An example of this was a lesson on Ancient Egypt in which children were asked to make an Egyptian face mask. Using research from books and internet sources, they then proceeded to make the face masks using a variety of materials. Careful monitoring of the class allowed prompt support to be given to individuals as and when required. A key component of this differentiated approach is the use of appropriate resources. As Bage (1999: 128) has emphasized, 'one key to making history accessible for all learners is to use a variety of historical sources: pictures, objects, music, film or site visits for instance, as well as computers, books and documents'.

In recent years the differentiation debate has placed a strong focus on the needs of gifted and talented children. Gifted children can display a range of characteristics including being imaginative and original, having enthusiasm for knowledge, learning quickly, having strong viewpoints, showing high levels of concentration and producing historical work of outstanding quality (O'Hara and O'Hara, 2001). Gifted children can provide considerable challenges for teachers in terms of persistent questioning and completing work quickly. The key task is to provide activities which can extend gifted children. This needs to be considered when planning.

Another great challenge for the history teacher is ensuring that the history curriculum is culturally relevant to all pupils. The United Kingdom and other western countries are very diverse multicultural societies. Large scale immigration in the 1960s and 1970s from the Caribbean, India and Pakistan, for example, has had a major impact on society in the United Kingdom as *Roots of the Future* (Frow, 1997) has emphasized. The National Curriculum unit 'Britain since 1948' provides ample opportunity to explore the symbolic arrival of the SS *Empire Windrush* from the West Indies in 1948, and the Commonwealth immigration which followed (www.standards.dfes.gov.uk/schemes2/history).

There are many exciting ways of exploring ethnic minority history, such as oral history and the use of museums which give recognition to minority groups. A valuable contribution to this area is also Black History Month, which takes place every October in the United Kingdom and provides an excellent opportunity for schools to celebrate the contribution of Black and Asian people to British society (www.black-history-month.co.uk). However, there is a need for this issue to be embedded in our history teaching all of the time and not just periodically. It is important for schools without ethnic minorities to recognize the importance of using their history curriculum to promote cultural diversity.

Assessment

Although assessment should be a fundamental and integrated part of the overall teaching and learning process, there is evidence that in Foundation subjects like history it can be given insufficient attention. In a Primary History report of 2000–1, for example, it was noted that: '...even in many schools where history is thriving, assessment is an area of relative weakness. This weakness begins with planning that does not clearly specify the objectives against which pupils' work will be assessed. In these circumstances, marking is often cursory and comments fail to help pupils see how they can improve' (Ofsted, 2002: 6).

A school's history subject-leader has a key role in ensuring that assessment is prominent within the history scheme of work and in the day-to-day teaching of this subject.

Assessment refers to measuring a child's level of performance using various strategies such as written tasks, but there are other inter-linked activities including monitoring, recording and reporting which should also not be neglected.

Given the importance attached to assessment, it is necessary for teachers to have a secure grasp of its purposes in relation to history. Children clearly need to be made aware of the progress they are making in their history work, and also ways in which they can improve. Much of assessment activity in history will be of a formative or diagnostic nature such as day-to-day marking or monitoring of children's work in history lessons.

A variety of assessment strategies is available to the primary history teacher. Traditionally much assessment in history has focused on written work but other aspects should not be neglected. Observing children and listening to them talk about their history work can provide a wealth of assessment evidence. Consider, for example, a lesson on 'Homes' where groups of young children are given objects to investigate such as a carpet beater or oil lamp. Children will be sharing their ideas on what they think the objects are and how they were used. Careful observation may indicate how effective their enquiry skills are and their understanding of concepts such as old or new. In recent years much greater recognition has been given to speaking and listening skills and this needs to be reflected in history assessments such as observations. Skilful questioning by the teacher either in a whole-class or group situation can also provide useful assessment opportunities.

Central to history assessment is the marking of children's day-to-day classroom tasks. For this to be effective, however, teachers need to be very clear about the learning outcomes for each task in terms of the historical knowledge, skills, understanding and attitudes promoted.

Let us now take as an example 'Seaside Holidays', a popular Key Stage 1 topic within the English National Curriculum. A commonly used activity is getting the children to compare seaside holidays now and in the past, such as the 1900s, using old and new photographs. Appropriate objectives for this work would be: to find out about seaside holidays in the past by using photographs; and to identify similarities and differences between seaside holidays now and in the 1900s.

When marking such a task a strong focus should be placed on the history content and assessing to what extent the child has met the learning objectives. This is why it is so important to be clear about learning outcomes when planning lessons or learning activities. Marking clearly needs to be positive and constructive with written comments highlighting achievements but also misconceptions and development points. With reference to the seaside holiday task, one particular child found out that visitors to the seaside in both the 1900s and the present day could travel by train. The teacher commended the child for identifying this similarity but also made a comment asking the child to think about how the train's appearance had changed over the years. Children clearly need to be advised on how they can improve and move forward. The marking of children's work is a sensitive activity with clear implications for their motivation and self-esteem. Excessive alteration to a child's work needs to be avoided and it is important to remember in the context of marking history that although use of English and presentation are important, priority should be given to assessing subject content.

Another important dimension is to make judgements about children's long-term progress in history. This summative evidence is valuable for reporting to parents and evaluating the school's overall history provision. An effective strategy for history summative assessment is to ensure that at the end of each history unit some form of assessment takes place which allows the children to show their progress in historical knowledge, understanding and skills. Summative assessment in the History National Curriculum is facilitated by the existence of various level descriptions which describe the performance of pupils at varying ability levels. At the end of Key Stage 1 (5–7 years), for example, most children are expected to be operating at level 2, the key features of which are defined as showing 'their developing sense of chronology', 'recognizing that their own lives are different from the lives of people in the past', 'beginning to recognize that there are reasons why people in the past acted as they did' and 'observing or handling sources of information to answer questions about the past on the basis of simple observations' (DfES/QCA, 1999: 29).

Eleven-year-old children at the end of Key Stage 2 are expected to be working between levels 2 and 5 with the majority achieving level 4. The following description shows clear progression with children now giving 'some reasons for, and results of, the main events and changes. They show some understanding that aspects of the past have been represented and interpreted in different ways' (DfES/QCA, 1999: 29).

Finally it should be stressed that assessment should not be viewed as solely the responsibility of the teacher. Primary education in recent years has witnessed an increasing focus on promoting skills of independent learning and this has influenced assessment practice positively with the growing popularity of pupil self-assessment. A common approach with younger children is to use a smiley face format but for older children there can be a more detailed approach in allowing children to assess what they have learned. Turner-Bisset (2005: 159), for example, suggests the use of concept webs and 'I can do' statements linked to the learning objectives.

Assessment also has a significant evaluative function within history both at classroom and whole-school level. Assessment of work might highlight children's misconceptions or resources which proved too challenging. Teachers can respond to issues highlighted by assessment with revisions in planning.

Resources

One of the best ways to allow children to be active historians and investigate real evidence is through artefacts. A potential difficulty of teaching history to young children is that it can seem quite a distant subject, but providing historical objects which they can hold and feel can make the past seem more concrete. History topics which focus on the past 100 years such as the Victorians, Homes and Britain since 1930 can be relatively easily resourced with artefacts. Parents and grandparents can often be a useful source but avoid taking responsibility for valuable items.

With topics more chronologically distant such as the Tudors, Romans and Ancient Egypt, access to original artefacts will generally not be feasible. Nevertheless, collections of replica items will often be available from local museum education services or local education authority resource centres. Across the primary age phase, artefacts can be used for a wide range of interesting activities. Barnsdale-Paddock and Harnett (2002), for example, have highlighted how Key Stage 1 children acted as curators and set up their own toy museum which helped their historical understanding as well as providing opportunities for play.

The teaching of history can also be enhanced by drawing upon an abundance of pictorial sources. Original paintings can provide a useful resource for a variety of National Curriculum topics such as the Tudors, as a subsequent case study shows. Portraits of individual people are also a good introduction to famous people. With Henry VIII, for example, there are several portraits available painted at different times of his life and it is interesting to contrast his appearance as a young king to what he was like in old age.

The widespread availability of photographs from the late-Victorian period onwards provides a superb resource for history topics over the last 100 years such as the Victorians or Britain since 1930. One of the most interesting aspects of the latter period is exploring

Britain and the Home Front during World War Two and photographs provide one of the best and most easily accessed resources. A recent publication by Kent County Council entitled *60 Years On… remembering and exploring Kent's wartime role* (2005) exemplifies this with an excellent collection of photographs from the archives of the Kent Messenger Group. Examples include local land girls, children decorating a bomb crater, Rochester boys being evacuated and victory dancing in Maidstone High Street in 1945. Historical photographs like these can be a rich source of information and focus of discussion for pupils of all abilities – but as with all historical evidence issues of reliability need to be introduced.

Other pictorial sources should not be neglected. Many posters were published by the British Government during World War Two as part of the war effort and are useful examples of historical evidence for the Home Front. There was a strong focus during the war on bringing women into the workplace, one particular poster proclaiming 'Women of Britain Come into the Factories' against a backdrop of a factory producing aircraft and tanks. A collection of British World War Two posters with their strong visual element and easily understood slogans can quickly allow children of all abilities to empathize with the events of the time, while also illustrating the potential bias and propaganda aspect of such material.

Television and video resources provide excellent support for primary history. The main providers of broadcast material are BBC (www.bbc.co.uk/info) and Channel 4 (www. channel4.com.learning). These also provide accompanying classroom resources including lesson-planning material.

Stimulating children's interest in history and encouraging them to really engage with the past is made much easier by good-quality television programmes which can so effectively and realistically take us to another time and place. The series *A Walk Through Time* with Tony Robinson in the Zig-Zag series is a good example of how skilful animation is used to take the children on a virtual walk through key periods in history, looking at topics such as food in an authentic manner. In contrast the Channel 4 series *All Change: The UK 1945– 1970 through home movies* imaginatively uses newsreel and amateur video footage to bring to life aspects of the 1950s and 1960s such as the rise of package holidays.

As with all resources, the effective use of television depends on the teacher. Programmes need reviewing before being shown to evaluate their suitability and highlight any preparation needs. Consideration also needs to be given to the role of children both during and after the viewing. Encouraging them to observe and listen is often preferable to making notes, while the use of the pause button and skilful questioning can help children grasp the key points.

> **Case Study**
>
> A Year 5 class studying life in Tudor times was split into small groups and given a painting of Baron Cobham and his family dating from 1567 showing a very wealthy family at their dining table. The children were asked to look carefully at the painting and to see what they could find out about the family simply from the evidence in the painting. They listed their ideas on flipchart paper and when they reported back key points were recorded on the interactive whiteboard. The groups raised many interesting points including the fine clothes and jewellery, the very pale faces of the people, food such as fruit and the strange pets including a monkey, parrot and bird tied to a perch! Questions from the teacher encouraged ideas to be put forward such as the wealth of the family and evidence that the Tudors must have had links with far-away places. Issues of reliability and bias were also discussed. This painting provided a useful starting point for more detailed research of Tudor life using books and the internet.

Conclusion

This chapter has sought to highlight key features and issues in the teaching of primary history. For trainee teachers it is important to be able to articulate a rationale for history in the curriculum and to develop their own philosophy for teaching the subject. Good practice depends on careful planning but documentation needs to be realistic. Planning is a skilful process and this is where teachers can use their creativity to select interesting approaches, learning activities and resources with due consideration of pupil needs. Quality history teaching, however, is not just about the essentials which have been covered so far, because there are wider dimensions such as cross-curricular themes which will now be considered.

References

Bage, G. (1999), *Narrative Matters: Teaching and Learning through Story*. London: Falmer Press.

Bage, G. (2000), *Thinking History 4–14*. London: RoutledgeFalmer.

Barnsdale-Paddock, L. and Harnett, P. (2002), 'Promoting play in the classroom: children as curators in a classroom museum'. *Primary History*, January, 19–21.

Bowen, P. and Hoodless, P. (2006), *100 History Lessons Ages 5–7*. Leamington Spa: Scholastic.

Claire, H. (2004), 'Oral history: a powerful tool or a double edged sword?' *Primary History*, Winter, 20–23.

Cooper, H. (2002), *History in the Early Years*. London: RoutledgeFalmer.

DfES (2003), *Excellence and Enjoyment*. London: DfES Publications.

DfES/QCA (1999), *The National Curriculum: Handbook for Primary Teachers in England*. London: HMSO.

Frow, M. (1997), *Roots of the Future: Ethnic Diversity in the Making of Britain*. London: Commission for Racial Equality.

Gardner, H. (1993), *Multiple Intelligences: The Theory in Practice*. New York: Basic Books.

Hoodless, P. (1996), *Time and Timelines in the Primary School.* London: Historical Association.

Hoodless, P. (ed.) (1998), *Teaching History and English in the Primary School: Exploiting the Links.* London: Routledge.

Hoodless, P. (2006), *100 History Lessons Ages 7–11*. Leamington Spa: Scholastic.

Kent County Council Corporate Communications (2005), *60 Years On… Remembering and exploring Kent's wartime role*. Maidstone: KCCCC.

Magorian, M. (1986), *Goodnight Mr Tom.* London: Pelican.

Marwick, A., (2001), *The New Nature of History.* Basingstoke: Palgrave.

Ofsted (2002), *Primary Subject Report for History. 2000/2001*. Ref. HMI 361.

O'Hara, L. and O'Hara, M. (2001), *Teaching History 3–11*. London: Continuum.

Sands, B. (2004), 'Planning a Victorian school day'. *Primary History*, Winter, 26–29.

Turner-Bisset, R. (2005), *Creative Teaching: History in the Primary School*. London: David Fulton.

Wallace, B. (2003), *Using History to Develop Thinking Skills at Key Stage 2*. London: NACE/Fulton.

Wood, L. and Holden, C. (1999), *Teaching Early Years History*. Cambridge: Chris Kington Publishing.

History: Beyond the Curriculum

Paul Bowen

'We live in a country that is richer than many others in the visible remains of the past but most of us are visibly illiterate.' W. G. Hoskins (1967: 32)

Introduction

In the previous chapter key aspects of teaching history in the primary school have been discussed such as the nature of the subject, planning, teaching strategies, resources and assessment. The focus now will be on exploring the broader context of primary history, and considering links with the wider curriculum. A particularly topical issue in primary education at the present is that of creativity, and the implications for creativity in history are explored. Related cross-curricular issues will be commented upon including citizenship, literacy and ICT. Looking at primary history in a wider context inevitably raises the issue of different modes of delivery. Should history be seen as a single subject or part of a more holistic, integrated topic approach which encompasses other curriculum areas alongside history? The value of out-of-school learning will also be highlighted because history should not be solely a classroom-based activity. Visits to places of interest such as castles, the use of museums and local history activities can all be exciting opportunities to bring history alive for children and to make it more relevant.

Creativity

In recent years we have witnessed a growing interest in the promotion of creativity within primary education, and it is important to explore the implications for history teaching. The emergence of creativity as a key issue is to some extent a reaction to the relatively rigid structure of content and assessment imposed by the National Curriculum. An influential contribution to the creativity debate was the publication of the report *All our Futures: Creativity, Culture and Education* (DfEE/NACCCE, 2001). This has been followed by many other discussions such as those by Jones and Wyse (2004). There is certainly debate about the precise nature of creativity because of its abstract nature and it is often described as having an elusive definition. Its close association with the arts can also make definition a complex procedure. *All our Futures* identifies four main characteristics of creativity including using imagination, pursuing purposes, being original and judging value. There is often agreement among commentators that for creativity to be promoted other conditions should be present, such as offering pupils some choice and scope for curiosity, encouraging risk-taking and allowing independent learning. The current focus on creativity might suggest that this is something new in primary education, but this would be inaccurate. Good-quality primary teaching has always included features which are now part of the creativity agenda.

How might creativity be specifically applied to the history classroom? The QCA (www. qca.org.uk/history/innovating/key2/wider_curriculum/creativity) identifies a number of ways in which history teachers can encourage pupils to think and work creatively:

- accommodating different approaches to learning
- making connections with learning in other areas of the curriculum
- making connections with personal experiences
- making learning vivid or memorable
- organizing unexpected challenges to pupils' thinking
- changing the direction of teaching
- helping children find their own problems or challenges
- making clear to children there are no right or wrong answers
- recognizing and valuing unexpected responses and outcomes from pupils.

In effect these features are what we would expect to be present in good-quality history teaching and they provide an excellent framework for creative lesson planning. Let us consider a few of the points above. 'Making learning vivid or memorable' is the challenge for the teacher and this is where imagination is called for. A class studying life in Britain during World War Two assembled artefacts including a working air raid siren which had helped to convey the fear and dangers of those times. On a recent visit to a school in Salzburg, Austria, I was intrigued to hear that a class had visited the famous fortress building one dark winter's evening and then returned to school, where they stayed overnight but also started follow-up work including model-making and creative writing. The children spoke most enthusiastically about this event and the work on display showed how successful the event had been in terms of learning. 'Making clear to children that there are no right or wrong answers' is a fundamental part of being an historian and adopting a critical standpoint. For older primary children studying civilizations such as the Egyptians, Greeks and Romans, there are opportunities for them to draw some conclusions about the positive and negative features of these societies. In Britain, for example, the Romans brought new standards in terms of roads, buildings, industry, art and culture, but this was accompanied by less desirable features such as military conquest and slavery. Similarly the magnificent architectural achievements of the Egyptians such as Khufu's Great Pyramid at Giza will hopefully encourage children to consider the position of the workers who were involved in the hard, manual labour of building it. Forming and expressing opinions about such issues using evidence is a key benefit of history.

Although history can clearly be taught as a single subject, and this is the predominant focus of National Curriculum history, it can also be delivered in a more integrated manner as part of a wider cross-curricular scheme. Indeed, there is a strong case for arguing that primary children approach learning in a more holistic way rather than in terms of individual subjects, which can be a somewhat artificial and limiting system of classification. More integrated approaches can include history being taught as part of an overall topic theme such as homes, ourselves or transport. Alternatively a predominantly history topic can be used to develop links with other aspects of the curriculum, an approach exemplified by the following case study.

Case study

A Year 4 class studied the life of the notable Victorian engineer Isambard Kingdom Brunel as an example of a famous individual. Although the focus was primarily historical, the activities chosen by the teacher involved opportunities for valuable cross-curricular work to be undertaken. In looking at the building of the Great Western Railway, which opened in 1841 between Bristol and London, the children used a map to follow the route, which enhanced their geographical skills.

An interesting lesson allowed children to compare trains at the time of Brunel, such as the steam locomotive *Firefly*, with present-day electric Pendolino trains. By carefully observing the similarities and differences in the style of these trains, children were clearly engaging with key aspects of art and design. The teacher was keen to encourage children to realize how railways dramatically changed the way of life in Victorian times. As part of this lesson Robert Louis Stevenson's poem 'From a Railway Carriage' was used to emphasize the speed of trains.

Case study (continued)

There were also useful links with English in terms of poetry as a form of communication and the vocabulary developed.

One of Brunel's finest achievements was the building of the Royal Albert Bridge across the Tamar estuary near Plymouth, which opened in 1859. Photographs were used to show children the main features of the bridge and this was followed by a bridge-making activity using materials such as construction straws. The class not only explored the history of the bridge but were also, through the bridge-making simulation and evaluation, gaining experience of design and technology issues (Bowen and Hoodless, 2006: 104).

Cross-curricular themes

Literacy

One of the most important cross-curricular links is with literacy. This has been the subject of recent publications, for example, by Hoodless (1998) and Bage (1999). Historical study is underpinned by a wide range of written sources and texts including fiction, rhymes, letters, diary entries, newspaper reports, advertisements, poems, biography and information texts which can promote children's awareness of information texts. With any history topic there are many interesting examples of these sources which can be used as a stimulus for activities which develop skills in both history and English. Take, for example, the use of books to research topics about Ancient Egypt such as the pyramids, gods, farming, food, writing or mummification.

To use non-fiction books efficiently requires use of indexes and contents pages so the children will not only be developing an understanding of life in Ancient Egypt and historical enquiry skills, but also important transferable literacy skills. Robert and Moses (2005), for example, have taken the topic of World War Two and assembled a fascinating group of written sources including school-logbook entries describing the evacuation, newspaper reports about bombing raids and posters proclaiming 'make do and mend'. A ration book, a recipe for cow heel stew and a song called 'Dig for Victory' highlight food shortages during the war, while Michael Morpurgo's novel *Friend and Foe* provides an insight into wartime life from a child's perspective. In using these sources children will be involved in activities such as reading, speaking, listening and writing, key communication skills which are a fundamental part of literacy. History can also provide an interesting context for developing speaking and listening skills. Oral history has rightly become very popular in primary schools because older members of the community can often talk with enthusiasm and interest about their own life histories and such diverse topics as World War Two, seaside holidays in the 1950s and the pop culture of the 1960s. Good practice with oral history involves children being given plenty of opportunities to ask questions, and it can be useful for them to think about these before the session. Claire (2004) has highlighted the value of this, but also recognizes some of the difficulties of oral testimony. Redfern (1996) provides comprehensive guidance on practical ways in which oral history can contribute to teaching and learning.

For younger children nursery rhymes can provide a very useful introduction to life in the past while also encouraging language development (Woodhouse, 2001). They are part of our cultural heritage and generally familiar to children, providing opportunities for singing, reciting and miming as well as discussion and questioning. Consider the famous example of 'Ring-a-ring o' roses'.

> Ring-a-ring o' roses
> A pocket full of posies
> Atishoo, atishoo
> We all fall down.

Traditionally associated with the Great Plague of 1665, it links neatly with the plague story and can help children engage with the topic, although a recent interpretation suggests that it has its origins in a nineteenth-century country dance. From a literacy perspective children are given experience of rhythm, rhyme and vocabulary. Historically questions can be asked about what the phrases mean and points made about marks on the skin which were a sign of the plague, symptoms such as sneezing, the use of posies to ward off the plague and the fact that many people died from the plague.

Citizenship

In discussing the wider context of history teaching in the primary school, some consideration of the theme of citizenship is highly relevant. Citizenship has become an important aspect of the English National Curriculum in recent years, but it is usually an aspiration for any education system and clearly has multinational relevance. Citizenship is about preparing pupils for their future role in society so that they can make a positive contribution.

Linked into this has been a campaign to promote the concept of global citizenship, a key issue which has been promoted by the charity Oxfam with the significant publication of *Global Citizenship: the Handbook for Primary Teachers* (Young and Commins, 2001). Oxfam sees a global citizen as a way of thinking and behaving, a way of life. It recognizes the Earth as a resource for life, and the need to safeguard it for future generations. Being a global citizen, however, is broader than this and includes tackling issues of injustice and inequality. The influential document *Developing the Global Dimension in the School Curriculum* (DfES, 2005), for example, identifies a number of global citizenship concepts to which history can make a very powerful and distinctive contribution, such as diversity, values and perceptions, conflict resolution and human rights.

Case study

A class of 11-year-old children were studying a topic on life in the Victorian period (nineteenth century) with a focus on the lives of children. A visit to Styal Mill near Manchester showed how, before compulsory schooling was introduced, many Victorian children worked in factories. The class investigated the growth of a free and compulsory school system following the introduction of the Education Act of 1870. Life in a Victorian classroom was explored, including simulating a typical school lesson of the time. In this topic the teacher was able to promote an understanding of Victorian schooling, but also citizenship issues of social justice and human rights. Although education today in the western world is seen as a basic human right, the class found out that this was not the case in Victorian England, where education was often the preserve of the wealthy. The emergence of a mass schooling system in the late nineteenth century helped address a major social injustice. Moreover, looking at the features of a Victorian lesson such as excessive strictness and punishment also highlighted important citizenship issues such as the rights of children. As part of the topic the teacher made the class aware that for many children in the world today education is still not a basic right, and fundraising took place to support the building of a school in Africa.

Information and communication technology (ICT)

One of the key developments within primary education in the last decade has been the progress of ICT to the extent that most classrooms have interactive whiteboards (IWBs). Heavy financial investment in ICT has often been accompanied by claims that this technology will transform teaching and learning in schools as well as the way we work. One commentator has referred to this developing context as 'a new age of discovery, and ICT is the gateway' (DfEE/QCA,1999: 97). An examination of the emerging relationship between primary history and ICT is valuable in terms of identifying the potential for good practice. There is, of course, the issue of defining what is meant by the term ICT. It can be an all-embracing term to include video, digital cameras, audio resources and computers, but the focus of this section will be on computing aspects.

When using ICT in a history lesson, the development of ICT skills is important; however, a key focus should be on how this resource can support teaching and learning in history. With the widespread availability of interactive whiteboards, there is an increasingly effective use of ICT.

How then can the use of computers enhance the teaching of history? ICT can allow children to communicate their knowledge and understanding of history in a clear, interesting and presentable fashion. Word-processing can be used for any written responses by pupils working individually or as a member of a team. The use of templates allows various types of written work to be easily undertaken, such as newspaper reports, diary accounts and letters. Word-processing is much more versatile than handwriting, and allows valuable editing and redrafting to take place. Another invaluable facility of the computer is the ability to source visual material and to use this to illustrate their written work. PowerPoint software, for example, is an excellent resource for children presenting the findings of group-based research projects.

Perhaps one of the best uses of computers in history is how, by internet access in particular, there is easy access to a wealth of resources – many of a visual nature. Museums and art galleries often now have excellent interactive websites of real value to the primary history teacher. The British Museum, for example, has a good Egyptian website (www. ancientegypt.co.uk/trade/index.html) including a section on the mummification process showing graphically how the brains were extracted via the nose! In contrast the National Portrait Gallery website (www.npg.org.uk) contains a searchable database allowing easy access to portraits of famous people such as the Tudor monarch Henry VIII and Mary Seacole, a West Indian who nursed soldiers during the Crimean War. The British Educational Communications and Technology Agency (BECTA) (2003) provides a useful list of history sites which are excellent resources for promoting pupils' skills of historical enquiry and interpretation of sources. It should be emphasized that with all these internet-based sources careful, critical evaluation is important to assess their suitability.

Another valuable use of ICT within history is the use of databases, allowing historical information to be easily handled and analysed. There are some online databases for historical topics, but it is also possible for teachers and children to generate their own. One example is a church graveyard survey where data such as year of death, age of death, gender, names and occupations can be inputted and analysed.

Perhaps of all recent ICT developments the growing use of interactive whiteboards or smartboards has been particularly beneficial for history teaching. The IWB and use of an electronic pen are a powerful teaching tool with the potential to improve pupil interaction in lessons. Moreover, the growth of this new technology has been accompanied by the availability of easily accessible history resources such as downloadable flipcharts. The National Interactive Whiteboard Network (www.nwnet.org.uk) has a wide range of these resources.

One of the examples is a flipchart looking at what it was like for children during World War Two. Useful maps, pictures, text and a timeline help set the context for the war, and key content of the topic such as the blitz, evacuation and rationing are explained with interesting pictures and text. Such a resource is clearly adaptable and could be used for whole-class teaching, or on an individual or group basis. Moreover, there is a strong emphasis on activities involving the children such as planning wartime menus for the week using rationing information, and adding information to the flipchart about how the war affected the local area. IWB resources like these require careful evaluation by the teacher before use, but they do offer many benefits in terms of quality of text, images and activities while also offering economy in planning time.

Finally, as with all effective teaching, good use of ICT is closely linked to the skill of the teacher both in terms of planning and executing the lesson. As BECTA (2003: 2) recognizes, 'ICT can enhance learning by helping teachers to demonstrate, explain and question, stimulate discussion and invite interpretations of what is displayed'. However, when ICT is being used in history, there is still a need for teachers to be constantly encouraging children's interaction with the media through skilful questioning and prompting.

With its distinctive methodologies and resources, history has a unique role to play in the curriculum and should be there on its own merits. What clearly is important is that children receive a broad and balanced education and history's emphasis on exploring people's lives in the past is an essential part of this.

Beyond the school

This chapter focuses on the wider aspects of teaching primary history and central to this must be a recognition that pupils should not learn history confined to the classroom. There is a wider learning environment outside the school which can stimulate children's interests in history and make it more meaningful.

Interaction with a range of experiences is clearly valuable in terms of learning and visits provide this diversity, allowing children to use their various senses and intelligences. Take, for example, a topic such as the Tudors where houses might be a focus of study. Books and internet resources will be valuable, but far more effective will be providing children with an opportunity to visit an actual Tudor building. They can actually see and take in the atmosphere of the building, observing in detail how the timber-framed house is joined together with large wooden pegs with wattle and daub used as infilling. Visits like this can promote historical understanding but also transferable, key skills such as observation.

The nature of visits to places of interest may vary enormously from fully guided activities to visits which are self-guided by the teachers and adult helpers. As with any effective teaching, careful planning is of importance and a pre-visit is essential to become familiar with the location, to identify possible activities and teaching points and to carry out a risk assessment. Children must be encouraged to use their observational skills when on location. If visiting a castle, for example, the main features such as the moat, gatehouse, keep and well need to be highlighted. Key questions need to be asked, such as: Why was this castle built here? What was it built from? Why might attackers find it difficult to attack? And: What would it have been like living in the castle?

Ideally children need to work in small groups supervised by adult helpers and as part of the planning process a briefing meeting with some written guidance is advisable. Group leaders have an important role to play, encouraging children to talk about what they can see and asking and answering questions. Children can make brief notes and drawings about their observations and a digital camera or camcorder is always useful to facilitate follow-up work. It is good practice at the end of a visit to briefly review with the class what they have found out and what has surprised or interested them.

Although self-guided educational visits of places such as castles and houses can be rewarding, many places of interest have well-developed education services which organize activities specifically related to popular historical topics. Both the National Trust and English Heritage have properties which provide rich experiences for children.

Case study

A Year 1 class was studying the topic seaside holidays. They were comparing the 1900s with the present day and looking at aspects such as the pier, beach, transport, entertainment and the promenade. The children had limited experiences of the traditional seaside town, and to enhance their learning a visit was arranged to Llandudno, a classic Victorian seaside resort. During the visit children went on the pier, walked the promenade, watched a Punch and Judy show and saw the many hotels as well as the activities on the beach.

Back in the classroom, old photographs of the 1900s had been enlarged and laminated, allowing comparisons to be made between now and then. The visit gave the children a much greater understanding of seaside resorts and changes over the past 100 years. The visit formed a stimulus for a range of activities including setting up a Punch and Judy theatre, designing a seaside postcard, model-making, creative writing and looking at souvenirs.

Museums

An important aspect of out-of-school learning in history is visits to museums, which are accessible to many schools. Traditionally museums had their collections displayed in glass cases which limited the potential for pupil interaction. However, over the past 20 years or so, great progress has been made in the educational use of museums. The appearance of new innovative museums and the redesigning of existing ones have been strongly influenced by a desire to make museums exciting and accessible places to visit. A recent national initiative has been the Museum and Gallery Education Programme promoted by the DfES and the Department of Culture, Media and Sport (DfES, 2003: 33).

The pioneering Jorvik Viking Museum is a good example, providing a highly interactive introduction to Viking York, not only in visual and audio terms but also through realistic recreation of the smells of the period!

Most museums have good educational services offering courses for teachers, practical workshop sessions for children, artefact collections for loan and visits to school by educational officers.

One of the most notable of the new breed of museums in the UK has been the opening of the Imperial War Museum North in Manchester. Visitors may note the sparseness of exhibits compared to many museums but this is balanced by a philosophy of encouraging personal and immediate interaction with the many issues of war. 'Big Picture' shows transform the main exhibition area into spectacular audio-visual presentations on themes such as 'Children and War'. A huge timeline looks at wars over the past 100 years and shows the effects on people's lives. Silos are innovative exhibition spaces which focus on themes such as women, technology and science. Timestacks contain the objects of war arranged thematically. Even the impressive museum building designed by Daniel Libeskind conveys the theme of war, based as it is on three shards or pieces from a shattered globe.

Local history

The value of educational visits to places such as museums and castles has been emphasized, but it is all too easy to neglect the immediate local environment, where there are often interesting visible remains of the past. In this section the nature and importance of local history will be emphasized. Local history as an academic subject is relatively young, owing much to the pioneering work of W. G. Hoskins at Leicester University in the 1950s and 60s. It is now a significant aspect of primary history, providing opportunities to promote historical knowledge, skills and understanding in a context familiar to children.

The essence of local history is a focus on the local community and landscape, and how these have changed over time. All schools are surrounded by local areas which have their own history, although obviously some might be more interesting than others. Developing an effective local history study, however, can be challenging for teachers compared with other history topics with a national or international focus such as Ancient Egypt or the Romans, where commercially-produced materials are available in abundance. Careful research, planning and preparation are called for on the teacher's part, but this can be a creative and rewarding activity with a sense of developing teaching resources which are original. A good starting point for a local study is exploring the area for buildings or features of interest and then looking in the local library for relevant publications which can provide an historical background, because it is essential for the teacher to gain a confident knowledge base. While a local history study may cover many historical periods, more distant times are generally less accessible in terms of information; in my experience one of the most feasible options is to look at an area in a Victorian context.

To illustrate how a local history study can be developed let me use the example of the hamlet of Crewe Green, close to the Cheshire campus of Manchester Metropolitan University, which I have studied with trainee teachers over a number of years.

Case study

A visit to Crewe Library revealed many local history publications about the town but few references to the small settlement of Crewe Green. A few old photographs were found, however, and these were subsequently supplemented by others from an online local history website. Some useful primary sources were located, including a large-scale Ordnance Survey map of 1902 (25 inches to 1 mile) showing great detail, including individual houses. Another valuable find was *Kelly's Trade Directory* of Cheshire for 1902, which included a section on Crewe Green. Produced in large numbers in the Victorian period on a county basis, each town or village has a detailed description about features such as history, farming, industry, schools and transport.

Additionally there are lists of private residents and a commercial section with information about businesses, shopkeepers and the like. Trade directories, therefore, constitute valuable evidence but as a teaching resource they are not very user-friendly in their original format and this is where teachers need to use their skills to transcribe, simplify and re-present the material for children. Finally census material was obtained for Crewe Green for 1881 and 1901. Government censuses have taken place every ten years from 1801 and examples such as 1881 and 1901 provide a fascinating insight into Victorian England with details of the people who lived in individual houses, their ages at death, their places of birth and their occupations.

One of the most important aspects of local history is getting the children out of the classroom to look at the history around them. It is surprising how often we can fail to recognize history on our doorstep.

The use of observational skills is fundamental to effective fieldwork and it is also important to consider what is expected of children during the actual fieldwork. Over-emphasis on a clipboard and worksheet approach can impede children's observational skills and interpretation of their surroundings. With children in small, adult-led groups, there is scope for observation plus interactive discussion promoted by some key questions from the adult.

The Crewe Green example provides interesting historical features which can be clearly linked with the documentary sources. The 1902 map showed Crewe Mill Bridge and the nearby corn mill with its millpond. Today there are no real visible remains of the mill although the millpond site is discernable. The 1881 census, however, informs us that the miller was Thomas Hilditch, who lived with his family in Crewe Mill cottage. On a visit to the nearby Crewe Green Church a brief survey of gravestones provides insights into Victorian Crewe Green such as occupations, infant mortality and common names. Interesting gravestones include those of a manager of Crewe Locomotive Works whose epitaph describes how he died 'worn out from doing his duty', and nearby is a memorial to Thomas Hilditch the miller. Close to the church gates is a group of cottages and the modern scene can be interestingly compared with a photograph of 1906 when one of the cottages won first prize in the local flower garden competition. Nearby stands a fine Victorian building which is identifiable on the map, and there is also telling visible evidence about the origins of the old school building. A sundial has an inscription which advises people to '*use well thy time*', while other inscriptions included '*what shall we render unto the Lord?*' and '*time, rewarding industry punishing sloth*'. These written sources provided valuable evidence of the religious origins of this school and also an insight into Victorian beliefs. This information can be cross-referenced with the trade directory entries where we are told that the school was opened in 1882 as a National School (Church of England) and built by the Earl of Crewe of Crewe Hall, the landowner.

This Crewe Green example shows the importance of identifying interesting fieldwork opportunities and supporting these with relevant historical sources. The next stage is planning activities for the pupils both in terms of fieldwork and follow-up classroom-based activities and this is an ideal opportunity for teachers to be really imaginative and creative. Creativity, as we have seen, is open to interpretation, but activities which have some originality, allow problem-solving, give opportunities for pupils to work independently, have cross-curricular dimensions and cater for multiple intelligences will be appropriate. The list overleaf shows some of the possible activities which can be used.

Example

Crewe Green local history study: pupil activities

- Producing a guide to Victorian Crewe Green in booklet or PowerPoint form
- Comparing old and new photographs using a digital camera
- Producing a classroom exhibition
- Comparing old and modern maps
- Model-making (church, school, cottages, etc.)
- Interviewing older local residents
- Art and craft activities, for example making decorative tiles
- Recording and analysing gravestone information
- Re-creating a Victorian school lesson
- Developing role-play scenarios about daily life in Victorian Crewe Green
- Researching Victorian themes such as transport and schools
- Creative writing of autobiographies, diaries and poems

The value of children investigating history away from the classroom has been prominent in this chapter, but in all these activities the children's safety needs to be of paramount importance. Risk assessment procedures have become much more formalized in recent years and it is essential that for any history visits teachers comply with all necessary requirements such as completion of a formal risk-assessment form. Proposed fieldwork routes such as a town trail need careful reconnaissance to identify potential risks and dangers such as road crossings and narrow pavements. Effective and safe trips out can be best achieved by using a high ratio of adults to children, for example 1:5. Close control of the children can then be achieved both in terms of behaviour management and learning. Arranging a briefing of adult helpers and written guidance about the trip and the history learning activities which will be undertaken is invaluable if maximum benefit is to be achieved.

Conclusion

This chapter has sought to explore the wider context of history teaching in the primary school and ways have been highlighted in which history can be made more relevant, interesting and stimulating for children using a variety of contexts both inside and outside the classroom. A wealth of resources is available for history teaching, but the creation of effective learning for children depends largely on the qualities of the teacher. It is about having sufficient knowledge and understanding of history topics to be able to teach confidently. Historical topics can be quite complex and a sound working knowledge gained through research will allow their full teaching potential to be realized. Teachers need to be able to plan sequences of lessons which link well and have clear learning objectives. They need to select and prepare resources. Perhaps one of the most challenging tasks is the need to match work appropriately to the varying levels of the class and the needs of individual children. This requires not only expertise in history, but also insights into how children's learning can be affected by such factors as intellect or social influences.

Developing these many qualities is challenging. Teachers need to be critical and reflective practitioners, committed to taking responsibility for their own personal development. Critical evaluation of their own history teaching using evidence such as the observations of others, pupil feedback, assessment evidence and learning from the practice of others are attributes of a professional, learning teacher. Of equal importance is maintaining an up-to-date interest in primary history teaching and new developments in practice. This might involve attendance at courses run by local authority history advisors and meeting colleagues from other schools. Personal professional development can also be enhanced by membership of organizations such as the Historical Association and through keeping up to date by reading new primary history publications and regular journals such as *Primary History*. Personal enthusiasm in history and a genuine professional interest can really enhance the quality of history teaching and in turn motivate and enthuse the children on their journeys into the past.

References

Bage. G. (1999), *Narrative Matters: Teaching and Learning Through Story*. London: Falmer Press.

BECTA, (2003), *Using Web-based Resources in Primary History*. Coventry; BECTA.

Bowen, P. and Hoodless, P. (2006), *100 history Lessons Ages 5–7*. Leamington Spa: Scholastic.

Claire, H. (2004), 'Oral History: A powerful tool or a double edged sword?' *Primary History*, Winter, 20–23.

DfEE/National Advisory Committee on Creative and Cultural Education (2001), *All our Futures: Creativity, Culture and Education*, London: HMSO.

DfES (2003), *Excellence and Enjoyment: A Strategy for Primary Schools*. Nottingham: DfES Publications.

DfES (2005), *Developing the Global Dimension in the School Curriculum*. Glasgow: Department of International Development.

DfEE/QCA (1999), *The National Curriculum: Handbook for Primary Teachers in England*. London: HMSO.

Hoodless, P. (ed.), (1998), *Teaching History and English in the Primary School: Exploiting the Links*. London: Routledge.

Hoskins, W. G. (1967), *Fieldwork in Local History*. London: Faber and Faber.

Jones, R. and Wyse, D. (eds), (2004), *Creativity in the Primary Curriculum*. London: David Fulton.

Redfern, A. (1996), *Talking in Class: Oral History and the National Curriculum*. London: Oral History Society.

Robert, I. and Moses, B. (2005), *The Second World War*. London: David Fulton.

Woodhouse, J. (2001), 'Teaching history through nursery rhymes at the Foundation Stage'. *Primary History*, January 27.

Young, M. with Commins, E. (2001), *Global Citizenship: The Handbook for Primary Teaching*. Oxford: Oxfam Publishing.

Modern Foreign Languages (MFL): Teaching the Curriculum

7

Gee Macrory

Chapter Outline

'It should be in the curriculum and it should be statutory... and there is no reason why the primary teacher can't do it!' Year 2 undergraduate

Introduction

For the first time, we have in England a National Languages Strategy (DfES, 2002). Arising out of the Nuffield Report (2000), a report of a government enquiry into our national capability in languages, the strategy has as its cornerstone early language learning, arguably one of the most significant and challenging developments to the primary curriculum in England since the introduction of the National Curriculum in 1988. From January 2010, all children in Key Stage 2 will be entitled to learn a modern language in curriculum time. More recently, Lord Dearing in his review of languages (DfES, 2007) has recommended that languages become part of the statutory primary curriculum, ideally by September 2010. As we move rapidly towards this date, it is imperative that we all face the challenges that this brings with understanding and confidence. The first question one might wish to address is whether this is in fact an appropriate initiative. What place does a modern language have in the primary curriculum?

The place of modern foreign languages in the curriculum

A salutary place to begin might be the simple statistics of the multilingual world in which we live. There are over 5,000 spoken languages in the world (Crystal, 1997) and fewer than 200 nation states. Thus, we live in a multilingual and multicultural world. Both the imperatives of global citizenship and the economy underline the need for us to communicate with speakers of other languages, an issue recognized at European and at national level. But why start early?

There is, of course, a long-held view that, quite simply, younger equals better when it comes to language learning. It may seem strange to address this part of the chapter by an apparent negative, but Lightbown and Spada (1999) actually list this as one of the myths about language learning! Indeed, there is research that suggests that in fact adolescents and young adults are the ones that excel at language learning, progressing at a faster rate than children and being better able to make use of memory skills and metalinguistic strategies (Snow and Hoefnagel-Höhle, 1978). On the other hand, advocates of an early start point to better pronunciation in young children (Fathman, 1975; Ellis, 1985). Overall, however, this is an area where the research is inconclusive (see Sharpe and Driscoll, 2000). So why not wait until secondary school? The answer is that there are many other sound reasons for beginning early. What might these be? There are several:

- Positive attitudes towards learning languages and towards other cultures: teachers surveyed about the benefits of early language learning rated these two highest (Driscoll *et al.*, 2004: 52).
- Content of languages curriculum: some of the basics which include such things as numbers, colours, talking about oneself, are much more suited to young children.
- Preparation for secondary school: for a number of children, one of the things they find daunting when they consider the demands of secondary school is the requirement to study a language for the first time. Schools themselves can see the benefits and some report that children arrive with a sound approach to language learning, motivated and uninhibited (Driscoll *et al.*, 2004: 72).
- Enjoyment: research suggests that this is an area that gives children much pleasure and satisfaction (Driscoll *et al.*, 2004). This is consistent with the government move towards promoting 'Excellence and Enjoyment' (DfES, 2003) in the curriculum.
- The possibility of learning languages in a more cross-curricular way: in primary school, the curriculum is more integrated than at secondary level, offering the possibility of reinforcing the new language in different parts of the curriculum.
- Inclusion: for some learners, languages have already been part of the primary curriculum. Children who live in certain parts of the country, are from areas that are less affluent, or who are learning English as an additional language, are less likely to learn a language in curriculum time (Driscoll *et al.*, 2004). Many children in private schools receive tuition in a language from an early age, or attend

private clubs after school. The entitlement should ensure an early start for *all* children, irrespective of background.

The European Commission is unequivocal in its endorsement for an early start, stating that 'it is a priority for Member States to ensure that language learning in kindergarten and primary school is effective, for it is here that key attitudes towards other languages and cultures are formed and the foundations for later language learning are laid' (Commission of the EC, 2003: 7). On the broader international front, initiatives within and beyond Europe remind us that the promotion of languages in England and Wales is part of a wider development. Not only are there initiatives at a European level (see Rixon, 1992; Blondin *et al.*, 1998) but beyond, for example, Australia (Clyne *et al.*, 1995), the Middle and Far East (Kim, 1998) and, perhaps most well-known and of long standing, Canada (Swain and Lapkin, 1982).

Some may argue that primary languages have been tried unsuccessfully in the past in England. The most well-known initiative was in the 1960s, and the apparent lack of success of this resulted in languages being put back on the shelf for some time (Burstall *et al.*, 1974). Sadly, some of the positive findings attracted less attention than they could have, notably the gains in listening comprehension. More recently, we have learned much of value from the 1993–94 Scottish national training programme (Low *et al.*, 1995), the CILT/DfES Good Practice Project (CILT, 2002), as well as from the continuing work by CILT since 2001 (Development of Early Language Learning Project), work done in primary schools (Ofsted, 2004) and in Pathfinder Local Education Authorities (Ofsted, 2005; Muijs *et al.*, 2005) about effective practice in primary languages teaching. Equally, reports of current provision in primary languages (Powell *et al.*, 2000 and Driscoll *et al.*, 2004) highlight key elements that are important to making an early language learning programme work in practice.

Planning

Subject knowledge

We have so far established some sound reasons for teaching primary languages and we need now to consider how we might begin to plan for teaching this. So what do teachers need to know? What kinds of subject knowledge are needed? Before we do, however, the Key Stage 2 Framework for Languages deserves some consideration here, given the high profile that it has so far been given by the government. Published in 2005, its three linear learning objectives are oracy, literacy and intercultural understanding, with two further strands – knowledge about language and language learning strategies – designed to 'cut across' these and support them. It places great emphasis on developing language learning skills and not simply the content of one particular language. In thinking about subject knowledge and planning we need to keep in mind the breadth of experience that the framework implies for children learning languages.

The subject knowledge issue that usually produces the most anxiety is the ability to speak a language well enough to teach it. This is a most understandable worry, and we will return to it shortly. First of all, perhaps we need to take a broader view of subject knowledge. What aspects of the culture are important for teachers starting out on language teaching? Some research into topics that may interest young children, such as food, school or what happens at certain festivals, can provide a useful starting point, and such information is not generally difficult to access. Most importantly, if we are serious about developing intercultural understanding and appreciation of diversity, as well as motivation and ability to learn languages, then we need to adopt this wider perspective ourselves! A teacher does not need to be an expert linguist to create an appropriate context that facilitates language learning.

Providing the right environment is very important and can be done without too much difficulty; posters of the target cultures and countries are invaluable – it is easy to forget that many children have no idea what they may look like. A French or Spanish corner where you encourage pupils to make contributions raises their awareness. When teaching Year 6, the variety of items that they brought from home – from postcards to yogurt cartons – was inspiring, as was their willingness to create friezes and mobiles for their classroom. Another aspect is that primary languages teaching allows us to capitalize upon other languages children speak so that the classroom becomes not just a 'French' one, but a multilingual and multicultural one.

This is not to say, however, that the issue of linguistic expertise is unimportant. It is clearly essential that children have appropriate models of language use. But before we become too worried, let us take a considered look at the situation. Few people nowadays have never studied another language. If we start with residual anxieties arising from our own schooldays, we need to audit our own knowledge honestly and carefully, to identify, crucially, what we *do* know, and to set ourselves realistic targets for developing that knowledge. We need to clarify what expectations the school has of us.

At the beginning, it may be that your role is simply to support what is happening in the school already, by the classroom environment and a positive spirit! Possibly you need to contribute by reinforcing in class some language another teacher has introduced. The support that this teacher can offer you is invaluable. Observing and taking part in the lesson yourself is a real opportunity to practise the language and to observe your pupils. Which pupils excelled? Which pupils need more support? What aspects of the pronunciation seemed to be problematic? You may be faced with the more daunting task of introducing some new language yourself. At least in the early stages of the curriculum, it is unlikely that you will have to introduce a great deal of new language in one lesson, and it is infinitely better to learn a small amount well than to adopt an overly ambitious 'across-the-board' approach to the language. A step-by-step approach that anticipates the next stage allows you to learn and prepare in a steady and systematic way. The important thing is to have a sound grasp of what early learners might need to cover. Tapes and videos of native speakers also are a great aid in the classroom, both for you and your pupils.

A further key element is an understanding of *how* children learn languages. Firstly, we need an understanding of how first languages are learned. Secondly, we need a clear view of the similarities and differences between first and subsequent language learning. When thinking about similarities, some key issues to consider include the fact that error is an inescapable part of language learning – it may help learners to recognize that across the planet and throughout history, no one has *ever* learned a language without making errors! Other similarities are the gradual build-up of vocabulary and grammatical structures, the way in which using language as often as possible helps to reinforce learning, and the way in which the frequency of hearing it helps to tune the ear and to enable learners to break up the stream of speech sounds.

There are differences too, of course. The degree of difference will vary according to a number of factors, but a key one here is age. Very young children will behave much more like children learning a first language. A three-year-old will willingly try out new sounds and engage in songs, rhymes and other activities without feeling self-conscious, whereas it is possible that the older child, say of eight or nine, will already have a degree of anxiety and an awareness of the disparity in competence between their first language(s) and the new one being introduced in the classroom. On the other hand, the older child has resources not yet available to the very early learner in the form of enhanced memory skills, an ability to consider the differences between languages and a beginning grasp of patterns and regularities in language that can serve as an aid to understanding.

We have already considered subject knowledge in a somewhat holistic way and in relation to the strands in the Key Stage 2 Framework for Languages. However, it can be helpful to begin to think about specific content: what topics and related vocabulary do we need? While the Key Stage 2 Framework for Languages does not suggest or prescribe topics in quite the same way, and thus gives a degree of freedom, we easily think of topics that might be of interest to young children – for example, their friends, hobbies and pets. It is not overly difficult to predict and prepare the vocabulary needed for these topics. What parts of the grammatical system do we need to be secure in? In the early stages, the present tense of commonly used verbs, the noun and adjective system and relevant articles and prepositions form a sound basis. Once started, the learning of the language is not necessarily as daunting as it seems. Keeping a clear view of what you need to teach and making good pronunciation and spelling a priority will also help you to focus your efforts in the right direction.

A further issue that is worthy of separate consideration is the teacher's use of the target language in the classroom beyond the actual lesson content. Ideally, young children – or, arguably, learners of any age – need to hear as much of the new language as possible. This helps to familiarize their ears to the new sounds and to build confidence in their understanding of the new language. Again, focusing as precisely as possible upon what you need is vital. It is relatively easy to draw up a list of simple greetings and routine instructions that you feel comfortable using. This could be as simple as the language for 'hello' and 'goodbye', 'how are you?' and some simple instructions such as 'stand up', 'sit down', 'put your hand up' and the words for 'write, look, copy, listen'. If this list is short to begin with, it can be added to as your confidence grows.

Principles underpinning planning

Some principles arise easily from the issues outlined above. How might we summarize such principles? Key elements include:

- Global citizenship should be our starting point, with an understanding that languages and cultures transcend national boundaries. Whatever language we choose, we should look at its use worldwide and by a range of peoples. For example, in deciding to teach French, there are many countries and cultures in the world where French is spoken, including Africa, Canada and countries such as Cambodia. The opportunities for enriching the curriculum are immense.
- Effective language teaching should foster intercultural understanding, value all languages and embrace the notion of linguistic diversity. The diversity of languages in many of our schools provides a perfect springboard for this. Where this is not already the case, the teaching of a language in primary school is the ideal means to promote this.
- Communication should be seen as a key aim. By this we mean the ability to understand others through the spoken and written word, and in turn to convey to others our own meanings.
- As far as possible, authentic contexts for communication need to be created. It is perhaps ironic that it is virtual communication that conveys the reality of another culture. The benefits of technology are impossible to overestimate. Communication through email and video-conferencing offers a reality that no textbook can match! Exchanges with a country where the new language is spoken, or meeting speakers of that language, are invaluable in conveying the living nature of language.
- There should be well-thought-out linguistic progression underpinning the languages curriculum. Prioritizing communication does *not* mean that teaching is not based on carefully planned and well-sequenced lessons.
- This progression should be based on our understanding of how children learn languages and the role of age (see below) in language learning.
- Learning a language should be interactive and based on using the language. Language is learned *during* use – we do not learn language and then use it. However, there is a role for metalinguistic

knowledge that is age-appropriate and very effective links can be made with mother tongue literacy knowledge. The Key Stage 2 Framework for Languages (DfES, 2005) offers a structure within which this can be done.

- There should be a balance of skills (oracy and literacy) according to age. At times, teachers express concerns that the written word may either demotivate or confuse children. Done judiciously, this can reinforce and enhance learning.
- Activities should appeal to a range of different learning styles, based on aural, visual and kinaesthetic approaches.
- Teaching needs to be based on an understanding of the role of error in language learning. We need to show sensitivity to the role of confidence in children's learning by recognizing that errors are part of language learning and by fostering a classroom climate that accepts error and encourages risk-taking.
- We need to encourage as much use of the target language in the classroom as possible – by the teacher as well as the children. We need to remember how little of the new language children may otherwise hear, and how few opportunities they may get to use it, in comparison with the way they learned their first language(s).
- Finally, we need a culturally and linguistically supportive environment. Part of this is the positive attitude to error mentioned above, but another important aspect is this: children should not simply be learning a particular language, but should be learning how to learn languages, so that they have language learning skills for life. They therefore need to think about *how* they learn as well as *what*. The classroom needs to support their learning by displays, books, dictionaries, videos, maps and other resources that reflect the culture as well as the language.

Developing objectives

As with all subjects, developing medium- and short-term objectives is crucial. When doing this in languages, it is important to recognize the differences between behavioural/functional objectives and linguistic objectives. These are both important and should relate closely to each other. A behavioural/functional objective might be something like 'children will learn to name fruits in French and to say which fruits they like'. The linguistic objective needs therefore to be 'vocabulary for fruit (listed) and j'aime/je n'aime pas'. The language to be taught needs to be sequenced over a number of lessons in a logical way and a variety of activities planned for that will allow the children to meet the intended outcomes.

Teaching strategies

Knowing *what* is one thing, but knowing *how* is another. Even those of us who might be fluent and confident in another language may well wonder where to start in order to teach it!

Presenting new language is a key element of language teaching. This needs to be done as clearly and unambiguously as possible. First of all, an accurate and clear model of pronunciation needs to be offered by the teacher. Let us suppose that we are going to introduce the names of some food items in the new language. It is important to contextualize the language that is to be introduced, and this can be done in a number of ways, such as through the use of pictures. A picture of a family eating a meal can focus the children's minds on the topic of food before you actually introduce them to names for the food items in the target language. When the new language is presented, visual aids can support the spoken word so that the meaning is clear. Visual aids might be pictures (traditional pictures or electronic displays on an interactive whiteboard), realia such as plastic food items for young children, or, for that matter, real food items. Handling items and smelling and/or tasting them enables children to use a range of senses in their learning.

A second issue to consider is how to provide opportunities to practise and use the spoken language, since language is learned through use. Children need the chance to hear the language and to repeat it. Getting the class to repeat new language together or in pairs or groups enables them to practise without feeling too exposed and individual repetition, either on a voluntary basis or at the teacher's request, can be a next step in the learning. Practice activities can include games, rhymes and songs, and for young children puppets and toys can serve as useful ways of overcoming shyness. Practice helps children develop good pronunciation at the same time as helping them to memorize the new language. Games such as 'noughts and crosses' or Pelmanism are easy to adapt to language teaching and can help to develop memory skills.

Inclusive practices

There will, of course, be a need to differentiate according to ability. Strategies for anticipating difficulties – for example pronunciation – and providing support, especially for children with special educational needs (SEN), will be needed and additional opportunities may be required to practise and reinforce the new learning. Different skills areas may require differing levels of support, so that for some children extra practise in listening may be needed whereas for others it may be support for spelling. On the other hand, some children may so quickly absorb the new language that you are left wondering what to do! This is where a resource box of worksheets, books, dictionaries and games can be very useful to allow the children additional opportunities to work independently. Often children are happy to peruse such material and at other times they may need a task to extend them, such as setting them the challenge to find and learn five new food items of their choice.

At times, there are activities that all can do but with different outcomes. For example, playing Pelmanism in groups, some children can earn points for saying the noun correctly, whereas others are encouraged to embed this in a sentence (*je n'aime pas la pizza*) in order to gain a point.

Assessment

Assessment of learning (summative assessment)

Assessment is very important and need not detract from the enjoyable aspects of language learning. This is a key issue if progression is to be monitored and is indispensable to transition to secondary school. As one primary teacher said, 'if we don't tell the secondary school teachers what the children have learned, how can we expect them to make effective transition arrangements?' There is a clear relationship between progression and assessment.

However, it is important to consider what it is that we are assessing when we assess language learning. One key issue, long a matter of debate, is whether we assess communication or accuracy or both? A second issue is that of assessing skills discretely. Does it make sense to separate out the four skills of speaking, listening, reading and writing? The non-statutory guidance for Key Stage 2 (QCA, 1999) gives us a set of levels for each of the skills, whereas the recently published *Languages Ladder* (DfES, 2005), based on the Common European Framework, takes a more holistic approach. The Junior European Languages Portfolio (CILT) provides a useful format for recording and acknowledging children's progress. However, assessing in languages is not just about summative assessment and recording – as with other subjects, assessment is part and parcel of the teaching and learning process, hence the importance of assessment for learning.

Resources

There are, of course, published/commercially available resources that are excellent and versatile. Commercially-produced resources include videos and DVDs, songs and rhymes on CD, and ICT-based resources for the interactive whiteboard. Big books, too, are increasingly available in a range of languages.

However, we must not overlook the role that general classroom resources – such as the OHP, acetates, tiddlywinks or beans for playing games like noughts and crosses, CD player, coloured pens, wrapping paper (for pass the parcel), linking cubes, bingo cards, toys and puppets, card for mobiles, friezes and displays – can play. In starting out, it is a wise investment of time to consider what you want to teach over an initial period of time and then think about the resources you will need. An audit of what is already available in school can be followed by the judicious selection of a small 'starter pack' of a good set of songs and rhymes, some books, posters and maps. If you are anxious about your own pronunciation, you may wish to prioritize CDs or DVDs that have fluent speakers of the language to use while you build up your confidence.

Conclusion

As a generalist primary teacher, you have much to offer. After all, the teacher is the key resource in any classroom and this is just as true in the languages classroom – taking it step by step should mean that there is no reason why the primary teacher cannot very effectively support the learning of modern foreign languages, whatever their initial starting point.

References

Blondin, C., Chandelier, M., Edelenbos, P., Johnstone, R., Kubanek-German, A. and Taeschner, T. (1998), *Foreign Languages in Primary and Pre-school Education: Context and Outcomes. A Review of Recent Research within the European Union.* London: CILT.

Burstall, C., Jamieson, M., Cohen, S. and Hargreaves, M. (1974), *Primary French in the Balance.* Slough: NFER.

CILT (2002), *The Early Language Learning Initiative: Report on phase 1, 1999–2001.* London: CILT.

CILT/QCA (2003), *Modern Foreign Languages and Literacy at KS 2 and 3.* London: CILT.

Clyne, M., Jenkins, A., Chan. I., Tsokalidou, R. and Wallner, T. (1995), *Developing Second Language from Primary School: Models and Outcomes.* Deakin: National Languages and Literacy Institute of Australia.

Commission of the European Communities (2003), *Communication from the Commission to the Council, the European Parliament, the Economic and Social Committee and the Committee of the Regions, Promoting Language Learning and Linguistic Diversity: An Action Plan 2004–2006.* Brussels, 24.07.2003 COM (2003) 449 final.

Crystal, D. (1997), *The Cambridge Encyclopedia of Language.* Cambridge: Cambridge University Press.

Department for Education and Skills (DfES) (2002), *Languages for all, languages for Life: A Strategy for England.* London: HMSO.

DfES (2003), *Excellence and Enjoyment: A Strategy for Primary Schools.* DfES0377/2003.

DfES (2005), *National Voluntary Recognition Scheme for Foreign Languages – The Languages Ladder.* London: HMSO.

DfES (2007), *Languages Review.* London: HMSO.

Driscoll, P., Jones, J. and Macrory, G. (2004), *The provision of foreign language learning for pupils at KS2*, DfES Report: ISBN 1 84478 306 5.

Ellis, R. (1985), *Understanding Second Language Acquisition.* Oxford: Oxford University Press.

Fathman, A. (1975), 'The relationship between age and second language productive ability'. *Language Learning*, 25, 245–54.

Ioannou-Georgiou, S. and Pavlou, P. (2003), *Assessing Young Learners.* Oxford: Oxford University Press.

Jones, J. and Coffey, S. (2006), *Modern Foreign Languages 5–11: a Guide for Teachers.* London: David Fulton Publishers.

Kim, J. R. (1998), 'Elementary education reforms in Korea'. *The Language Teacher.* www.jalt-publications. org/tlt/files/98/oct/kim.html (accessed 15 August 2006).

Lightbown, P. and Spada, N. (1999), *How Languages are Learned*, 2nd edn. Oxford: Oxford University Press.

Low, L., Brown, S., Johnstone, R. and Pirrie, A. (1995), *Foreign Languages in Primary Schools: Evaluation of the Scottish Pilot Projects 1993–1995 Final Report.* Stirling: CILT.

Muijs, D., Barnes, A., Hunt, M., Powell, B., Arweck, E. and Lindsay, G. (2005), *Evaluation of the Key Stage 2 Language Learning Pathfinders.* DfES Report RR692.

Nuffield Foundation (2000), *Languages: The Next Generation.* London: Nuffield Foundation.

Office for Standards in Education (Ofsted) (2004), *Ofsted subject reports 2002/2003: Modern foreign languages in primary schools.* London, TSO.

Ofsted (2005), *Implementing languages entitlement in primary schools: An evaluation of progress in ten Pathfinder LEAs.* Ref.no.HMI 2476.

Powell, B., Wray, D., Rixon, S., Medwell, J., Barnes, A. and Hunt, M. (2000), *Analysis and evaluation of the current situation relating to the teaching of Modern Foreign Languages at Key Stage 2 in England.* University of Warwick: Centre for Language Teacher Education.

Qualifications and Curriculum Authority (QCA) (1999), *The National Curriculum Handbook for Primary Teachers in England: Guidelines for Modern Foreign Languages at Key Stage 2 (non-statutory).* London: QCA.

Rixon, S. (1992), 'State of the art article: English and other languages for younger children: practice and theory in a rapidly-changing world'. *Language Teaching*, 25 (2), 73–93.

Sharpe, K. and Driscoll, P. (2000), 'At what age should foreign language learning begin?' in K. Field (ed.), *Issues in Modern Foreign Languages Teaching.* London: RoutledgeFalmer.

Snow, C. and Hoefnagel-Höhle, M. (1978), 'Age differences in second language acquisition'. In E. M. Hatch (ed.), *Second Language Acquisition: A Book of Readings.* Rowley, Massachusetts: Newbury House.

Swain, M. and Lapkin, S. (1982), *Evaluating Bilingual Education.* Clevedon: Multilingual Matters.

Further reading

Cameron, L. (2001), *Teaching Languages to Young Learners*. Cambridge: Cambridge University Press.

Driscoll, P. and Frost, D. (1999), *The Teaching of Modern Foreign Languages in the Primary School*. London: Routledge.

Ebenlos, P. and Johnstone, R. (eds) (1996), *Researching Languages at Primary School: Some European Perspectives*. London: CILT.

Sharpe, K. (2001), *Modern Foreign Languages in the Primary School: the what, where and why of early MFL teaching*. London: Kogan Page.

Singleton, D. (1989), *Language Acquisition and the Age Factor*. Clevedon: Multilingual Matters.

Useful websites

www.nacell.co.uk
Educational resources
www.cilt.org.uk
(See CILT Young Pathfinder Series)

Modern Foreign Languages (MFL): Beyond the Curriculum

8

Gee Macrory

Chapter Outline

'The whole thing has been brought to life for them!' Teacher in local school partnered with a school in France

Introduction

In the first chapter on teaching modern languages in the primary school (Chapter 7) we looked at the place of this subject in the curriculum and considered what might be needed in terms of subject knowledge and subject pedagogy to create effective language teaching lessons and to plan for assessment. In this chapter, we are going to take a broader look at the kinds of language learning opportunities we might want to consider for the children in our schools. We will begin by thinking about possible models of provision for the primary school. However, models of provision need to address the principles of good practice set out in Chapter 7. We will thus be referring to such issues as global citizenship, communication in language teaching and other elements of effective teaching and learning in primary languages.

Models of provision and cross-curricular themes

Most people embarking upon a career in teaching will be familiar with a secondary school approach to teaching languages. While this is true of all subjects up to a point, we generally also have our memories of primary school upon which to draw. This is usually not the case with modern languages as for most of us this will be a subject we embarked upon only at the age of 11 or thereabouts. What are the implications of this? A key issue is the nature of the secondary curriculum in Britain, which is historically very compartmentalized. Children's timetables set out discretely a sequence of lessons such as history, maths, art and French. The language (let us say French for argument's sake) will be taught at set times several times a week and will typically not be referred to by other teachers in other lessons.

Perhaps for many children the defining feature (certainly one of the most important) of secondary school itself is the fact of having a different teacher for every 'subject'. There are, of course, distinct advantages in this discrete approach: for example, it permits the teacher to be highly skilled in one area, to have an overview of the whole age range and the understanding of progression within a particular subject area that comes with this, and allows her or him to plan a carefully sequenced programme of language teaching that is progressive, recursive and developmental. This means that it is often easier to address the issue of linguistic progression. Furthermore, children can concentrate on one subject at a time when they are in a lesson and this often takes place in a dedicated classroom environment with subject-specific resources and facilities. The important issue of intercultural understanding and awareness of global issues can of course be embedded in the teaching and learning of the language. The teaching of French through what French Muslim children do to celebrate Eid can sit as comfortably in the curriculum as German lessons on what children in Austria do at Easter. Interactive activities can include a balance of skills and appeal to different learning styles, and the teacher can do much to create a supportive environment: maximizing use of the target language, adopting a sensitive approach to error, providing access to technology and ensuring that the physical classroom environment reflects an enjoyment and awareness of other languages and cultures.

The familiarity of this model may predispose us to adopt this approach when in a primary school. As is the case with older children, there are the advantages and possibilities set out above. And if the teacher introducing languages to the primary school is someone from the local high school this will be an obvious way to start; and for those learning from such a visiting teacher an equally obvious model to take up. However, there are also some disadvantages to this.

The linguist Eric Hawkins famously described this model of secondary school language teaching as 'gardening in a gale' (1981), meaning that the language learned in the lesson was swept away by the 'gale' of English that surrounded the children the minute they left their language lesson. Even several lessons per week represent only a small amount of time, with the result that new language can be quickly forgotten. Furthermore, this approach can locate the language in the children's minds within a notion of a school subject, rather than a real and useful skill for life. Sincere attempts to acknowledge and include the range of linguistic and cultural backgrounds within a teaching group, and to make reference beyond the confines of a particular language and its most well-known geographical location, may suffer from the pressure of covering the syllabus in a limited amount of time and thus may even be seen as tokenistic.

The primary school context, on the other hand, offers a more integrated environment within which language learning and teaching can take place. By this I mean that the same teacher is usually responsible for all areas of the curriculum and able thus to identify greater opportunities for language learning. Even if there is one person responsible for discrete elements of delivery, class teachers can work alongside and with such colleagues to provide a coherent and integrated approach. What might the advantages of a more cross-curricular approach be? Firstly, and perhaps most obviously, there is the frequency with which new (and old!) language can be reinforced and consolidated. The children do not have to wait until a designated day and lesson to practise some new grammatical structures or vocabulary items. More than this, however, the other parts of the curriculum offer myriad opportunities to include the language as part of the lesson. Thus another potential advantage is that language learning need not come wholly at the expense of the time needed for other subject areas. Some examples follow.

Maths

Mathematical operations with the numbers taught in a language lesson give valuable practice of both maths and the language itself. Here, the language is being used for real communication. Even simple mathematical operations can convey the notion that the language has a real purpose. These can even serve as a way of reinforcing or revisiting previously taught elements of the maths curriculum, which may be particularly supportive of the needs of children with learning difficulties in this area.

Geography

Maps, flags and other aspects of the target country or countries can be included in the geography lesson. The kind of language needed for some topics in geography is often descriptive and can easily be supported by visuals. Topics such as weather can be delivered in the target language, and learning reinforced by producing weather mobiles for the classroom. Part of geography is developing an awareness of the lives of others, and there are excellent visuals available (for example, www.oxfam.co.uk) of children's lives and experiences around the world that can easily be presented in another language. There are clear links here to citizenship too.

Music

Children enjoy singing but we can go well beyond this. Having to recognize items in the target language and imitate these gives the opportunity for listening comprehension at the same time as developing other skills. Having to follow instructions in the target language can act as an incentive and activities including such things as counting and clapping can develop a sense of rhythm that is useful both for music and for tuning into the stress and intonation patterns of a new language.

Physical education

As in music, following instructions to learn or practise skills can be a great way to both focus attention and practise the new language. Children can of course practise *giving* the instructions as well as understanding them. Learning rules for a new game can be done in the target language too. While much will be done orally, reading and writing activities could also be developed where age- and stage-appropriate.

Drama

Plays of famous stories or festivals can easily be created through the device of direct speech. Carefully chosen vocabulary and structures in speech bubbles combined with lively visuals can create an accessible play script. On other occasions, simple props and contexts can give children the opportunity to use the language they know with real spontaneity. For example, a common activity is ordering or choosing food and drink in a 'café'. Short activities simply to allow children to speak and to encourage confidence include, for example, asking them to say something – anything! – about an item you hold up. This could be saying the name of the object, requesting it, saying what colour it is and so on. More advanced language learners can take two or three items either of their choice or the teacher's and create a dialogue based on it. This can be great fun as well as a real learning opportunity. Although errors will naturally happen, both teachers and learners need to keep at the forefront of their minds that this is inevitable and part of the learning process. A positive perspective on error can liberate learners from anxiety and let them adopt a playful, experimental approach that gives them a chance to use the language.

English

This offers a host of possibilities. Speaking activities can highlight pronunciation. For example, the consonant cluster 'pf' as in *Pferd* (German for 'horse') simply does not exist in English. Stress and intonation patterns can be compared and discussed. Learning another language can enhance grammatical awareness and understanding – noticing the order of words is invaluable, whether this is the verb needing to be at the end of the sentence in German or the adjective coming after the noun in numerous other languages. There are invaluable opportunities to focus the children's attention on important aspects of literacy, such as spelling. Apparent similarities such as 'ch' in both French and English can give rise to discussion of its different pronunciation in the two languages. Equally, differences can prompt children to reflect with renewed awareness on the conventions of English and for that matter any other languages they are familiar with. This might include accents, an area where ICT can be very supportive, as the effective use of the keyboard allows children to see that, for example, *é* or *ç* are letters in their own right, rather than seeing accents as something that you 'sprinkle' on top of or underneath otherwise familiar graphemes! Teaching techniques such as cutting and pasting or dragging text can also be combined with teaching about word order.

Art

This is another area that lends itself very well to integration with languages. At its most obvious, it can provide an easy way to introduce colour terms. These can be used to describe pictures, give instructions or teach children about colour mixing. Art, of course, is not just about colour. Shapes, sizes and directionality can be included, as can personal opinions about pieces of work.

History

A lesson on clothes in earlier periods could introduce new language or reinforce vocabulary taught previously. Use of the past tense in the target language sits very appropriately in history of course!

Science

There are numerous ways to integrate this with languages. The solar system, for example, can be so easily illustrated with real objects or pictures. Growing plants and talking about the need for rain and sunshine can link effectively to conversing about the weather also.

This is by no means a comprehensive coverage of integrating languages into the curriculum. There are many opportunities and clear advantages – we have already noted the way in which this approach helps to create time in the curriculum and to reinforce the language frequently and regularly for the learners. However, this is not simply a practical consideration but also a pedagogic one. In addition to the value of frequent opportunities to be exposed to and to use the target language, children can engage in real communication about meaningful things.

As we have pointed out earlier, it is through use that language is learned. We do not learn it simply in order to use it later. The cross-curricular approach thus addresses many of the important principles of good practice we outlined in Chapter 7. As inspectors have noted, 'learning some content through the medium of the language can be a good motivator for children in addition to offering increased opportunities for language practice and use, as it can increase the sense of purpose … creative ways of linking language learning to other areas of the curriculum … contributed strongly to pupils' progress (Ofsted, 2005: 8). For other ideas, see Muir (1999) and Jones and Coffey (2006).

There are, however, at least two possible objections to this approach. From a subject content point of view, depending upon the age of the children and their level of attainment in a given subject area, it could result in a mismatch of content and language. For example, at the beginning stages of language learning, children's limited command of numbers in the new language may constrain the mathematical operations they can perform with them. It will make all the difference if the numbers one to ten are being taught to very young children where there will be a better match of content and language than would be the case with older children. The other issue is that of linguistic progression. A more integrated approach could potentially be a 'messier' one! From the point of view of the language to be learned, it could be spread more widely, be more disjointed and it could be difficult to plan and monitor progression. This is where planning comes in.

We are not suggesting that language learning is a neat and incremental process. Indeed, this is not the case with first language learning either (Macrory, 2001; see also Lightbown and Spada, 1999). Far from it – children will learn some parts of the grammar more quickly and easily than others, will make progress, then regress, make errors of all kinds and adopt (consciously or unconsciously) wrong hypotheses about the linguistic system. However, by careful planning, we can avoid unnecessary confusion, and assist children to see links. In Chapter 7, I talked about linguistic progression *within* a lesson. In the same way, we can plan across the curriculum over a period of time. So, for example, if we are going to teach a vocabulary set such as colours for younger children, this can be judiciously built into the art lesson, the robes that monarchy wore in previous times in the history lesson and a description of the solar system.

With more advanced learners, the past tense could be incorporated into the history lesson, but also used in a short report of an experiment in science and an account of an event in English. Instructional language can be focused on preparing some food, then perhaps in games and later in a music lesson.

So far we have considered the possibilities that the nature of the primary school curriculum offers to languages teaching, enabling a more holistic approach than has traditionally been the case at secondary level. Largely, however, this is a way of reinforcing and complementing the language teaching taking place. An even more integrated approach than this can be taken, whereby a subject or indeed a number of subjects are taught wholly through the medium of the target language. This is often known as Content and Language Integrated Learning (CLIL) where, crucially, the *content* is taught through the medium of the new language. Proponents of this approach argue that there are both educational benefits to learning new subject matter in another language and linguistic benefits from learning meaningful content (see, for example, Coyle, 2000 as well as examples of good practice in the Dearing Report, DfES, 2007). While the most well-known example is probably the Canadian immersion teaching, there has been recent interest in a number of European countries (European Commission, 2006). However, contextual issues vary hugely from one country to another, so that, for example, some countries may accord greater time and status to the issue of learning languages, a key factor in the success of particular approaches to the curriculum. An obvious concern is that the effective learning of the content itself may be jeopardized by the teaching of it in an unfamiliar language. There is not the scope to consider this issue in depth here, but it is important to recognize that there is a continuum of possibilities in terms of models of provision for primary languages (see Johnstone, 1994; Driscoll, 1999; Tierney and Gallastegi, 2005; Jones and Coffey, 2006).

Creating this integration between the curriculum and the language, however, does not need to remain within the classroom.

Beyond the classroom

A whole-school approach to language learning takes the early language initiative one step further. This has the added advantage of bringing into the initiative not only all the teachers but additional adults such as teaching assistants and so on. It also brings the place of language in the school to the attention of parents, carers and other visitors. It is important to reiterate the way in which this can contribute to the promotion of linguistic and cultural diversity more broadly. Some effective strategies that can be tried are suggested below.

Displays

Perhaps this is an obvious place to start but it is no less valuable for that. Displays that highlight the language itself can reinforce reading and writing in that language and the role that children play in their production can instil a sense of pride and purpose as they work on appropriate presentations. Displays can draw attention to the range of places where the new language is spoken as well as, of course, to any other languages spoken in the school. The cultural impact that positive images of people and places can offer should never be underestimated. The up-to-date information that can be provided about the countries is a valuable source of current world knowledge for children and their parents. As with all displays, they need to be changed at appropriate intervals and should reflect current events and festivals. They can also be interactive, seeking comment from people and asking questions. One successful display was a giant French advent calendar in a school, constructed on the floor-to-ceiling gym equipment in the hall. The relevant door was opened each morning at assembly by one of the children, and everyone had the opportunity to practise the date and the name of the Christmas-related item concealed behind it.

Assemblies

These can be an occasion to allow children the opportunity to demonstrate their knowledge in the new language and of the new culture, whether this is four-year-olds introducing their teddy bears or older children introducing their best friends. With the whole school as an audience this can be a real opportunity to practise presentation skills. Other activities appropriate to assembly time include songs and poems – always popular! Finally, visitors from abroad can play an invaluable role in giving children first-hand experience of their lives.

Real events using the target language

One primary school successfully created a café in a classroom and, after an assembly to which carers, parents and governors were invited, the latter were served drinks and snacks all in French. On other occasions, cookery lessons conducted in small groups in the school kitchen in the target language provided a service to all the teachers who were subsequently treated to the results, provided they used the target language in accepting the offerings from the kitchen. The head teacher too looked forward to the knock on the door that brought his weekly treat.

Beyond the school

So far in this chapter we have examined how we might reconsider the model of language learning typically associated with secondary schools in this country. The scope that primary schools have for extending learning outside the boundaries of subject and classroom and across the whole school is immense and can bring about real engagement on the part of the staff and parents as well as the children themselves. This in turn can contribute to sustainability of the initiative, an issue identified in previous research (Driscoll *et al.*, 2004). Yet we can take this a stage further by looking beyond the school itself.

In Chapter 7, I identified a number of issues as key to good practice, including first and foremost the notion that our children must grow up to be citizens of the world, open-minded and outward-looking. Hand-in-hand with this important objective is the ability to communicate with other people and other cultures and recognize the role that authentic contexts for language learning can play in developing such skills and awareness. As far as possible, then, children should be encouraged to step outside the classroom, either in reality or in a virtual sense, in order to engage with other children in other countries.

It could be argued that global understandings and intercultural communication can be effected without necessarily learning another's language. This is undoubtedly true, as otherwise we would be limited to the actual languages we can speak. On the other hand, the ability to speak to someone in *their* language and not just our own is a powerful intellectual and emotional engagement that can lead to a high degree of empathy. This in turn can lay the foundations for intercultural understandings at a broader level. In order to do this and in order to create authentic contexts for language learning itself, there is no substitute for contact with other speakers of that language.

A large number of schools now have links with schools in other countries and this provides the children with opportunities to engage in real communication with people their own age (as well as giving staff invaluable professional development opportunities). In order to illustrate the potential benefits of this, we will look at a case study of a group of schools in the north-west of England, each of which has a partner school in France.

Case study

The 20 schools in this particular project (funded by the Teacher Development Agency and the British Council) are drawn from five different local authorities. Set up in 2005 following a two-day visit by a member of staff to a partner school in France, each school has established links between a class group here and a class group in their partner school. As each school (and each teacher) created a personal and individual partnership, the details vary from school to school: in terms of the year group, frequency of exchanges, whether letters, emails or gifts are exchanged and whether the communication is from French to English or vice versa. Research with ten of these schools suggests that there is a positive impact in several ways (Macrory and Beaumont, 2006).

Case study (continued)

Firstly, as evidenced by the quote at the beginning of this chapter, 'the whole thing has been brought to life for them!' There is a clear sense in which the children are very engaged by the experience being a 'real' one. For many, finding out how similar French children are to themselves was at least as important (if not more so) as studying the differences. One teacher described his children as 'really, really excited … it has given them not just the language but an idea of what it is like for children in France and the differences and similarities'. Furthermore, the ways in which teachers then used the letters from the French children or the artefacts sent became important vehicles for teaching about culture and, in subjects like geography, a tendency to use the relevant area of France as a means of teaching geographical concepts. The teachers therefore reported an increased tendency to adopt a more cross-curricular approach; in addition, the role that letters and emails played resulted in more reading and writing work than before.

Most interesting, perhaps, was the independence that many children showed in their learning. Instances of children seeking to understand and use novel words and phrases were reported by their teachers, as was the way in which some children had learned new language through their exchanges that the teacher had not explicitly taught them. This suggests that the introduction of such a link can potentially alter the dynamic between teacher and child, and provide an element to the provision of language teaching that is truly communicative and promoting of intercultural understanding. Clearly, technology has a hugely promising role to play in such developments, with the internet and video-conferencing able to open doors hitherto closed – or as Jones and Coffey (2006: 130) describe it, 'a window on the world'.

Exciting as this is, it nevertheless raises important issues for teachers. The research project also highlighted some possible avenues for further investigation, such as the potential differential impact of such exchanges upon children of different ages, backgrounds and abilities. Of equal interest might be the long-term impact of this experience upon motivation, attitude and later language learning at secondary school as well as on their intercultural understanding. What we cannot deny is that language teaching in the primary school is a rapidly developing field and that this has implications for teachers who are involved. Thus the ability to reflect upon experience is underlined more than ever.

Reflecting upon language learning and teaching

The reflective practitioner is by no means a new concept but what it means in practice arguably varies according to contextual factors. In this particular case, we need to ask ourselves *what* we should be reflecting on and *how* we go about it. As a beginning teacher involved in this new curricular initiative, there may be several areas upon which to focus.

- Your subject knowledge, both linguistic and cultural: how do you audit this and how is your provider and/or school helping you with this? In terms of subject knowledge, we need to include the actual language and also experience of the culture. What kinds of targets might we set? These could be limited to a small set of linguistic and cultural objectives, possibly related to an area or areas that you have been asked to teach; they might be more ambitious and include a planned trip to the country. Consider carefully *how* you evaluate your progress, as thinking about your pronunciation, confidence, range of vocabulary, grasp of grammar and so on will in turn help you with monitoring and assessing the progress of the children you teach.
- Your teaching of discrete lessons: your more general skills in self-evaluation will also serve you well in modern language lessons. However, in addition to considering the appropriateness of objectives, pace, transition, classroom presence, classroom management and so on, try to tease out the elements of the lesson that are particular to language teaching. These include your modelling of good pronunciation and spelling, the children's accuracy, fluency and recall of the language, the balance of the four skills of speaking, listening, reading and writing, grammatical progression, your and their use of the target language throughout the lesson, your use of visuals and realia and your use of appropriate opportunities for assessment as well as how well your lesson links to documentation such as the National Curriculum and the KS2 Framework for Languages. You should think about the children's learning and their interest and motivation. Consider asking them – and their parents – for some feedback.
- A further issue to review and evaluate is your progress in consolidating your teaching of the language across the curriculum. Review your progress in cross-curricular teaching, reflecting upon the appropriateness of the match between content and language and whether the activities allow for the range of ability, learning style and background of your children.
- Now consider whether you have made a contribution at a whole-school level. What was it, why did you choose it and what impact did it have? What will you do next and why?
- Are there links with a school abroad? If so, review how much you know about this, establish who is in charge and arrange to be present when an exchange is taking place. Consider how you might evaluate the impact upon the children. For example, perhaps you could interview a small number of children to find out what role this is playing in their learning. If there is no such link, consider setting one up. The website www.globalgateway.org.uk will help you find suitable schools.

Conclusion

The questions above should serve as a means to help you evaluate your own progress in this relatively new but rapidly growing field. Considering them in isolation, however, is not enough. You need to think about how this part of your role as a teacher relates to all the other aspects of the job, and in parallel with this, how the children's progress in language learning relates to their overall progress. The 'data' you gather as you do this will equip you to answer the more fundamental questions that I addressed at the beginning of the earlier chapter. The principles of good practice to which I referred are offered to you as starting points. Ultimately, those to which you adhere need to arise from your own experience and your engagement with that experience. In other words, you need to work towards your own answers to those questions and not mine.

References

Coyle, D. (2000), 'Meeting the challenge: developing the 3Cs curriculum', in S. Green (ed.), *New Perspectives on Teaching and Learning Modern Languages.* Clevedon: Multilingual Matters.

DfES (2007), *Languages Review.* London: HMSO.

Driscoll, P. (1999), 'Modern foreign languages in the primary school: a fresh start', in P. Driscoll and D. Frost (eds), *The Teaching of Modern Foreign Languages in the Primary School.* London: Routledge.

Driscoll, P., Jones, J. and Macrory, G. (2004), *The provision of foreign language learning for pupils at Key Stage 2.* DfES Report: ISBN 1 84478 306 5.

European Commission (2006), *Content and Language Integrated Learning (CLIL) at School in Europe.* Brussels: Eurydice.

Hawkins, E. (1981), *Modern Languages in the Curriculum.* Cambridge: Cambridge Educational.

Johnstone, R. (1994), *Teaching Modern Languages at Primary School.* Edinburgh: The Scottish Council for Research in Education.

Jones, J. and Coffey, S. (2006), *Modern Foreign Languages 5–11: a Guide for Teachers.* London: David Fulton Publishers.

Lightbown, P. and Spada, N. (1999), *How Languages are Learned*, 2nd edn. Oxford: Oxford University Press.

Macrory, G. (2001), 'Language development: what do early years practitioners need to know?' *Early Years,* 21 (1), 33–40.

Macrory, G. and Beaumont, M. (2006), 'Partnership in Primary Languages: Implications for learning, teaching and training'. Paper presented at the British Association for Applied Linguistics Annual Conference, University of Cork, Republic of Ireland.

Muir, J. (1999), 'Classroom connections', in P. Driscoll and D. Frost (eds), *The Teaching of Modern Foreign Languages in the Primary School.* London: Routledge.

Ofsted (2005), *Implementing languages in primary schools: An evaluation of progress in ten Pathfinder LEAs.* Ofsted: HMI 2476.

Tierney, D. and Gallastegi, L. (2005), 'Where are we going with primary foreign languages?' *Language Learning Journal,* 31, 47–54.

Music: Teaching the Curriculum

Kate Buchanan

'I was born with music inside me. Music was one of my parts. Like my ribs, my kidneys, my liver, my heart. Like my blood. It was a force already within me when I arrived on the scene. It was a necessity for me – like food or water.' Ray Charles (1930–2004), American pianist and singer (Charles, 1978)

The place of music in the curriculum

Music is taught in schools because it is a natural human behaviour with a range of unique qualities. It also part of the compulsory curriculum (in England and Wales). In recent years, researchers have been working together from the fields of education, science, psychology and social sciences to help us improve our understanding of the role and relevance music has in society. Psychologists have shown that music is helpful in the development of a child's individual cognitive capabilities (Papousek, 1996) and provides opportunities for social interaction.

'Music provides for a child a medium for the gestation of a capacity for social interaction, a risk-free space for the exploration of social behaviour that can sustain otherwise potentially risky action and transaction' (Cross, 2001). In studies of neuroscience, it is becoming clear that music is associated with specific brain architecture and indicates that we are hard-wired for music. Evolutionary musicology and bio-cultural studies are revealing evidence that music may have been integral to the development of early humans. 'Without music, it could be that we would never have become human' (ibid.).

By understanding its evolutionary, cultural and social functions as well as its contribution to aesthetic and artistic education, we can begin to recognize the importance that music has in the primary curriculum.

Music can be expressive of many things – passion, playfulness, humour, sadness, strength, love, patriotism. It can be spontaneous, surprising, predictable, exciting and intuitive. It can create feelings of grief, wonder, dismay, admiration, happiness, awe. Many of these it shares with other art forms but one unique aspect is its relationship with time; we listen through time and it is literally 'of the moment'. Performing music with others or listening together can create meaningful and memorable social interaction. At times of distress it can create a bond of affection, a wordless exchange of emotion which is unique to music. In times of struggle music can help us through. In times of happiness music is there to enhance celebration. It is these emotional and aesthetic qualities that are important and the real reasons for equipping children with the skills to experience music for themselves as performers, composers and listeners.

Children come to school with an impressive range of musical abilities. As observed by Ray Charles, the music **is** inside. The extent to which pupils have absorbed or engaged in music varies. Infants who have been sung to are more likely to have developed a greater awareness of music than those who have not; other children may have absorbed a wide range of musical influences from home, television, computers, playgroups and nursery. Schools should be able to build upon these and present children with opportunities to explore and engage in musical experiences in various ways.

The benefits teaching music brings

Defining the benefits is not easy – many of us working in schools have observed the sheer pleasure and elation children experience when performing or listening to recordings of their own work. Research has demonstrated that learning music can improve children's spatial awareness, motor skills, self-esteem and achievement in mathematics and language (Rauscher *et al.*, 1997). The so-called Mozart-effect which appeared in slogans such as 'Music Makes You Smarter' provided interesting evidence but some of the claims in the media proved exaggerated. Nevertheless, some studies (for example, Michael Wallick's in Ohio, USA) suggest that teachers' commonly-held fears about pupils' learning being negatively affected by their withdrawal for specialist music tuition are unfounded – and that such tuition may enhance achievement in reading, writing, mathematics and citizenship. But it is not for academic achievement that music is taught. According to Music in the National Curriculum for England (DfEE/QCA, 1999): '…we teach music in schools because it is a powerful, unique form of communication that can change the way pupils feel, think and act'.

Schools which value music are often highly rated and many make claims that musical schools are happy schools. Music brings people together and can create shared experiences across generations and sectors irrespective of cultural, political or social divisions. See Chapter 10, 'Beyond the Curriculum', for examples of projects which show some of the benefits of musical activities outside the classroom.

What is in a music curriculum?

In the lead-up to the development of a national curriculum, music educators had the opportunity to decide what should be included. There was general agreement that pupils should sing, play instruments, listen and move to music. Three areas remained contentious: creative music-making (or composition), listening, and notation. Composing was seen by many as belonging to advanced studies in higher education, listening was seen as solely concerned with music appreciation, while others saw musical literacy and notation as a core skill. The critics doubted that composition (or invention) could be achieved by children as young as five years old and some bemoaned the fact that music appreciation and the acquisition of musical literacy through learning Western classical notation was not made a requirement.

After much debate in music education circles and following a number of revisions, the 1999 (current) version for England states: 'Teaching should ensure that "listening, and applying knowledge and understanding", are developed through the interrelated skills of "performing", "composing" and "appraising"'. (DfEE/QCA, 1999).

Scotland (Scottish Office Education Department, 1992) opted for music as part of the Expressive Arts curriculum encompassing inventing (rather than composing); Wales (QCAA Wales, 2000) adopted three strands of performing, composing and appraising. In the revised Northern Ireland curriculum implemented in 2007 (Department of Education for Northern Ireland, 2007), music combines with 'art and design' to form an arts curriculum with three strands: (1) working creatively with sound; (2) singing and performing; and (3) listening and responding.

Music from different times and cultures

All curricula in the UK refer to the importance of listening to a range of music. In Scotland and Wales special provision is made for the musical traditions of each nation. The primary curriculum for music in England (DfEE/QCA, 1999) encourages a breadth of study through 'a range of live and recorded music from different times and cultures (for example, from the British Isles, from classical, folk and popular genres, by well-known composers and performers)'. The bracketed examples are included in the description for Key Stage 2 (KS2).

Today, the music likely to be encountered in primary schools spans a wide range of styles and genres including gospel, samba, African drumming, MC-ing, jazz, folk, rock and pop, and classical. Prior to the 1970s, the emphasis was on Western classical music and arrangements of folk songs. The inclusion of popular music, jazz and 'World' music first appeared in secondary schools in the 1960s but it took time to become an accepted part of the curriculum. Many musicians and teachers felt this was long overdue not only because of pop music's relevance to young people but also because it gave opportunities to explore different modes of learning (see **Teaching and learning styles** below).

Musical styles

All styles of music are valid in the curriculum. The only proviso is that a teacher can enthuse about it, know something about it and communicate it with commitment. Until the 1980s, classical music was considered by some as the only valid style for inclusion in the curriculum. This provided barriers to generations of teachers who had not pursued a classically-based music education and who perceived their lack of knowledge as a barrier to teaching about the music they knew and loved. This increased the polarization between the music that children experienced in school and the music enjoyed out of school. Fortunately this limiting of styles is no longer the case and the curriculum should lead to a greater sharing and engagement with a wide range of musical styles of interest to pupils and teachers.

As a vehicle for listening, moving and responding, all music has relevance to children. In terms of playing and singing, the level of complexity in terms of technical difficulty, length and lyrics may need to be taken into account. The lyric content is often what determines appropriateness to a particular age group and not the musical content.

Through self-reflection and by understanding music's value and impact on a personal level, teachers can be encouraged to develop confidence in music. Follow the seven-step process overleaf to develop an awareness of your interests, understanding, strengths and weaknesses.

Step 1

Start with the music that you have grown up hearing and/or that has meaning to you. Make a list of what you listen to, how it affects you, when and where you listen to it.

Step 2

Note anything of interest, e.g. listening to rock music before going out for the evening; listening to music which brings back memories of a sad/happy/joyful/important event; performing at church or youth clubs; jamming with friends; creating soundtracks/clips/ backings on a computer.

Step 3

What were your early experiences of learning or performing music? Where did these happen – at home, at school, in the community? Make a list of positive/negative experiences.

Step 4

Review the complete picture: it is likely that your own experiences will highlight clear preferences for certain styles of music.

Step 5

Consider the emotional or functional uses of music in your life. Your engagement with music when you were at school may have been positive, memorable, negative or non-existent.

Step 6

Consider the challenges which you need to overcome from your early experiences in learning about music, e.g. improvisation; playing by ear.

Step 7

Identify your strengths and weaknesses in terms of musical competencies (e.g. singing and song repertoire, rhythm and beat, expressive understanding, instrumental skill, leading and directing).

Maximizing listening

As well as identifying the musical styles and genres which are important to a teacher responsible for music, an inclusive approach can also be encouraged with all staff. The following example shows how a school has created an inclusive approach to listening.

Case study

School A in South London has a policy where all staff are encouraged to nominate their favourite music for playing as children walk into assembly. This includes all staff in the school: school-keeper, cleaner, secretary, cooks, classroom assistants and other support staff, head teacher and teachers. Sometimes during assembly, the member of staff who chose the track will tell the children why they chose it and what they like about it. On the occasion of my visit, a song by Norah Jones is playing as children walk into assembly. It is clear that all the staff are enjoying it. The list is up for the next few weeks and showed an interesting variety of staff interests including *Moonlight Sonata* (Beethoven), *Telling Stories* (Tracy Chapman), *Long Walk to Freedom* (Ladysmith Black Mambazo), *The Simpsons Sing the Blues* (Various), *The Pink Panther* (Mancini).

Performing music

This involves pupils presenting informal and formal performances through singing and playing their own and others' music. Performing can involve a whole class, small groups and individuals. Through performing to different audiences within school and in external contexts we can observe improvements in self-esteem, confidence and communication skills. Singing and playing instruments (mainly percussion) are the primary means of acquiring skills in performance and can be shared within the class or become part of a presentation to a wider audience, for example in assembly. Every music lesson should involve performing in one form or another: singing or moving to a song or piece of recorded music, playing instruments or participating in body percussion. Being active is the key here: young children need little prompting to move energetically when listening to a lively piece of music or tap along in time.

Spontaneous movement should be encouraged and actions can be devised to accompany singing. The whole school might participate in performances during an arts week, members of staff might prepare some of their favourite songs, and pupils may perform alongside visiting musicians. Other examples are explored in subsequent sections.

Listening and appraising

Listening is without exception the most important activity in developing skills and understanding in music. Good listening requires time and space, a sense of purpose and guidance. Listening to a musical style which is unfamiliar can be mediated by a helpful 'listen out for the low bit towards the end', or 'the backing rhythms change halfway through' or 'that's a bassoon playing at the beginning'. If we think about our own listening in this way, we will be better placed to provide guidance.

If children are sharing examples of favourite music brought from home, it may be that they can enlighten the teacher and the class about a particular folk song or song from the shows chosen by a member of their family. Appraisal implies active listening with a specific purpose in mind and is a way of coming to know and understand music. Purposeful listening can be helped by planning activities which are interrelated and feed off each other, leading to new things or helping to refine what has gone before. Appraisal (critical listening) is necessary in both performing and composing and is pursued in more depth in **An integrated approach** (see below).

Composing

Composing as part of the primary music curriculum is relatively new. Although a number of educators promoted its inclusion as long ago as the 1920s and 1930s, it was not until 1992 that composing appeared as a strand of the primary music curriculum. During the 1960s and 1970s John Paynter and others (1970) explored the role that creative music-making might have in school music. Many interesting projects were developed and music psychologists evolved ways of tracking pupils' development in music, including the very young. Research clearly demonstrated that children have an immense capacity for music and are able to invent (compose) and control musical elements in a sophisticated way.

Composing within the primary music curriculum enshrines an attitude that everyone has the potential to be musically creative. It starts simply with exploring and experimenting with sound. This leads to developing skills in controlling and manipulating and finally the process of reviewing and refining. In the early stages, frameworks can provide safe and unthreatening ways to explore vocal and instrumental sounds. Experimenting with sound effects, putting together short sequences, playing sounds in turn are all starting points in the process of learning to compose. Later stages of composition might include writing lyrics, creating rhythmic patterns and accompaniments, making a multilayered computer-generated piece based on repeating patterns, songwriting, producing sound effects for a play and so on.

The key to the development of composing is the parallel development of listening skills. Choosing instrumental/vocal sounds and combinations and making decisions about the speed, volume and length of a particular phrase or section depends on the ability to listen. Pupils at the end of primary schooling who have had opportunities to listen to all kinds of music, compose pieces and songs and record samples of their work have acquired a huge range of transferable skills such as teamwork, cooperation and working to a brief or deadline as well as recorded evidence of their achievements.

Planning

Planning effective musical activities depends on time allocation, expertise, enthusiasm and resources. A well-resourced school will have a good collection of songbooks, a range of percussion instruments, schemes of work adapted or written for the school's specific circumstances, computer software to support composing, audio and/or video recording equipment, sufficient and appropriate space to store and access equipment and resources and, finally, access to appropriate spaces for practical activities (a hall and/or a dedicated music space – both indoor and out).

Planning for music is likely to be linked to the school's existing schemes of work. The best schemes allow for flexibility of approach and leave room for teachers' individual strengths and interests. The National Curriculum recognizes the need to develop musical skills over time. The Ongoing Skills section in the Qualifications and Curriculum Authority's (QCA) published Schemes of Work (2000) stresses the importance of regular singing and rhythmic work including movement. These are the most fundamental and probably the easiest to plan and organize.

Singing needs no special equipment or resources (although some may welcome CD backing tracks – see section on **Leading singing** below). Creating song lists which are gradually added to by the children and staff is a simple way to build up a repertoire. Music benefits from repetition – the song list may comprise a core of favourites which is expanded over time and reflects the interests of the pupils and staff.

Rhythm work needs regular and frequent practice and although best achieved through a combination of singing, body percussion, movement and instrumental work, can also be taught without any special equipment. Rhythm games, actions, movement and body percussion can be used to complement singing activities and extended into all kinds of creative composition work (see below: **An integrated approach**). Rhythmic development supported by movement and singing needs to be at the forefront of musical experience. The 'other' musical elements (namely timbre, dynamics, tempo) provide the expressive qualities of music – they cannot be hived off as separate entities. Think of any song or piece of music and you will recognize this. Some pieces of music may have a clearer rhythmic impact while others rely more on contrasts of sound. A number of publications have tried to compartmentalize the musical elements but this gives a misleading idea of how music works. Effective music teaching integrates all the elements and shows pupils how they work together within performing, composing and listening.

Instrumental skills are harder to plan for, especially if resources are limited. Most primary schools have a range of percussion instruments, xylophones, metallophones and keyboards. Some schools have visiting instrumental teachers who provide specialist input. Recent developments in whole-class instrumental teaching are providing new models which draw on the best practice of class and small group teaching. See Chapter 10, 'Beyond the Curriculum', for further details. Instrumental playing which grows out of vocal and simple percussion work ensures effective progression and establishes a solid foundation in the aural, manipulative and cognitive skills.

Music sessions need to have a beginning, middle and end. As music is a journey through time, it is important that the planning takes account of this. For example, a warm-up activity may be based on the same rhythm patterns used later as the focus of instrumental work. The final section may provide opportunities to review and appraise the transformation of the rhythms first heard in the warm-up. Despite the current trend for setting out the aims and objectives of a lesson, a journey of discovery where one activity leads seamlessly to the next with minimum verbal instruction is offered as an alternative strategy. Class music sessions may include a warm-up activity (for example, vocal warm-up or rhythm work), performing (songs and/or body percussion and/or instrumental playing), composing in groups (for example, vocal, songwriting, percussion, computer-generated) and final sharing. Pupils should have opportunities to record their compositions and performances and explore different media through links with drama, art and dance. This presents additional challenges in terms of planning and organization and may be part of a special project during the year.

An integrated approach

Activities which integrate the three interrelated areas of listening, composing and performing achieve the best results. Such activities also give opportunities for holistic assessment. Composing can encompass the simple to the complex: re-ordering a sequence of sounds is an example of the former. Thus, every performing activity can become a composing activity with a small creative leap.

In the following example we see how an appraising activity is the stimulus for creative work. Listening and understanding underpins each stage of development. The activities involve the use of different technologies.

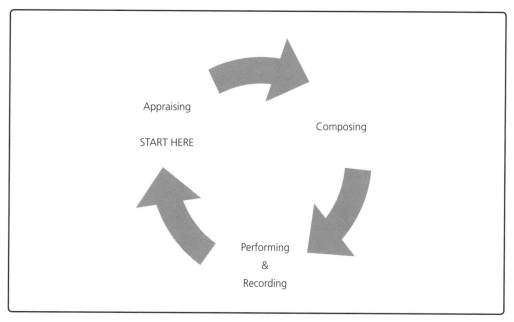

Figure 9.1 Appraising – composing – performing and recording

Case study

A group of Year 5 pupils listen to a variety of songs based on different themes and in different styles. Some are chosen by the teacher to reflect her interests; others are current favourites of the children. She takes some care to avoid lyrics which might be deemed inappropriate. The teacher asks the children to think about the ways the songs are organized (musical form) – some use a verse/chorus format; others have a solo voice (call) followed by the group (response); some have rapped sections; others have instrumental sections (no vocals). She asks them to consider the meaning of the songs, express preferences and analyse the way the lyrics work: some rhyme and/or use alliteration and assonance, others do not; some have a central theme, others tell a story. The teacher demonstrates a couple of contrasting lyrics on the whiteboard which the pupils could use as models for their own songs.

Pupils work in small groups, choosing a theme and inventing their own lyrics. Some pupils make up melody lines at the same time; others work with a keyboard to try out ideas. Over the next two sessions, pupils develop their ideas, present 'work in progress', receive feedback from their peers, review and refine their work. They record their own performances of the songs, receive further peer and teacher feedback of both the performance and composition, and then re-record them.

Leading singing

Singing is an essential part of any music curriculum. It can present challenges in terms of what songs to teach and how to teach them. If leading singing is a new experience, it is advisable to start with songs already known and familiar and then gradually extend to new songs. Learning how to lead singing in school is best done by observing someone who is an experienced practitioner. In the absence of this, some general pointers are offered here:

- Know your material well.
- Warm the voice up through humming, buzzing and other vocal experimenting supported by physical movement.
- Provide a model by capturing the feel and spirit of the song (this is as important as singing the 'correct' notes).
- Use an OHP or whiteboard to display lyrics for songs that are complicated or have many verses; otherwise teach by rote.
- Try out different strategies for different types of songs and age groups, e.g. the youngest children can 'catch' the song through continuous repetition of the complete song with ever-changing body movements/actions.
- Sing short sections (or chunks) and have the class repeat them back.
- Provide a clear model of the song in your delivery and support the singing with movement/actions/ rhythms.
- As a general rule, avoid teaching the words first. Aim for a multisensory experience.
- Be aware of the power of non-verbal communication such as gesture and facial expression.
- Use a backing CD to support the melody or provide a backing if necessary or if appropriate when performing the song.
- Avoid singing along to recordings of songs from the shows and other commercial recordings which are often too high for anyone to join in with comfortably.
- Nursery rhymes need treating carefully. Many of the melodies of so-called traditional rhymes were composed in the Victorian era with little consideration of the range or complexity. For example, *Humpty Dumpty* has a huge vocal range, big leaps and is awkward to sing.

Teaching strategies and learning styles

Styles have changed in the teaching of music over the last 20 years, in part due to a greater understanding that music is best learned through active practical involvement but also through a recognition that teaching strategies needed to adapt to the wider range of musical styles and genres.

Musicians from aurally-based traditions learn music differently from classically trained musicians. Music teachers trained in classical music primarily learn music by learning to read it whereas jazz, folk, pop and traditional musicians of many countries generally learn through listening and playing. Examples of the drummer apprentice in West Africa, gamelan novice in Indonesia or bass guitarist in a rock band provide useful points of reference. The music is 'picked up as you go along' rather than taught. The musicians learn from each other through imitation, repetition and experimentation. They listen and copy, they compose as they perform: the riffs, melody lines and lyrics; instrumental sections often come out of the process of performing. Teaching strategies based on this approach to learning are likely to be the most effective. The teacher can provide opportunities for pupils to learn in this way by modelling, creating safe environments for group exploration and experimentation and facilitating opportunities to practise skills and perform.

Assessment and progression in music

Assessment in music is subjective and depends on the listener. We generally know when a performance is 'together', sounds good and engages us. This provides us with a starting point for assessing children's musical performances and compositions. The National Curriculum provides a list of descriptors over five levels which offer guidance in making judgements. Assessment in musical performance and composition needs to be considered holistically. Considering individual components is a bit like considering individual words in a sentence without looking at their overall meaning.

For example, a rhythm played accurately but with limited expression will demonstrate a lack of understanding of the expressive qualities of dynamics, timbre and tempo. The electronic sounds of a click track or metronome illustrate how a rhythm on its own lacks expression. By adding the expressive use of dynamic and changes in timbre, a repeated rhythm will acquire musical quality. The snare drum rhythm played throughout Ravel's orchestral piece *Bolero* demonstrates clearly the expressive use of a repeated rhythmic phrase.

Pupil assessment is best done by creating a portfolio of evidence drawn from different musical experiences. Teacher and pupil feedback on their own and others' work can provide ongoing formative assessment. Evidence can be stored through audio and video recording to add to pupil profiles. Combined with pupil notebooks, peer and teacher comments, profiles can be used to demonstrate musical experiences and learning over time and allow for differentiation and individualized learning.

The 'National Curriculum in Action' website provides examples of how to make judgements at the end of a key stage in music. The following list highlights the key areas. Profiles show:

- strengths and weaknesses in performance across a range of contexts and over a period of time
- learning that has been demonstrated confidently across a range of different experiences and through a variety of different activities

- understanding of a variety of genres, styles and traditions
- a range of forms of communication and situations
- different ways of demonstrating the same aspects of musical learning.

In terms of progression, a recent report from Ofsted (2005) highlighted the need to build on previous experiences from Key Stage 1 to Key Stage 2 and improve links with other types of provision, for example whole-class instrumental teaching (see Chapter 10, 'Beyond the Curriculum'). Pupils should have opportunities to observe others' work in class or have joint celebrations, for example in assembly or at special events.

The impact of technology

Technology has been slow to impact on primary music-making. While every primary teacher is a teacher of ICT, its use in music at Key Stage 1 is not compulsory although it is encouraged. At Key Stage 2, the requirement in England specifies that the breadth of study must include 'using ICT to capture, change and combine sounds' (DfEE/QCA, 1999).

Ofsted (2005) commented that there is a need to consider a wider range of technologies beyond those which are screen-based to include materials on interactive media and the use of backing tracks and digital recording facilities. With the developments in technology, it is possible to listen to any type of music from around the world anywhere and at any time. It has become more cheaply and more widely available and the download culture has changed the way we consume music. Technology by its nature is dependent on access to equipment and resources.

The British Educational Communications and Technology Agency (BECTA) produced a list (2003) of the types of equipment which might be used in an ICT entitlement in music:

- computer software and CD-ROMs
- electronic means of communication (email and the internet)
- equipment for making and replaying sound recordings (e.g. microphones, cassette/minidisc recorders)
- equipment that can alter sounds to give 'special effects' (e.g. add echoes)
- electronic musical instruments (e.g. keyboards) that can produce a range of alternative timbres.

In addition, the BECTA website provides examples of using and investigating sounds, refining and enhancing performances and compositions, extending knowledge and awareness of styles and advice on the use of web-based resources.

The internet provides opportunities to listen to all kinds of instruments from around the world and to find out about singers, songwriters, composers and bands. Music organizations provide sound clips linked to graphics and animations which can bring the virtual reality of a symphony orchestra, rock band or Indonesian gamelan into the classroom. There is a range of software programmes available commercially which enable pupils to compose on-screen; in the early stages pupils choose sounds and create sequences through to sampling sounds, editing and composition using multiple layers. Editing programmes such as 'Audacity' are available free from the internet. ICT and music needs to be purposeful, engaging and help children make connections. An animation project can provide immediate access to the creation and manipulation of sound and image involving drama, movement, dance, sound design and art.

Conclusion

Music is a multifaceted art form and is a powerful means of expression and communication. All of us establish strong preferences for particular pieces or styles of music. Music teaching and learning thrives when teachers and pupils have opportunities to engage with the familiar and also be encouraged to explore the unknown. Musical skills are developed over time and need sustained and regular engagement in order to progress. Extending an understanding of how music works through creative exploration, experimentation and performance presents us with opportunities for an engagement which lasts far beyond the primary years.

In summary:

- a holistic approach to music teaching and learning is the most effective way to support the development of skill, understanding and knowledge
- starting with the musical preferences of the teachers, support staff and pupils will lead to greater engagement in music-making
- effective development in music requires regular and sustained activity
- music creates unique opportunities for shared artistic, social and educational growth.

References

BECTA (2003), 'Entitlement to ICT in Primary Music'. http://schools.becta.org.uk (accessed 23 Sep 2006).

Charles, R. (1978), *Brother Ray: Ray Charles' Own Story*. New York: Doubleday.

Cross, I. (2001), 'Music, mind and evolution'. *Psychology of Music*, 29 (1).

Department for Education and Employment (DfEE) and Qualifications and Curriculum Authority (QCA) (1999), *Music: The National Curriculum for England*. London: HMSO.

Department of Education Northern Ireland (2007). *The Revised Northern Ireland Primary Curriculum*. Belfast: T. S. O.

National Curriculum in Action, www.ncaction.org.uk/subjects/music/index.htm (accessed 23 Sept 2006).

Office for Standards in Education (Ofsted) (2005), *The Annual Report of Her Majesty's Chief Inspector of Schools 2004/05: Music in Primary Schools.* London: TSO.

Papousek, H. (1996), 'Musicality in infancy research: biological and cultural origins of early musicality', in I. Deliège and J. Sloboda (eds), *Musical Beginnings: Origins and Development of Music Competence.* Oxford: Oxford University Press.

Paynter, J. & Aston, P. (1970), *Sound and Silence.* Cambridge: Cambridge University Press.

Qualifications and Curriculum Authority (QCA) (2000), *Schemes of Work for Music Key Stages 1, 2 and 3.* www.standards.dfee.gov.uk/schemes.

Qualifications, Curriculum and Assessment Authority for Wales on behalf of the National Assembly for Wales (2000), *Music in the National Curriculum in Wales*. Wales: QCAAW.

Rauscher, F. H., Shaw, G. L., Levine, L. J., Wright, E. L., Dennis, W. R. and Newcomb, R. (1997), 'Music training causes long-term enhancement of preschool children's spatial-temporal reasoning'. *Neurological Research*, 19, 2–8.

Scottish Office Education Department (1992), *National Guidelines 5–14: Expressive Arts.* Scottish Office.

Music: Beyond the Curriculum

Kate Buchanan

Chapter Outline

'They teach you there's a boundary line to music. But, man, there's no boundary line to art.'
Charlie Parker, American jazz saxophonist, 1920–1955 (in Porter, 1999)

Introduction

This chapter considers the wide range of opportunities for learning and experiencing music outside the curriculum through project and cross-curricular work and explores ways of recognizing and valuing a range of project work and out-of-school learning. The chapter provides snapshots and case studies to inspire reflective thinking and further professional development.

Extending boundaries

The saxophonist Charlie Parker reminds us to ignore imaginary lines and boundaries. By recognizing that pupils are engaging in music – as listeners, consumers and participants

– outside school, it enables us to expand our understanding of how music is learned and experienced in formal and informal contexts. The technological revolution provides us all with access to music from all parts of the world and with ever-increasing speed and ever-improving sound quality. Children and young people are increasingly sharing music via the internet, both as listeners and creators. They are able to define and express their identity through the choices of music they engage with and explore particular interests unbounded by a curriculum. Children may also have opportunities to explore music within the context of their family and cultural heritage: family celebrations, street festivals, local and national events all provide opportunities to engage in music on many different levels. As teachers, we need to recognize and value the richness of these experiences and understand how they can be of benefit to pupils, ourselves and our schools.

Developing relationships

Schools have opportunities to develop relationships with a wide range of organizations and individuals to complement and extend curriculum activity in music. They include amateur bands/ensembles, choirs, arts/music/street festivals, music services, professional orchestras and ensembles, community musicians and other education providers. The following example illustrates the unique contribution of a composer-led project which took its inspiration from a local art gallery:

Case study: crossing the boundaries

A project involving community musicians and composer Hugh Nankivell began with a visit to Huddersfield Art Gallery. The paintings were the stimulus for all kinds of composition work including a vocal piece based on an abstract picture called *Day Painting*, a song called 'Mysterious Arena', the adding of instrumental parts to a song and writing poems and stories. The project culminated in a performance to the school and parents.

Pupils' comments

Amy says her favourite part of the project was the concert because her mum and sister were watching. Daniel enjoyed it when everyone played instruments in 'The Ballad of Hill Town'. *'He's a very musical man, he can play everything!' 'A brilliant experience.'*

Teacher's comments

The children really grew in confidence and were willing to sing alone or in pairs and to try out new ideas. Hugh was very inspiring – seemingly able to play every instrument put in front of him!

Access and funding

Funding for external projects comes from education authorities, funding councils and charitable trusts, many of which collaborate with schools to provide access to high-quality music-making from a range of genres. Project work of this kind is by no means nationally available: while some schools may regularly attend performances or have visits from musicians from different traditions and cultures, others do not. It largely depends on local networks, regional and national priorities, and the funding climate. This imbalance has been identified in the recent Music Manifesto (2006): one of its five key aims is an entitlement for all pupils to 'a wide range of high quality live music experiences'.

Project work and educational outreach

Many schools have opportunities to participate in projects initiated by external providers or they may be initiated by the schools themselves. Partnerships are often developed over time, providing links to a richness of musical experiences from school-based creative projects and whole-school performances to visits to venues hosting a range of workshops and musical performances.

Symphony orchestras, performing groups and musicians in receipt of public money, for example through Arts Council England, are required to demonstrate an engagement with a range of audiences. Since the late 1980s, orchestras and opera companies in the UK have explored new and innovative ways of engaging with diverse audiences including primary children. Many of these organizations target young audiences through outreach projects in educational and community settings. Some focus their energies on a specific geographical location and others take on residencies as part of a touring programme. For example, The South Bank Centre in London works closely with its resident orchestras and ensembles including the London Philharmonic Orchestra (LPO) to build schools' programmes and develop outreach projects. The Sage, Gateshead: A Home for Music and Musical Discovery is one example of a purpose-built venue providing all kinds of performances and activities focusing on learning and participation.

African and Caribbean Music and Dance Week and *Tam O'Shanter* are examples of cross-curricular projects which provide opportunities for developing cultural awareness and continuing professional development.

Case study: African and Caribbean Music and Dance Week

A primary school in Northampton organized a week of African and Caribbean culture building on curriculum work undertaken in Years 2 and 5. Additional funding for gifted and talented pupils in music in Years 5 and 6 provided an opportunity for African dance and drumming workshops from *Music for Change* – an educational charity that promotes awareness, understanding and respect for cultural diversity through music and the performing arts in order to achieve beneficial change. Volunteer parents with African and Caribbean roots contributed sessions on storytelling, cookery and costume.

Other music and dance workshops were provided for other classes throughout the week as well as a session for staff (teachers, teaching assistants and other support staff), funded through the school's professional development programme. The drumming group from the local secondary school provided an African drumming performance for all KS1 pupils, organized by the school's advanced skills teacher. The week culminated in a celebratory performance of all those involved comprising African and Caribbean drumming, song, dance and storytelling to an audience of other children, family and friends.

Case study: Tam O'Shanter

Inspired by Robert Burns' (1759–1796) *Tam O'Shanter*, Malcolm Arnold (1921–2006) composed an orchestral overture. The characters and events in the poem are vividly portrayed and include a section where Tam visits a cemetery and watches a group of witches dancing on tombstones. As part of a project involving a violinist and clarinet player from the LPO, Year 2 pupils listened to live examples from the piece, following the narrative structure. Over four weekly workshops the Year 2 pupils participated in musical games, listening and dance activities and worked in groups to create their own movement sequences, rhythmic patterns and drone accompaniments on xylophones. At a special assembly, the pupils performed their own versions of the story and the witches' dance. The following week the whole class attended a free schools' performance including *Tam O'Shanter* at the Royal Festival Hall, South Bank Centre, London which included 'their' musicians performing in the orchestra.

What is the impact?

- Children provide role models for learning by showcasing their skills to others
- Teachers have opportunities to expand their subject knowledge (e.g. orchestral music, African music)
- Staff and pupils extend their understanding of specific genres of music in an authentic way through high-quality specialist input
- Parental involvement is recognized and valued

Sharing sounds

Sonic Postcards explores the use of technology and links to other curricular areas and provides a vehicle for social and cultural exchange.

Case study: Sonic Postcards

Sonic Postcards is a UK-wide education project devised and delivered by Sonic Arts Network (www.sonicartsnetwork.org). It is a unique and innovative project that enables 9–14-year-old pupils to explore and compare their local sound environments through the exchange of sound postcards with other schools via the internet. The project focuses on the impact of sound on our lives and the possibilities for creativity through the manipulation of sound with technology. As with an ordinary postcard, it offers the opportunity for people to exchange information about their local environments, providing windows into a variety of places, lives and cultures, from urban to rural, suburban to coastal. Pupils create Mp3 files which can be emailed, podcast, burnt onto CD, uploaded onto an iPod or downloaded from the Sonic Postcards website. A sonic postcard is a composition of about one to two minutes in length which has been created by pupils using recorded sounds – these sounds can be natural environmental sounds, man-made sounds or spoken word. The activities provide a range of cross-curricular links with ICT, geography, English and citizenship.

What is the impact?

- New approaches to creative learning through the use of technology
- Pupils and staff learn new skills together, e.g. downloading software, sampling sounds, making and manipulating recordings
- Teachers develop confidence in the use of technology and e-learning initiative
- Opportunities to develop links and partnerships with other schools

Music services and learning beyond the school

Music services provide a range of instrumental tuition in schools and at music centres ranging from African drumming to the more traditional instruments including violin, guitar and flute. Other activities include opportunities for pupils to participate in instrumental and vocal ensembles, for example jazz, big bands, orchestras, string groups, wind bands, vocal groups, choirs, pop/rock groups and holiday music courses. They provide visiting specialist tutors for schools as well as working directly with pupils and their families. Many music services make direct charges and some are able to offer bursaries to those pupils identified as gifted and talented.

Children who achieve a high level of specialist instrumental skill usually do so through sustained study over many years and often through one-to-one tuition. It is sometimes difficult to integrate children with high levels of instrumental skill into curriculum activity. Their skills need to be recognized and valued and where possible incorporated into curriculum activity. Pupils can become role models and provide peer to peer support. They need to be challenged by musical objectives differentiated by outcome. For example, a proficient keyboard player in a small group composition task can be asked to interpret a graphic score on the piano or electronic keyboard using a combination of chords and melodies; the violinists described in the case study below could be encouraged to perform their compositions to the rest of the class; a rock drummer can provide a backing for whole-school singing activities. By valuing their achievements, we can help motivate other pupils if handled sensitively. We are quick to praise achievement in sport. Let's do the same in music!

In places where parents can afford it or where schools make it a priority, many pupils can benefit. The picture is not the same in all areas. It is clear from a research report commissioned by the Associated Board of the Royal Schools of Music (ABRSM) in 2006 that this provision is available for a minority of our children. The report cites that just 13 per cent of children in the state sector were receiving any kind of instrumental tuition. This is in stark contrast to a figure of 50 per cent of pupils in private schools.

Since 2000 Ofsted has included instrumental tuition delivered by music services in its inspections. The report from 2002 reflects on effective strategies, teaching style and the integration of musical and technical learning.

The teacher in the example below:

- values pupils' creative work
- incorporates appropriate technical vocabulary, e.g. phrases, note names
- helps develop pupils' awareness of good use of the body to avoid physical strain
- encourages peer learning and support
- supports the development of listening and memory skills.

Case study: characteristics of good instrumental music tuition

In a session for Year 4 beginner violin pupils, the two girls and one boy begin by playing from memory a short piece each has composed at home. They listen carefully to each one and the tutor helps them to describe the shape of phrases and range of notes. They continue with a bowing exercise and the tutor encourages them to make strong, clear movements in the air. They play patterns in the note range they have already learned in first position, listening carefully to ensure firm bowing and secure intonation. Each pupil plays a different short piece from notation in the tutor book and they play all of them as a group, with the tutor adding a keyboard accompaniment. A new note is introduced by the tutor on his violin. They all find it and he shows them a new pattern to practise at home. The lesson ends with the pupils playing two favourite pieces: the tutor adds a second, accompanying part to the first piece and the whole group plays the second as a round. (Ofsted, 2002)

Instrumental tuition

Tuition for instrumental learning has generally taken place outside the curriculum. As we have seen above, its delivery has been by specialist visiting teachers or at after-school centres, many of which are run by music services. The opportunities for instrumental tuition have been available to a small number of pupils, to which parents were expected to contribute. It was therefore heartening in 2000 when the Secretary of State (Ofsted, 2004) made a promise that 'over time, all pupils in primary schools who wish to will have the opportunity to learn a musical instrument'. In order to deliver this promise, the Wider Opportunities initiative was established in 2002 and provided first access for pupils in instrumental tuition at KS2. It provided an impetus for music services to explore new models of delivery through a series of pilot programmes. Instrumental tuition has traditionally focused on the techniques of learning to play an instrument and marginalized other areas of musical development such as composing.

Twelve of these programmes were evaluated by Ofsted in 2004 in a report entitled *Tuning in: wider opportunities in specialist instrumental tuition for pupils in Key Stage 2*. It provides compelling evidence of the value of whole-class instrumental tuition which adopts a more holistic approach to musical development and links strongly to curriculum music. A further Ofsted report in 2005 backs this up: whole-class teaching provides 'a more effective, stronger and better integrated programme of musical experiences and opportunities'. It also recognizes that it is 'providing professional development for school-based staff (teaching assistants, class teachers and music coordinators) and music service tutors'.

Case study: SoundStart: whole-class instrumental tuition

Thirty pupils in Meadowfield Primary School near Warrington are learning to play wind, brass and percussion instruments as part of a project entitled *SoundStart*. Led by three members of instrumental teaching staff from Warrington Music Service, weekly sessions comprise a broadly-based curriculum of instrumental playing, singing, moving, improvizing and composing. Pupils take their instruments home and, despite initial misgivings, none of these instruments has been damaged or lost. The class teacher attends every class and the classroom assistant is learning to play the flute from scratch with the pupils. Reports from both the class teacher and the head teacher describe increased concentration, improved literacy scores, better teamworking and cooperation. This is in addition to the evident pleasure, sense of achievement and fun which I observed on my visit to the school.

Reflecting on practice

Developing children's learning beyond the curriculum requires teachers to have a broad view of their own role both as a teacher and learner. Many teachers lack confidence in music because they feel that their own abilities are limited. In the previous chapter, we explored the nature of musical understanding and argued that a narrow definition was unhelpful. If we enjoy listening to music and wish to share that with our pupils, we need to start from our interests and strengths as well as recognizing that we can learn from new experiences and develop technical, musical and team-based skills.

Reflecting on our own practice is essential to identify strengths and weaknesses as well as areas of particular interest. Teachers with little or no experience of the classical Western tradition either as a listener or performer need no longer feel marginalized. Since pop music first appeared in the curriculum in the 1960s, there has been a cultural shift away from the classical canon. With the increased emphasis on creative approaches to music-making, many music teachers reliant on reading music notation have had to re-appraise their own musical achievement and engage in ongoing personal and musical development.

Continuing professional development

Schools, education authorities, publishers and other organizations provide in-service courses in primary music. They range from one-off workshops to longer-term courses although they are currently not part of any integrated structure of continuing professional development. During the 1980s the music provision in Initial Teacher Education (ITE) was drastically reduced. Prior to this, many ITE courses provided sustained opportunities for trainees to develop their skills in music. Following the cuts, many teachers were under-prepared for the challenges of teaching music. Publishing houses sought to provide resources for generalist teachers ranging from sing-along CDs, schemes of work and interactive computer software. Opportunities to engage with ongoing professional development have been few and music is often not identified in a school's long-term planning as an area for development.

There are many schemes in different parts of the country which have sought to address the challenge of equipping teachers who lack confidence to develop their musical and music teaching skills. The example below provides a snapshot of an effective way of delivering in-school training.

Case study

Pamela is a primary teacher with a responsibility for special educational needs and an interest in language development. An opportunity arose for Siân, an experienced music teacher from the local music service, to provide in-school training. A six-week project was negotiated which gave Pamela opportunities to observe Siân teaching her class. The activities included leading vocal activities and singing, circle work, instrumental playing and composing using picture notation. From session 4, Pamela was given opportunities to lead some of the activities and receive feedback from Siân.

Feedback from Pamela: This was a really useful way to develop my understanding of what can work well with this age group. Seeing how to introduce and develop ideas, maintain a sense of flow in the lessons, involve individuals in leading and directing the class and how to use percussion instruments in a manageable way were all useful strategies I learned from Siân. The materials were great and showed me how I could adapt some of the work I do in English into music and vice versa.

> **Case study (continued)**
>
> **Feedback from Siân:** This was a great opportunity to plan in-service training to suit an individual's needs. I was pleased to be able to gradually step back in the later sessions and allow Pam time to try out ideas. She began with repeating my activities and as her confidence developed, she was able to extend this with her own starting points.

Conclusion

Musical learning has no boundaries and is experienced in all kinds of situations. As educators, we have an important role in adopting an inclusive approach and recognizing the wide range of musical experiences encountered by pupils and staff both inside and outside the classroom. Instrumental and vocal music teachers, often an untapped source of energy and expertise, are increasingly working more inclusively and there are examples of collaborative teaching with classroom teachers. Developments of this kind and projects involving visiting musicians require schools to adopt an open and flexible approach. But the benefits to the school of looking 'beyond' are many. Engagement in music can help to raise achievement, increase self-esteem and motivation and provide opportunities for shared artistic engagement. Listening to and/or participating in musical performances are experiences which often stay with us for a very long time, especially when they are shared with others. They can provide us all with enriching, sometimes transformational experiences that we remember for the rest of our lives.

In summary:

- acknowledging and celebrating musical learning outside the school environment is essential in a holistic approach to musical learning
- professional musicians, including composers, bring a unique range of sounds and experiences for pupils and staff
- professional development needs to provide opportunities to develop skills, knowledge and expertise as well as opportunities for artistic and aesthetic engagement
- music technology is providing opportunities for creating and sharing music across the globe
- instrumental/vocal learning is most effective when integrated into the curriculum.

References

Associated Board of the Royal Schools of Music (ABRSM) (2006), *Annual Review 2006*. London: ABRSM.

Music Manifesto (2006), 'Making every child's music matter'. *Music Manifesto Report Number 2*. London: TSO.

Office for Standards in Education (Ofsted) (2002), *Local Education Authority Music Services: Survey of Good Practice*. London: HMSO.

Ofsted (2004), *Tuning in: Wider Opportunities in Specialist Instrumental Tuition for Pupils in Key Stage 2*. London: TSO.

Ofsted (2005), *The Annual Report of Her Majesty's Chief Inspector of Schools 2004/05*. London: TSO.

Porter, E. (1999), 'Dizzy atmosphere: the challenge of bebop'. *American Music*, 17, (4), 435.

Useful websites

www.musicmanifesto.co.uk
Music Manifesto
www.abrsm.org.uk
Associated Board of the Royal Schools of Music
www.lpo.org.uk
The London Philharmonic Orchestra (LPO)
www.thesagegateshead.org
The Sage, Gateshead
www.southbankcentre.co.uk
The South Bank Centre, London
www.musicforchange.org
Music for Change
www.sonicartsnetwork.org
Sonic Arts Network
www.sonicpostcards.com
Sonic Postcards – a creative project created by Sonic Arts Network

Physical Education: Teaching the Curriculum

Alison Heap

Chapter Outline

'The challenge to physical education and sport is to promote and foster active lifestyles which are likely to be sustained into adult life.' N. Armstrong (1998: 8), academic and researcher

Introduction

One of the main concerns for western societies at the advent of the twenty-first century has been the issue of childhood fitness and obesity. As children become more restricted in their freedom, and more sedentary in their habits, the role of physical education (PE) in the primary school would seem to be ever more relevant. As teachers we recognize our commitment to children's academic, physical, social and emotional development, and recognize the impact good PE teaching can have on all of these. Whether you perceive yourself to be good at sport or not, as a generalist primary school teacher you have a statutory responsibility to address the requirement of the Physical Education National Curriculum (PENC), and address it to the best of your ability.

In this chapter emphasis will be placed on issues related to practice and the implementation of the curriculum rather than subject knowledge. However, it is recognized that this may be the area of PE in which you are less secure. Websites have therefore been included to support this.

The place of physical education in the curriculum

If we consider the quote above it is evident that the effective teaching of the PENC has implications for the lives of children beyond the lessons they participate in during their years in the primary school. If we wish to encourage children to remain healthy and engage in physical activities throughout their lives, it is important that their PE lessons in the primary school are positive experiences.

This has implications for both our practice in PE, and our philosophy towards PE. While participation and the development of skills are important, enjoyment, satisfaction and enthusiasm must also be recognized as positive outcomes for PE lessons (DfES, 2004).

You are probably aware that until the 'fitness and obesity crisis' PE was a rather lowly subject in the school curriculum, and PE specialists were frequently, and unfairly, the butt of unkind comments about their intellectual ability. Given the historical background to the subject's development this is hardly surprising.

Prior to 1953 primary schools engaged in physical *training* (PT) rather than physical *education*. This was a strongly regimented form of physical activity based essentially on practising skills until they were perfected, and engaging in major games (for example hockey, rugby, soccer and netball). Emphasis was placed on copying, competence and competition.

With the introduction of *Planning the Programme: Physical Education in the Primary School* (HMSO, 1953) PE adopted a more child-centred model of teaching physical activity. The PE curriculum became broader and included more emphasis on creativity and movement. In schools that recognized the value of PE children benefited from this change, but it was not until the introduction of the National Curriculum in 1989 that PE gained statutory status and became a recognized foundation subject, rather than an optional extra taught only on sunny Friday afternoons.

Despite the introduction of the PENC, government initiatives to promote literacy and mathematics in 1998 resulted in PE, like other Foundation subjects, suffering from a decreasing time allocation.

However, the political profile of PE is currently high, and the notion of developing a more active and health-aware nation is a key feature of government policy.

What are the aims of teaching physical education via the physical education curriculum?

In its most simple form the aims of PE have long been:

- education in movement
- education through movement
- education about movement.

In 2005, a position statement in PE released at the National Summit on Physical Education stated that: 'The aim of physical education is systematically to develop physical competence so that children are able to move efficiently and safely and understand what they are doing. The outcome – physical literacy – is as important to children's education and development as numeracy and literacy.'

Why do we need to teach physical education?

PE recognizes and builds upon children's natural desires to play, to be active and to explore the world. While it is recognized that PE contributes to the health of a child, it is less recognized that the range of psychomotor skills developed through PE is an excellent conduit for building self-esteem, confidence and competence in more general physical activities – such as playground games. It is through these that many children develop their skills at turn-taking, negotiating and abiding by rules, all of which are attributes children need to learn so that they can socialize effectively.

As a consequence of the diversity of the content of the PENC, which includes such areas of activity as dance, games, gymnastics, swimming, athletics and outdoor and adventurous activities, children have the opportunity to engage in a range of quite different forms of physical activity. While not all children may enjoy all of these areas of activity, there are few children who like none, particularly when it is taught well. When combined with the activities provided through after-school clubs and other physical activities now available to them, children will, hopefully, remain active throughout their lives.

Planning

As a beginning teacher you will now be engaging in all three levels of planning. During your Initial Teacher Training (ITT) you will have spent much of your time immersed in planning documentation, so this section will contain only the points and issues salient to PE.

Necessary prior knowledge

All levels of successful planning are based upon your prior knowledge and understanding. This knowledge goes from the holistic to the specific and deserves consideration.

- You must understand the value and contribution of PE to children's education, health and well-being.
- You must have a sound understanding of the curriculum and knowledge of the six areas of activity (athletics, dance, gymnastics, games, outdoor and adventurous activity [OAA] and swimming).
- You must have subject knowledge and awareness of the core basic skills specific to each of the six areas of activity.
- You must have the pedagogical knowledge to know how to adapt these basic skills so that they are appropriate to the learning of the children you are teaching.
- You will need to know how to adapt your class management strategies and teaching style to physical environments other than the classroom (the hall/gym, field, swimming pool, outdoor space).
- And, perhaps the most significant, you need to understand the development of children, and be familiar with growth patterns to ensure safe practice, and enable you to give a structured framework for planning, delivery and assessment.

If you do not feel confident in any of these areas it is suggested that you seek help and advice. Schools are aware that in ITT there is a lack of dedicated time for training in PE, and often the PE subject-leader or a more competent colleague will be willing to support you, or team teach with you. Most local education authorities (LEAs) also provide in-service education in PE, and much of this is targeted at newly qualified teachers (NQTs).

Long-term planning

More than for any other subject, PE planning at this level requires collaboration with teaching colleagues. Programmes of study, the allocation of teaching space, and access to equipment should be managed by the subject-leader. These will all have an impact on the whole-school timetable, and you will need tact, assertiveness and professionalism for the necessary negotiations.

Medium-term planning

It is for this level that units of work are planned. Units are based on one of the six areas of activity. As each area is covered in one academic year, a unit is usually one half-term in length. It is at this level of planning that progression through the unit is organized. Progression requires children to be challenged according to their age and ability. Tasks should become increasingly difficult and promote the development of quality performance. However, it must always be remembered that while quality of performance is age-related, it is not age-dependent. Although all children will develop and mature physically, they will not all have the same level of competence.

Progression in quality can be achieved through tasks and learning experiences that will require:

- accurate body alignment or placement
- increased tension in actions
- improvement in coordination
- improvement in control
- increased understanding of movement principles.

It needs to be recognized that it takes skill and experience to match children's learning experiences with the appropriate level of challenge. Thoughtful consideration at the medium-term planning stage will support your short-term planning immensely. If done well, medium-term working documents can be adapted and modified as a result of your ongoing assessment and serve as the basis for future planning.

At this level it is also sensible to identify any safety issues that might need to be addressed. For example, how will you supervise 35 children in the swimming pool, or set up large apparatus in the hall with a class of small children? (www.standards.dfes.gov/schemes)

Short-term planning

Short-term plans are those that inform single lessons. As you will be aware, they provide the structure and organization for your lesson, and will show *how* you intend to deliver the content. Like your medium-term plans, they are working documents and as a practitioner you need to teach each lesson knowing:

- **The aim of your lesson** – what is the broad, non-specific target of this unit?
- **The objective of your lesson** – what is the specific purpose of this lesson?
- **The children's prior experiences** – what can the children already do that I can build on?
- **The engagement of children in your lesson** – what learning experiences and tasks will I provide for the children so they can succeed in their attainment of the learning objective?
- **The equipment you will need** – which equipment will I need, and how will I move it to and from my lesson safely?
- **The role of the teaching assistant** – which group will the teaching assistant work with, and how will they work with them?
- **The outcome of your lesson** – what criteria will I use to measure how successful we were in meeting the objective?

If you have considered all of the above, it is up to you (or school policy) how you will document your short-term planning.

Planning for progression in basic movement skills

The PENC does not directly emphasize the development of the basic movement skills, but from an early age, it includes them as part of the more complex activities. However, the importance of the basic movement skills cannot be over-emphasized, and it is these that will be developed within each PE lesson that you plan. Progression can be achieved and supported by:

- increasing the variety of movements through movement concepts
- allowing children to work with partners or groups
- providing tasks that demand better balancing or coordination skills
- using tasks that require increasing strength, flexibility or stamina
- providing situations which require quick decision-making
- planning tasks that require children to move from single to combined movements
- encouraging the use of abstract, rather than concrete, ideas
- encouraging the use and understanding of increasingly advanced techniques.

Progression in tasks and lessons must match the development of children's basic movement skills if they are to be successful. Recognition of who, what, when and how assessment will be done is therefore an important part of your plan.

Teaching strategies

Case study

Michael teaches a class of Year 3 children. During the year he and the children have worked hard on their PE, and have enjoyed participating in this process.

Evan joined the class just after the Easter vacation, and has settled in well but, unlike his peers, he does not seem to enjoy PE. He participates in all the activities he is asked to do, but lacks enthusiasm and always seems tentative when asked to do something new or unfamiliar.

As a reward for all their hard work in PE during the year, Michael decided that during a games session the children could play their favourite game, which is unihoc. As the children went to collect their unihoc sticks he noticed Evan sitting by himself. When asked to get a stick, for the first time ever Evan refused to do as he was asked, and then refused to play. So Evan watched as the children broke into their teams and Michael supervised.

> **Case study (continued)**
>
> Through further investigation Michael found that the child had had the experience of unihoc in a crowded, unruly hacking game of 17-a-side. During this game he had spent most of his time trying to avoid a raucous crowd brandishing their sticks, fearful he was going to be hurt. This experience reinforced for Michael the need to consider carefully not only what he taught, but also how he taught.

A positive and safe learning environment

Safety and security

A positive learning environment is one in which all children feel safe and secure. It is vital that teachers always provide a safe environment – not just for challenging activities – and recognize their 'duty of care'. Children must also learn to be responsible for their own safety, and that of others.

In some cases the risk management procedure may need to be used. Help and support in making decisions about all aspects of safe practice can be found at www.baalpe.org.

As Evan's experiences show, a negative experience can have a profound impact on children's engagement. In Evan's case the fear was of being hurt, and in PE there is a potential for this. In PE lessons children *must* be supervised at all times. If you must leave the room/field the children must stop, sit down and wait until another adult can supervise them.

It is important that you know who the first-aider in your school is, and where they can be found – or better still become a first-aider yourself.

Children will also be reluctant to participate in PE if they do not feel safe from being humiliated or ridiculed. If children are being humiliated because of their physical appearance, this needs to be addressed through the system appropriate to your school. If children are being ridiculed because they are not very physically competent, this also needs to be addressed, as does your provision for differentiation.

Appropriate clothing

Safety also comes from participants being appropriately attired. Children need to be able to move freely, but should not be wearing clothes that could catch on equipment. When possible, children's feet should be bare during PE lessons inside. When outside, footwear will depend on the activity, and must allow children to move easily and safely. There is also no reason why children cannot wear warm clothes outside for PE during cold weather. Children should be encouraged to layer clothes so they can be removed as their bodies warm up.

As long hair can get caught on equipment and interfere with movement it should be tied back. Many swimming pools now insist that all people entering the water wear swimming hats. If this is the requirement, it must be complied with.

For safety reasons all jewellery should also be removed.

Teachers should also modify their dress. PE will require you to demonstrate, and be able to move quickly, so appropriate clothes are necessary. (Issues concerning changing facilities are addressed in Chapter 12.)

The work space

When inside a hall or gym, objects that children could bump into must be removed. This might include pianos, tables, doors that open inwards and stored equipment.

Fields can be more problematic. While clothes will protect children from prickles and nettles, mole holes, dog fouling, broken glass and other unsavoury items must be removed before children use the area.

The use of routines

Knowing when and how things will happen can make children feel secure, and strong routines are particularly useful for children with behaviour problems or disorders such as those on the autism spectrum or Attention Deficit Hyperactivity Disorder (ADHD). Moving from one learning environment to another can be very disruptive for some of these children, which then leads to disruption in your lesson. They need to be made familiar with the routine, and reminded first thing on the mornings when change will occur.

Parents need to be informed if you intend changing the routine for PE on the class timetable. In this way they can still provide their child with their PE kit.

Time management

Time management for active lessons can be difficult, and it must be remembered that the time children take to change is included in your PE time. To use this time more productively, this can be the time when you explain the lesson's learning objective.

If you are teaching the younger children it is often possible to organize lunch supervisors to change at the end of the lunch break, and be ready for their lesson straight after lunch.

For older children, whole-class changing targets can be set, and incentives can be used for individual children. You can also use changing time to organize groups before you start a lesson. Different ways can be used for grouping. These could include:

- the children's birthday months
- the colour of their socks
- counting along a line 1, 2, 3, 4, 1, 2, 3, 4.

Use of demonstration

In PE lessons demonstration can be an important teaching tool. If you are unable or unwilling to demonstrate, children are usually willing to oblige. All children should have opportunities to demonstrate, even if they only have part of the action correct. Comments such as: 'Well done, Jake, show us how your feet are in the right position' will hopefully encourage others to place their feet in the right position, and inspire Jake to put greater effort into the rest of the movement.

Differentiation and the use of extension work

In PE it is unusual for children to engage in different activities. Differentiation usually occurs within the activity.

In modified activities the tasks might be adapted to make them easier or more difficult.

In parallel activities children will be involved in the same activity, but would be using different equipment.

In inclusive activities the activity remains the same, but different conditions apply.

This kind of differentiation may change according to the activity or the needs of the children. For some children with special educational needs (SEN), separate activities may be presented to children dependent on their needs.

Providing feedback

Feedback, based on observation of children's participation, can be one of the most important interventions used in PE. The DFES (2004), in their document *Every Child Matters* recognizes that positive feedback rather than negative guidance is an effective way of increasing both motivation and enjoyment. This does not mean, however, that all levels of children's performance and effort are accepted as appropriate. Consider the statements/ questions below:

- I liked the first part of that movement Kalik; how are you going to finish it?
- That was a good try. What do you think might happen if you put your left foot forward a bit more?
- Sam, well done. I could see that you were watching the target really carefully as you threw the ball that time.

- That's great! That's great! Keep going … well done!

All of the feedback above was positive, yet some of it was expecting children to consider how they might improve either their skills or their effort. With a repertoire of positive feedback strategies teachers can bring about a transformation in learning.

Inclusive practices

With the increasing recognition of children's human rights and the introduction of the 'Every Child Matters' agenda (DfES, 2004), inclusive education is now expected to be implemented in all schools. Schools now have a statutory responsibility to provide equal opportunities for all of the children attending the school. This includes the recognition of gender, cultural and racial issues, and addressing the needs of children with special educational needs and disabilities.

Gender issues

While gender issues can still be prevalent in secondary schools, they are less evident in primary schools (Bedward and Williams, 2000). In recent years the negative impact of the gender-differentiated PE curriculum has been increasingly recognized. Though there are still schools that persist with children playing games along traditional lines, they are aware that this does not constitute good practice. Where it does persist it is frequently the result of teachers feeling unqualified to teach unfamiliar games, for example a male teacher teaching netball.

Children themselves may also reject the playing of games they consider 'inappropriate' and evidence indicates (Arnot *et al.*, 1998) that while views are becoming less gendered, boys' roles are still more rigidly prescribed than those of girls, and that they are less willing to play girls' games than girls are to play boys' games. If these attitudes are evident in a school, it is the responsibility of all teachers within the school to challenge such assumptions.

Cultural and religious issues

There are some cultural and religious issues that are quite specific to PE, and they cannot just be ignored as they were prior to the legislation introducing inclusive practices.

Benn (2000) argues that the root of much of the conflict between PE and Islam lies within the 'rituals' and 'traditions' of both cultures, particularly once children reach puberty. At this stage dressing modestly is required for both boys and girls. Boys should be covered from the navel to the knee, which is not usually problematic, even when boys are swimming. Girls do have dress issues as they should have their bodies, arms and legs covered. In most primary schools Muslim girls (and teachers) are able to wear tracksuits which are suitable for most activity except swimming. Swimming costumes for Muslim girls and women are now available, and increasingly being used.

In some schools with a high percentage of Islamic children, children attend the swimming pool in single-sex groups.

Teachers also need to be aware of such religious practices as fasting at Ramadan. During this time children who are fasting will neither eat nor drink between sunrise and sunset. Concessions therefore need to be made with reference to the level and amount of rigorous activity required of these children.

Children with special educational needs (SEN)

The entitlement of children with SEN or a disability to participate in the teaching of mainstream PE lessons is supported not only by the 'Every Child Matters' (2004) agenda, but also by the Special Educational Needs and Disability Act (2001), and the Disability Discrimination Act (2005). Cheminais (2006) includes a broad definition for disability: 'A child or young person is disabled if they have a physical (including sensory), intellectual or mental impairment which has a substantial and long-term adverse effect on their ability to carry out normal day-to-day activities' (p. 40).

In terms of the specific legal provision for inclusion in PE, teachers and schools have new duties:

- not to treat disabled children less favourably
- to make reasonable adjustments to ensure that disabled children are not placed at a substantial disadvantage compared to able-bodied peers
- to contribute towards improving accessibility arrangements by
  o improving access to the physical environment
  o increasing curriculum and out of hours learning
- to take action to improve educational outcomes for disabled children to address underachievement
- to promote disability equality in order to eliminate unlawful discrimination and harassment, and promote equal opportunities and positive attitudes towards disability.

For a beginning teacher this is daunting, but consider the statement in the government's SEN document *Removing Barriers to Achievement* (2004), which argues that 'we want to see all teachers having the skills and confidence – and access to specialist advice where necessary – to help children with SEN to reach their potential' (3.9). While it is expected that you will be teaching children with SEN from the start of your professional life, there should always be support for you within your school. Both the PE subject-leader and the special educational needs coordinator (SENCO) have a responsibility to provide you with support and access to in-service courses and PE advisory teachers. You should also not underestimate your own skill and knowledge.

Bailey and Robertson (2004) recognize the problems related to addressing the diversity of SEN we may confront as teachers, and suggest some basic principles that can be adopted:

- **Understanding the child's disability**: You will need a general understanding of the disability so that you have some awareness of the kind of issues you will need to address.
- **Assessing the child's specific needs**: Even children with the same disorder can have quite different physical abilities and needs. Information about these will be on the child's SEN documentation. You should also have access to parents/guardians, and members of any multiprofessional team supporting the child.
- **Support in your planning**: If you need to, seek help with your planning for inclusion. It is during the planning stage that you will need to consider any special equipment, support from other adults and teaching strategies you may need to adopt.
- **Be flexible in your teaching of the child**: Experiment with your differentiation. If you consider the tasks you have provided are inappropriate, change them.
- **Communicate with the child**: Discuss what you are going to do with the child; they may have suggestions to make.
- **Do not patronize the child**: These children are like any other children in your class; they need recognition when they perform to the best of their ability, encouragement when they make an effort and chastisement when they behave inappropriately.

Assessment

We are all aware that assessment is integral to effective learning and teaching, but it probably will not surprise you to know that assessment in PE is not always done well (Clay, 1998). Assessment is frequently found difficult by teachers because the collecting of evidence is difficult, and also because teachers are sometimes unaware of what they should be assessing. So assessment in PE can be specific to the subject.

Piotrowski (2004) argues that it is only through the assessment of PE that we are able to have evidence of children's physical development, fundamental movement abilities and motor skills, which gives relevance to the assessment process.

As in other curriculum areas the two main forms of assessment for this curriculum subject are formative assessment (assessment for learning) and summative assessment (assessment of learning).

Formative assessment (assessment for learning)

Formative assessment is the level of assessment that informs our ongoing practice. It is an integral part of the planning, teaching, assessing cycle you are already familiar with. Effective formative assessment begins with effective planning. With a specific and precise learning objective, and clear lesson outcomes, the assessment focus of the PE lesson and often the form of assessment will be evident. In PE most formative assessment is based on observations, or through children's peer- and self-assessment. Peer- and self-assessment involve both teacher and child/children in reviewing and reflecting on progress. These two forms of assessment usually work in conjunction, and should be done as an integral part of the lesson. They can also be part of the positive feedback process discussed earlier.

While all children's efforts can be monitored during the lesson, the recording of assessment evidence should be done on a limited number of children. These recordings of your evidence should be used to form a profile of each child's physical progress. For recording documents for each area of the PE curriculum refer to Hopper, Grey and Maude (2000).

Summative assessment (assessment of learning)

The compiled evidence in children's PE profiles serves effectively as summative data. Many schools are now also collecting evidence using digital cameras and video clips which are included in profiles.

You will be aware that there is a statutory requirement to report to parents annually. While a PE profile will support these discussions, it may be necessary for you to use language and terminology that parents will understand.

PE profiles can also be an integral part of target setting, especially for children with SEN. Used in conjunction with SEN documentation they will give ongoing, year-by-year evidence of a child's physical development.

Conclusion

For many children PE lessons are the highlight of their week. It is a time when they can expend their energy and even excel. Missing PE should never be used as a punishment as this degrades its place as a valuable and unique part of a child's education.

Within the PE learning and teaching context it is possible to discover skills and abilities you never realized children (or you yourself) had. Although teaching PE is a serious business, it must also be invigorating and enjoyable for you and the children in your care.

References

Armstrong, N. (1998), 'Physical education, sport and the promotion of children's health and well-being', in A. J. Sargeant and H. Siddons (eds), *From Community Health to Elite Sport.* Proceedings of the Third Annual Congress of the European College of Sport Science, 15–18 July. Liverpool: CHCD.

Arnot, M., Gray, J., James, M. and Rudduck, J. (1998), *Recent Research on Gender and Educational Performance.* London: The Stationery Office.

Bailey, R. and Robertson, C. (2004), 'Including all pupils in primary school physical education', in R. Bailey and T. Macfadyn (eds), *Teaching Physical Education 5–11.* London: Continuum.

Bedward, J. and Williams, A. (2000), 'Girls' experience of physical education', in A. Williams (ed.), *Primary School Physical Education: Research into Practice.* London: RoutledgeFalmer.

Benn, T. (2000), 'Towards inclusion in education and physical education', in A. Williams (ed.), *Primary School Physical Education: Research into Practice.* London: RoutledgeFalmer.

Cheminais, R. (2006), *Every Child Matters: A Practical Guide for Teachers.* London: David Fulton.

Clay, G. (1998), 'Physical Education: Action, play and movement'. In J. Riley and R. Prenctice (eds), *The Curriculum 7–11.* London: Paul Chapman/Sage.

Department for Education (1995), *Physical Education in the National Curriculum.* London: HMSO.

DfES (2004), *Every Child Matters: Next Steps.* London: Department for Education and Skills.

DfES (2004), *Excellence and Enjoyment: A Strategy for Primary Schools.* Department for Education and Skills.

DfES (2004), *Removing Barriers to Achievement: The Government's Strategy for SEN.* London: Department for Education and Skills.

HMSO (1953), *Planning the Programme: Physical Education in the Primary School.* London: HMSO.

Hopper, B., Grey, J. and Maude, P. (2000), *Teaching Physical Education in the Primary School.* London: RoutledgeFalmer.

National Summit on Physical Education (2005), 'A position statement in Physical Education', *British Journal of Teaching in Physical Education*, 136, (1; 2).

Piotrowski, S. (2004), 'Assessment, recording and reporting', in R. Bailey and T. Macfedyn (eds), *Teaching Physical Education 5–11.* London: Continuum.

Useful websites

www.baalpe.org
British Association of Advisers and Lecturers in PE
www.culture.gov.uk
Department for Culture, Media and Sport
www.standards.dfes.gov/schemes
DfES
www.efds.net
English Federation of Disability Sport

12

Physical Education: Beyond the Curriculum

Alison Heap

Chapter Outline

'Look at that, Sir (beaming enormously, Lily points to a quite smooth but very high cliff face). I've just come down that, Sir. I was terrified – and it was great.' A Year 6 child while on a residential visit to an outdoor education centre in Wales

Introduction

As a keen young advisory teacher I decided to run a one-day course for primary school teachers with the grand title of 'Gymnastics in the primary school'. I booked the venue and sent out pamphlets advertising the course to all of the primary schools in the county. I planned the course in great detail and ordered coffee and lunch… two teachers attended, both of whom were keen and well-informed teachers of physical education (PE), and I spent several days reflecting on my failure. Why had this happened?

Teachers' perceptions of physical education

After much thought and discussion with colleagues I realized that this embarrassing experience was a valuable lesson, and decided to have another attempt. This time the course 'PE for the petrified' was over-subscribed, and most of the participants were there because they recognized that their teaching of PE was not very effective. The title was the only thing I had changed.

So why are so many primary school teachers so reluctant to teach PE and engage in physical activities with children? It would seem that most teachers are aware of the value of PE but few had enough sustained initial teacher training in the subject and consequently do not feel secure in their practice. Many have concerns about the management of behaviour and losing control of difficult classes. In our increasingly litigious and media-driven society the risks of children being hurt are rightly perceived to be an inherent danger in this subject.

In recent years the inclusion of children with special educational needs has contributed to the diversity of the physical abilities of children in our care. The Special Educational Needs (SEN) and Disability Act (2000), the Disability Discrimination Act (2005) and government initiatives such as *Excellence and Enjoyment* (DfES, 2003) and *Every Child Matters* (DfES, 2004) have all confirmed the rights of children with SEN to participate in all activities alongside their peers. Addressing the needs of these children safely and effectively may also concern many practitioners.

Confidence in teaching PE is therefore the main issue, and confidence comes with knowledge, experience and practice.

Like any other subject in the primary curriculum, PE needs to be planned, taught resourced, and assessed (as discussed in Chapter 11). As practitioners our role in the teaching of PE is to develop children's skills, recognizing that development will be defined by the experiences and abilities of individual children, not by their chronological age; recognizing that while most children may be able to throw a ball, most children can learn to throw a ball further, straighter, harder and more accurately: as we will see below.

> ## Case study
>
> Joe and Ruby are working as partners in a PE lesson where they are developing their overarm throw. Although they are only six or seven metres apart, both children are unable to throw the ball far enough to reach their partner, and Joe tends to lose his balance after each attempt. Their teacher has noticed these problems and using guided discovery strategies (see Chapter 11) asks the children to explain what might be causing Joe to topple over. Once they have recognized that the placement of feet could be the cause of the problem, they are allowed to experiment, and find more effective ways of standing as they throw the ball. After ten minutes of trial and error these same two children are able to explain and demonstrate to their teacher which stances work best and which ones do not work so well.

The teaching strategies used in teaching PE are the same as those used in other subject areas – encouragement, questioning, evaluating, modelling, demonstrating…

Building a positive and relevant physical education environment

Just as many teachers are reluctant teaching PE, many children also view the subject with reluctance. Not being picked for a team, having their attempts at a forward roll laughed at, and hours spent cold and damp on the sports field are the negative associations many children have with PE. As with other areas of the curriculum, children need to find PE enjoyable, purposeful and relevant if they are to engage in it with enthusiasm.

Cross-curricular themes

Cross-curricular planning provides the practitioner with a context for a range of PE activities. Some of these activities will provide opportunities to teach specific aspects of the PE curriculum. Let us consider some of these.

Music

Children can devise dances that will fit their own musical compositions or the music of a famous composer.

History

Children can be taught the skills and tactics necessary to play Victorian street games. They can learn to how to use a hula-hoop, long skipping rope, stilts, two juggling balls, or any of the toys used by children in the past.

Geography

The skills needed to participate in an orienteering event can provide a very practical context for map reading and understanding of the cardinal points. This is useful knowledge even in these days of satellite navigation systems.

Mathematics

PE will provide opportunities to make explicit young children's spatial concepts and help them develop their understanding and use of the associated prepositions (between, behind, after, before). It will also support the teaching of symmetry, estimation and the use of coordinates to older children.

Science

Through PE children will be able to examine the different physical effects of running, jumping and throwing on their bodies, and find out a great deal about forces.

These are obviously only a small example of how PE activities will enhance and support other subject areas. They may be done during PE lessons, or during the lessons of other subjects, or at other times of the day when children have opportunities to engage in physical activity.

Practising through the use of games and access to equipment

An important part of enabling children to effectively develop the skills taught in PE depends on their opportunities to practise. Finding the time for this in already crowded classroom hours is almost impossible – but what about playtimes and after school? The relationship between children needing to practise and wanting to practise depends on how positively they view practising. Being able to develop their skills through involvement in enjoyable games, and having access to the necessary space and equipment, will encourage children's participation and involvement in activities that support the development of skills.

The playground equipment available should include both fixed and portable apparatus, and systems should be in place for the supervision of fixed apparatus and the distribution and return of portable items.

The time allocation for physical education

It is now recognized that the amount of time many children spend on physical activities and sport is insufficient for them to achieve or maintain an adequate level of physical fitness. In 2002 the Physical Education School Sport and Club Links Strategy (PESSCL) was launched by the Department for Education and Employment (DfEE) and the Department for Culture, Media and Sport (DCMS). The original aim of the strategy was to increase the percentage of schoolchildren in England who take part in high-quality PE and sport both within and outside the curriculum for a minimum of two hours a week. The target set now seeks to involve 85 per cent of children, all of whom should have access to at least four hours of high-quality PE and sport each week (this will include two hours of timetabled PE, and two hours beyond the school day).

Apart from schools, key providers involved in this strategy include education authorities, organizations associated with sport, Ofsted and health organizations.

This initiative is now supported by both the 'Excellence and Enjoyment' (2003) and 'Every Child Matters' (2004) agendas.

The role of physical education in social and emotional development

As in all primary subjects, PE provides opportunities for addressing children's social and emotional development. PE provides a very practical context in which children can learn to negotiate, win, lose, take turns and share equipment. The social and emotional dimension in the playing of games must always be recognized. Once games that will enhance and support skills development have been taught, children can then be encouraged to invent their own games, and negotiate their own rules for these. This, and the implementation of the games, will ensure that all children experience situations where fair play is expected and, if necessary, enforced. It is important that a consistent approach to fair play is adopted throughout the school, and that it is recognized as desirable that older children are expected to model it for younger children.

One of the greatest issues that confronts and concerns many children results from having to get changed for PE. For children from many cultures, changing in front of male and female peers, even in the infant classes, is totally inappropriate. It is also inappropriate in the junior classes as children's bodies are beginning to undergo the changes of puberty. This now increasingly occurs in girls as young as eight and must be addressed sensitively and with discretion. The issue also has implications for the role of the supervising adult – especially male adults.

As part of their PE policy schools must find ways to provide children with adequate facilities for changing; and this does not include the toilets.

Beyond the classroom

The school sports day

School sports-days, where they still occur, should be the one day of the year that **all** children are able to demonstrate and celebrate their developing skills and fitness.

In some schools, however, the model is still very traditional. In these places the competitive and athletic children revel in glory, while the less enthusiastic and less competent sit in the sun, hot and bored, greasy from sun-cream, slightly ill from too much over-diluted orange squash, and dying to go to the toilet which is inaccessible over the road. For these children school sports day often confirms the pointlessness of PE.

Field events are, by their nature, competitive, and children who enjoy these events should have the opportunity to participate in them on such occasions.

Children for whom such events are anathema are still entitled to display the progress they have made in PE. This can be done through the use of a carousel of non-competitive team events, each one of five minutes' duration. Each event will require children to use the skills they have been developing and practising. These might include:

1. Bowling a ball between two cones from behind an appropriate baseline.
2. Guiding a ball in and out of four cones using a hockey stick.
3. Completing a gymnastics routine involving forward rolls, balances on a beam and star jumps.
4. Skipping, hopping and jumping relays.
5. A throwing and catching game (leader ball).
6. Throwing a ball at a target.

Teams could be multi-age, which would also encourage older children to support the younger children, and the more competent to support their less competent team members. As well as giving evidence of their skills development, these children would also be able to exhibit their teamwork and understanding of fair play.

Using the playground effectively

Part of ensuring that children engage in games, vigorous activity and other skills development (for example hopping, skipping and throwing) will rely on the ability of **all children** to access the space in the playground. Cold or even wet and icy weather should not prevent children from having access to this space before and after school, and at recess and lunchtimes; nor is it acceptable for a few boys to dominate the space playing football, while the girls and younger children cower on the edges of the playground. As early as the 1970s this was recognized as a form of gender inequity, and in some schools the practice is still evident.

However, in many schools innovative divisions of the playground have taken place to address gender inequity and ensure that a greater diversity of physical activity can take place. Part of the playground may be used for games, and other parts are reserved for less active play. These latter spaces frequently have playground decorations such as grids, snakes and number lines that encourage skill development such as hopping and jumping. In these areas walls often have artwork that can be used as targets to encourage aiming, throwing and bowling skills. Space might also be made available for children with skipping ropes, both individual ropes and long ones for group skipping.

In those playgrounds where space is severely restricted it might be necessary for school managers to consider implementing changes to the school's timetable, so that playtimes can be staggered. If possible this solution should avoid an infant/upper school divide, and managers should attempt to ensure that mixed age groups have playtimes together.

Others who can engage children in physical activity

Teachers are understandably reluctant to relinquish responsibility for their classes, but as concern for children's physical health and fitness grows, adults other than teachers are increasingly becoming involved in this aspect of children's lives.

Lunchtime in the playground

Lunchtime should be a time for children to socialize and engage in vigorous physical activity, after the sedentary work of the morning. It is a matter of concern that some schools are restricting this time because of negative playground behaviour rather than adopting a positive, educational approach.

It can no longer be assumed that children will come to school knowing games, skipping rhymes, or the protocol of playing. Consequently, lunchtime in the playground can be a lonely and possibly frightening experience for some children. Many schools are now providing training and support for lunchtime supervisors so that they are better able to engage with children and teach them these things, and provide children with playground equipment to use during this time. While this is a positive step, it will only be successful if all practitioners are seen to support the lunchtime supervisors. This might include teachers and lunchtime supervisors working together or liaising to teach playtime games, and adopting a consistent and mutually supportive approach to the management of behaviour.

The before- and after-school facilities

With the increasing need for child care, and the implementation of the Extended Schools agenda in England (2003), many schools have before- and after-school care facilities. These are usually managed by registered providers, and part of their agenda should include the supported provision of physical activity for children.

These providers must have basic PE equipment and access to the outdoor facilities. For many children who are highly supervised and no longer allowed to play outside when they are at home, this is their main opportunity to engage in noisy, extended and vigorous outdoor physical activity. It is one of the few times children can choose what they would like to do, and have the space, apparatus and peers they need for energetic physical play.

Case study

In one large and challenging inner-city school, staff and parents were concerned with the increase in both violence and obesity in the children. The need for a concerted effort to address these issues was identified at a Parent Teacher Association (PTA) meeting. They recognized that good quality after-school physical activity was required. They also identified the three main problems they would face – the kind of activities children happily participate in, money for apparatus and equipment and people who could coach and supervise the children. The inevitable small sub-committee was set up consisting of parents, teachers, children and invited members of the local community.

The kind of activities children would participate in

As part of the PSHE programme children were consulted about the proposal. They were asked to consider what physical activity they would like to engage in, and what equipment would be needed.

These included a climbing frame, rollerblades, ping-pong equipment and even 'somewhere to make dens'.

Raising money for apparatus and equipment

As well as the usual summer fêtes, Christmas fairs and car boot sales, the committee found other sources of funding. The whole community began collecting sports equipment vouchers from their local supermarket. Local sporting clubs, businesses and councils were all asked to support the project, and several local businesses were willing to sponsor events and

> ### Case study (continued)
>
> the purchase of clothing and equipment. One parent found several organizations that could be applied to for funding, and, with several more experienced colleagues, prepared and submitted several successful proposals.
>
> **People to coach and supervise the children**
>
> As a result of the fund-raising activities, liaison between the school and its community was strengthened, and members of the community began to come forward with offers of support. Some volunteers had specific coaching skills to offer, and others were willing to give their own time to help supervise children.
>
> Committee members also became aware of older children in the local secondary school who were completing or had finished their sports-leader qualifications, and a programme for training their own Year 6 children as play-leaders was introduced.

The outcomes of this initiative were positive. Children with little experience of outdoor play were able to begin to develop the basic physical skills and levels of fitness expected in healthy children. For example, skating and riding bicycles in a safe environment were activities valued by the children, their parents and carers.

School clubs

All primary school children have an entitlement to physical education through the curriculum, although many children benefit from the opportunity to engage in a wider range of physical activities. While it is a rite of passage for trainee teachers and Newly Qualified Teachers (NQTs) to use the coaching certificates they gained during their initial teacher training and coach and manage netball or football clubs, many schools now encourage non-teachers into schools to provide coaching in a wide range of sports. These might be professional coaches and instructors, or amateur enthusiasts with basic coaching qualifications. The sports most frequently included are tennis, judo, ballet/dance, karate, swimming – but many more are possible, depending on the school's facilities.

For maximum benefit to be gained from the experience and expertise of non-practitioners, liaison with the school's teaching staff and especially the PE subject-leaders is essential. Visiting coaches and instructors will require prior knowledge of children's experiences and abilities, and need to be made aware of any children who may need particular attention or support. They will need to know where necessary facilities and apparatus are located and be familiar with school procedures such as the system used for dismissing children if the club is after school.

It is also important that risk-assessments are completed, especially if children might be working with unfamiliar apparatus. This should be completed by a member of the school staff as well as the visiting club leader.

This aspect of provision for children should not be under-rated, as many children will still be involved with these sports long after they have left school.

Quality assurance of non-practitioners

We have seen that the role of the non-practitioner involved in children's physical activity in schools is diverse. With current requirements to ensure children's safety and security it is incumbent on all schools to check carefully that all non-practitioners:

- are adequately trained, and if providing sports coaching, have the appropriate coaching qualifications
- are police checked
- have some knowledge of first aid
- have any insurance cover that might be required.

Beyond the school

Some of the most innovative opportunities for children to engage in purposeful and enjoyable physical activity take place beyond the school gate. Such activities are often reliant on the commitment and enthusiasm of teachers who are willing to give their own time to support children in these endeavours.

Competitive games and activity between schools

For many children, competing in school teams can be a source of great satisfaction and pride. Playing competitively in inter-school games requires children to develop their skills beyond those taught in general PE lessons, and to do this children must be willing to show commitment to their team by attending training sessions.

Because of the competitive nature of inter-school games it is frequently only the children perceived to have talent and ability who are selected for the most prestigious team. This does not mean that they are the only ones who participate in competitive games. Other teams should also be available to cater for the less able. In primary schools it is increasingly common for such teams to include both boys and girls. Although some teachers, coaches and parents may still disapprove of this, all children have the right to participate in all sporting events.

Residential outdoor activity centres

So why would primary schools and teachers go to the effort, expense and disruption of encouraging their older children to go on a residential outdoor activity week? Consider the case study below.

Case study

This is more about Lily, who you met in the quote at the beginning of the chapter. What you read there was a very positive outcome for that child, but a lot of people contributed to that proud finale.

Lily is a bright, intelligent child. She comes from a loving, but very protective family who have to some extent denied Lily access to taking risks either physically or socially, or developing her skills and physical potential.

During the first three days of her five-day visit to the outdoor centre, her teacher and the staff at the centre carefully observed, monitored and encouraged Lily. Her classmates saw what was happening and also began to encourage her on all the activities they undertook together. On morning four, the day of the abseiling, Lily was truly terrified.

Half of the class and her teacher went down the cliff, and then it was Lily's turn. She didn't have to go. She knew that because the abseiling leader told her. But he also told all of the children exactly what to do, and noted that she was listening. His colleague demonstrated the techniques described, and he made sure Lily knew that he thought she could do it. Lily trusted this adult. She felt valued and although she was frightened she was willing to take this risk.

As Lily went over the top of the cliff with an outdoor leader on a separate rope nearby, the sound of the children above and below Lily was deafening.

You are aware of the outcome of this event, a very significant and memorable event for Lily. However, this event did not just happen. Lily's class teacher knew her well, and the leaders at the outdoor centre were skilled at both the activities taught and working with children. Together they worked to encourage this child to challenge herself, and recognize the positive aspects of physical education and strategies involved in risk-taking.

While taking children on residential visits to outdoor activity centres can be immensely rewarding, it is also hard work, and planning needs to be done with the children and their parents before you leave.

- Parents and guardians must be fully informed of sleeping, eating and activity arrangements before they decide to give permission for their child to attend.
- The collection and checking of letters from parents or guardians giving permission for the children to participate must be done prior to the visit.
- Dietary needs and medication routines must be planned for.
- In some cases parents or guardians might also need to attend the residential visit to support their child.
- A contact list including all parents and guardians must be taken.
- Both female and male teachers must be provided for the supervision of the children.
- All children must be made aware of the safety rules, and the consequences of non-compliance.
- Safety rules must be adhered to.
- Teachers must remain professional at all times during these visits.

Taking children on such visits is an enormous responsibility, but it provides an opportunity to find out a great deal about the children we teach, and it provides a unique context for learning.

Conclusion

It has been the purpose of this chapter to explore ways of engaging children in physical activity beyond the constraints of the PE lesson. While the knowledge and understanding that you received during your ITT in PE will be valuable in your implementation of this subject, your enthusiasm and enjoyment will be just as important. You do not have to be brilliant at PE to teach it well – just willing to have a go.

References

DfEE (1990), *The National Curriculum: Handbook for Primary Teachers in England*. London: Department for Education and Employment.

DfES (2003), *Excellence and Enjoyment: A Strategy for Primary Schools*. Nottingham: Department for Education and Skills Publications.

DfES (2004), *Every Child Matters: Changes for Children*. Nottingham: Department for Education and Skills Publications.

Useful websites

www.sportscoachuk.org.uk
Sports Coach UK

www.sportengland.org.uk
Sport England

www.bst.org.uk
The British Sport Trust

www.ccpr.org.uk
The Central Council of Physical Recreation

www.ndta.org.uk
The National Dance Teachers Association

www.pea.uk.com
The Physical Education Association of the United Kingdom

www.youthsporttrust.org.uk
The Youth Sport Trust

13

Religious Education: Teaching the Curriculum

Elaine McCreery

Chapter Outline

'The essence of education is that it be religious.' Alfred North Whitehead

'We had the sky up there, and we used to lay on our backs and look up at them, and discuss whether they was made or just happened.' Mark Twain

Introduction

Religion is a universal human phenomenon. Almost every society throughout history has had a religious understanding of the world. Religion has shaped the world we live in and continues to do so today. As our awareness of ourselves as a global community develops, the more we are introduced to the vast range of religious perspectives in the world. For millions of people, religion is a fundamental part of human experience and a force which gives meaning to and guidance for the lives they live. For others, religion has ceased to feature as a dominant aspect of their lives, but these people too live in societies whose laws, calendars and culture are informed by religious tradition. There are those too who, while rejecting formal religious practices, still recognize a spiritual understanding of human experience, and the growth in 'New Age' practices demonstrates humankind's continuing search for the 'transcendent'.

Within such a context it would seem imperative that children growing up in today's world are introduced to the variety and complexity of humankind's religious quest. Many of the children we teach belong to specific religious communities, others do not. But all children will be in the process of beginning to ponder life's enduring mysteries. Where did we come from? Why are we here? What happens to us when we die? Religious education (RE), therefore, seeks to help them on their own personal journey through life. RE gives children the opportunity to reflect upon their own beliefs, values and lifestyle and at the same time begin to explore the beliefs, values and lifestyles of others.

Religious Education should not be confused with religious nurture. Within families and communities children are taught the beliefs and practices of their own tradition. They are encouraged to follow in the family's footsteps and embrace the tradition for themselves. These children will become familiar with the stories, traditions and lifestyle of the religious community to which they belong. Such nurturing is the preserve of the family and its community: it is not part of our aims for RE in school. RE does not seek to convert or sustain children within one faith tradition. Instead it offers children the opportunity to learn about and from the religions of the world in a way that may enrich their own lives.

The place of RE in the curriculum

Knowledge and understanding

One of the main aims of RE is for children to develop their knowledge and understanding of religion. They will begin to understand what 'religion' is all about and begin to explore some of the major religious traditions of the world. One of these traditions may be their own, but even children without formal attachment to a tradition will begin to develop an understanding of the world, their place within it and how they relate to others and their environment. Through RE children begin to ponder those questions that are of perennial interest to human beings and can explore the similarities and differences between the responses that different communities have made to such questions.

Skills

RE is not about transfer of blocks of knowledge. An important part of the process is the development of skills with which children can handle such knowledge. RE helps to develop skills of critical thinking and reflection. It enables children to make informed judgements about the world around them, to discuss issues of importance and to listen and respond to the opinions of others.

Concepts

Religion is essentially an adult activity and the RE we offer children must enable them to make sense of the abstract concepts within religion. To this end, through RE, children will begin to develop their 'religious literacy'. They will begin to understand the vocabulary and grammar of religion so that they are able to articulate their own thoughts and enter into dialogue with others. One of the best ways to explore religious concepts with young children is to try to make links with their previous knowledge and understanding. For example, study of 'reconciliation' within Christianity might begin with a discussion of 'being sorry' or 'forgiveness' in which children share experiences from their own lives. Another way is to use children's literature to generate discussion relating to specific religious concepts. The story of *Dogger* by Shirley Hughes contains themes which link to 'loss', 'sacrifice' and 'special objects'.

Attitudes

A further concern of RE is the development of positive attitudes towards the self, others and the world around us. RE involves examination of values, how they originate and how they impact on our daily lives. RE is a moral endeavour in which children begin to examine their relationships with others and consider their responsibilities to others. In this way, RE makes a significant contribution to children's spiritual, moral, social and cultural education (SMSC), personal, social and health education (PSHE) and to citizenship.

Planning

When planning for RE, one of the first considerations is: which religions are to be covered? Some religious schools prefer to teach only their own tradition. In England and Wales, the majority of schools are required to follow a syllabus supplied by the local authority and these are multi-faith in content. It is recognized that trying to cover too many religions at once may cause confusion for the children. An in-depth study of two or three traditions is therefore preferable to a quick tour of more. Many schools begin by looking at the religions that are represented either in school or the local community. Clearly if schools recognize themselves as part of a global community, then this extends the possibilities.

From this, many schools develop their long-term planning for RE to take into account children's ages and abilities. Some have a whole-school approach in which topics are allocated to different age groups. Schools may then choose to explore the traditions in one of three ways. They may focus on one religion at a time, studying it in some depth. Alternatively they may use a thematic approach by looking at features common to several traditions, for example worship, festivals and so on. Another approach is a cross-curricular one which extends RE into other subject areas or builds the RE into a theme such as 'Special Places'. It also makes sense if long-term planning reflects the religious calendars so that festivals can be studied at the time when communities are celebrating them. Long-term planning should demonstrate progression, that is, topics introduced in the earliest years at school need to be revisited and built upon later as can be seen in Figure 13.1.

Which aspects of religion should be covered is determined by the ages and abilities of the children. These features include the practical aspects such as sacred writings, festivals, food laws, lifestyle and so forth but should also include study of the beliefs that underpin such practices, for example, understanding of the nature of God, ethical issues and belief in life after death. A useful guide is to consider the experiences of the children for whom you are planning. If they were growing up in any religious tradition, what experiences of that tradition are they likely to have had? What stories might they be introduced to? What would they know about prayer?

Medium-term planning in RE needs to take into account the time and resources available. It is tempting to try to cover too much over, say, a six-week period and this can lead to superficial treatment of the material with not enough opportunity for children to reflect on their learning. The activities chosen should allow for a variety of approaches making use of children's senses, skills and background knowledge. Figure 14.2 in the next chapter shows how it is possible to incorporate a range of subject areas with different demands being made of the children and a variety of skills being developed.

Time Of year/ age of children	Autumn Term 1	Autumn Term 2	Spring Term 1	Spring Term 2	Summer Term 1	Summer Term 2
4–5 years	Who am I?	Caring for babies	Friends	New life In Spring	My home	No RE
5–6 years	Harvest Time	Christmas customs	No RE	New beginnings	Neighbours	A Jewish Boy called David
6–7 years	Growing up	Hanukkah customs	Who was Jesus?	Easter customs	No RE	Why do Christians go to church?
7–8 years	Belonging to a community	Growing up in Hinduism	Visiting a Hindu Temple	What is the Bible and what does it mean to Christians?	Who were Jesus' friends?	Stories that Jewish children hear
8–9 years	Special places	What does Divali mean to Hindus?	Studying Jewish artefacts	What does Easter mean for Christians?	Caring for the world	Religion in our neighbourhood
9–10 years	What do Christians Believe?	What does Christmas mean to Christians?	Visiting a Synagogue	What does Passover mean to Jewish people?	Special journeys	Art and Religion
10–11 years	What do people believe about God?	What is the Qur'an and what does it mean to Muslims?	Questions and Answers	How do Christians follow Jesus' teachings?	Living as a Muslim	Understanding the world through religion

Figure 13.1 Long-term planning for religious education

When planning a lesson in RE, it is important to address two kinds of learning objective. It should be made clear what the children will be learning *about* that particular religion and also what the children might learn *from* it in relation to their own lives. Consideration also needs to be given to children's learning needs and their previous experience of that religion (or others). This will guide the teacher as to the most useful teaching strategies and content. Note that an emphasis on reading and writing activities might not allow some children to demonstrate their religious understanding if they have difficulty with these. A variety of activities making use of a range of skills will allow the majority of children to access the material. These principles are exemplified in the example overleaf.

Example

Lesson: Introducing a Muslim Child

Age group: 6–7-year-olds

Objectives:

Learning **about** *religion:* The children will understand that being a Muslim affects your everyday life.

Learning **from** *religion*: The children will appreciate that there are similarities to their own lives.

Previous Experience: The children have made diaries in which they have recorded their activities for a week. They have discussed the similarities and differences among different children.

Resources: Video: *Water, Moon, Candle, Tree and Sword* (Channel 4)

Content:

1. Remind the children about their diaries and how similar and different they were from each other's.

2. Explain to the children that they are going to see the daily life of a boy from a Muslim family. Ask them what they already know about Muslim children. If there are Muslim children in the class, this could be quite a lot! Make a list for the children to see. Encourage them to identify ordinary things – not necessarily linked to religion, e.g. 'Muslim children go to the park'. Ask them while watching the video to check if their list needs adding to and to look for similarities between the boy's life and their own.

3. Show the video, judging how much the class can take in at a time. Stop and start if necessary.

4. After the showing, ask the children what they learned, adding or editing from the original list.

Pause to think

Evaluate this lesson outline and reflect on its content and strategies in relation to your own practice.

Teaching strategies

Since the 1960s there has been much study of how to teach RE most effectively (Grimmitt, 2000). Various approaches have been advocated over the years, ranging from a knowledge-based approach commonly called a 'phenomenological approach' to an 'experiential approach', emphasizing children's spiritual development. Although these approaches often have different starting points and priorities, the main feature is a concern that RE is not just about presenting the 'facts' of particular religions, but encouraging children to engage with the material in a meaningful way that allows them to reflect upon what they are introduced to.

What is also recognized is that RE needs to be presented in a stimulating, immediate way using, where possible, first-hand experience and a range of resources. A further feature is the emphasis on giving children opportunity to respond to the material, using discussion, or their own creative responses. Religion is a complex human phenomenon and any material needs to be presented with children's ages and abilities in mind. Rather than trying to introduce children to the whole of a religion, it is preferable to present them with a child who is growing up within that tradition. In this way links can easily be made between the child's life and their own, and they can consider what it might be like to grow up in a different family. It also helps to avoid stereotyping and vague generalizations about the religion being studied. Some religious concepts are difficult for many adults to understand and so it is important to identify which aspects of religion are most suitable for study, given the age of the child.

Below are some examples of the type of strategy commonly used in RE.

Teaching RE through story

Story is one of the most ancient ways that humankind has found to reflect on experience. Within religions, stories serve many purposes and all the major world religions have their own collections. Such stories may reveal something about the nature of God, may explain something about the world we live in or may give guidance on how one might live the good life. The aim of RE is to introduce these stories to children to help them understand a little about how others understand God and the world around them.

The challenge for teachers is to make the stories accessible and give children opportunity to interpret the stories and find meaning in them. Breuilly and Palmer (2001: 3) recommend discussing the text, 'allowing the children themselves to offer comment and raise questions' about the story. Some religious stories may not be suitable for very young children due to the abstract concepts, language or alien context. The teacher needs to make sure they understand the story themselves and can handle questions that might arise from it, before they decide to use it with children. In the case study below, the teacher ensures that her presentation of the story and the discussion that follows helps the children to understand something of how Christians believe God wants them to live.

Case study

Julie is a teacher in a state primary school and this year she is teaching 9- and 10-year-old children. In RE the class has been finding out about who Jesus was and what Christians believe about him. As part of their study the children look at the story of the Good Samaritan (Luke 10) to understand what Jesus taught about 'loving our neighbour'. Julie set the scene by explaining that Jesus told the story in response to a challenging question from a Jewish teacher. She then asked the children to close their eyes and imagine a TV screen in their minds which would show the story as she told it. Julie had prepared herself for the session by reading the original text from the Bible and reading up on how Christians understand the story. She had made a list of questions she wanted to ask, and that the children might ask. She had also considered possible answers to the questions. She told the story in her own words, allowing time for the children to imagine the scenes.

The discussion that followed developed from the children's responses to the story and focused the children's attention on how they treat other people, particularly those they don't like. By the end of the session the children reached the conclusion that for Christians, everyone is their neighbour and they should try to love all people, giving help where it is needed.

Teaching RE through artefacts

One way of bringing traditions into the classroom and thus giving children first-hand experience is by using religious artefacts. Many religious traditions use objects in worship, as reminders of God's presence and as bridges to understanding God. Allowing children time to handle and examine such objects gives them opportunity to understand the part an object plays in the tradition and can help teach them about respect for others' sacred objects.

Teaching RE through places of worship

Worship plays a central role in many religious traditions and each has places that are associated with worship. Worship may take place in the home or in a special building. However, for many, it can also take place at any time, anywhere. Many traditions also have places of pilgrimage – towns, rivers, mountains, which have special significance and which people try to visit.

Many schools will have access to the buildings associated with worship like synagogues, churches and temples. A visit to one of these offers wide opportunities for studying aspects of that tradition. The emphasis in such study should be on the significance of the building for members of that community. The building itself is not as important as what goes on there. Making use of a visit for RE will be explored further in the next chapter.

Teaching RE through images

Within many religions there is a tradition of using visual images to convey meaning. These can be valuable resources for helping children to explore religion. Children can be encouraged to examine art work, photographs and other images to identify what religious teaching the artist was trying to convey. Children might therefore consider why beautiful mosaics adorn many mosques, or why the image of Jesus varies from country to country.

The use of ICT in RE

There are many opportunities to make use of ICT in RE. The internet contains many sites useful for background information on religious traditions and also ideas for the classroom (see list at end of chapter). Many sites offer 'virtual tours' of places of worship and places of interest. The internet can also be used to link children up with children from other schools, areas and countries to discuss their religious and cultural traditions. Databases, digital cameras, as well as word-processing can all be linked to aspects of RE.

Teaching RE through discussion

An important way of teaching RE and one which follows clearly in the tradition of religious debate is through discussion. It is important that children have an opportunity to express their opinions about the content they are covering, both to clarify understanding and compare views. Given the opportunity, many children are eager to discuss serious issues and RE can offer them the space, security and vocabulary to express their thoughts and feelings. Children should understand that there are few hard and fast answers in RE, but that the process of thinking about and discussing religion is a significant feature of it. Children should be encouraged to raise their own questions and offer each other answers. They should be given time to think about their work and share their thoughts with other members of the class. In this way the children learn not only some valuable skills but recognize that they are able to reach their own conclusions about the material they have studied.

The teacher's role during these activities is very important as such discussion may generate strong feelings and views which need to be handled carefully. To this end rules need to be established which are then reinforced before any discussion. The children should know the expectations for behaviour during discussion and feel safe and confident to express their views. Equally, children should not feel pressured to contribute, particularly in relation to sensitive issues. The teacher needs to keep a focus to the discussion and manage it so that all children have the opportunity to contribute if they wish. At the same time the teacher needs to handle their own views about the topic – how far do you reveal your own views? Can you deal with children's views that oppose your own? Are there some issues about which there is no debate, for example: 'we do not permit racist language in this school'?

Assessment

Assessment in RE has been a contentious issue in recent years. While many can see the possibility of assessing children's knowledge of religions, the other aspects such as skills, values and personal development could be seen as problematic. What is clear is that there are some things we cannot assess – nor would we want to. It would be difficult to assess the impact that studying a religion has had on a child's life. Many of the activities we provide in RE offer opportunities for response – and we cannot require a child to respond, we can only invite them. Assessment in RE should be a tool with which teachers can check on the effectiveness of their teaching while monitoring its impact on the children. In the example below the learning objectives are re-written as assessment criteria to demonstrate what the teacher would be looking for by the end of the lesson.

Example

Learning Objectives

1. Children will understand why the home is a special place for Jewish people (*learning* **about** *religion*)
2. Children will be able to consider their own home as a special place (*learning* **from** *religion*)

Assessment criteria

1. Can the children explain why the home is a special place for Jewish people? (*learning* **about** *religion*)
2. Can the children reflect on the importance of their own home? (*learning* **from** *religion*)

Content of the lesson

The children will be introduced to the Mezuzah (small box containing text and pinned to doorways in the home), and the celebration of Shabbat each week.

Example (continued)

Activities will include:

- handling and discussing Jewish artefacts and what they signify
- discussion of what our homes mean to us
- designing a wall hanging for our home.

Evidence (*What am I looking for in their work/responses?*)

Written work – What have the children chosen to write on their wall hanging? Does it demonstrate that they have considered the significance of home to them?

Discussion – during the lesson – can the children articulate their thoughts about their own home?

– at the end of the lesson - can the children explain what the artefacts are, how they are used and what they signify?

Pause to think

How might you build opportunities for the children to be involved in self-assessment into the assessment practice outlined above?

Inclusive practices

Among the chief aims of RE are those that pertain to children's developing sense of identity and to relationships with other people. Of all the subjects in the curriculum, RE has possibly the most responsibility for inclusive practice; it lies at the heart of everything we are trying to do in RE. RE encourages children to be self-aware, recognize their own uniqueness and develop their sense of identity. At the same time RE celebrates diversity, encourages respect for others and an appreciation of the contribution individuals can make to society. This means that our approaches to RE recognize the value of the individual, whatever their physical capacities, gender or racial and cultural background.

To do this our approach to RE must concentrate on developing positive attitudes towards others. This means ensuring that we avoid stereotyping groups of people, and that we make use of a wide variety of resources drawn from a range of traditions. We must be conscious of the language we use, avoiding sweeping generalizations and being aware of gender-specific terms. We must demonstrate to the children that other points of view are equally valid to their own, and that difference is not something to be afraid or ashamed of.

Some parents can be nervous of a world religions approach to RE. They may not be very knowledgeable themselves and may be suspicious of religions they are unfamiliar with. Other parents may be hostile to religion or may have strong views that it should not be part of a school education. As teachers we need to be sensitive to these feelings, ensuring that where we can, we communicate to parents the purpose and value of what we are doing. In England and Wales, parents have a legal right to withdraw their children from RE lessons.

Conclusion

Religious education is an important part of children's education, helping them to understand both their own perspective on life and that of other people. It needs to be approached confidently and sensitively, recognizing that religion plays a significant role in some people's lives. At the same time, religion can be controversial and it is crucial that we teach children the skills to deal with challenging issues. Ultimately, good RE teaching and learning is not so much about what content we teach, but about the way we approach it. Our aim must always be to help children understand this aspect of the world they live in.

References

Breuilly, E. and Palmer, S. (2001), *Religious Education 5–7 and 7–11*. Leamington Spa: Scholastic.

Grimmitt, M. (ed.) (2000), *Pedagogies of Religious Education*. Essex: McCrimmon.

Hughes, S. (1977), *Dogger*. London: Bodley Head.

Resources

Ashton, E. (2000), *Religious Education in the Early Years*. London: Routledge.

Bastide, D. (2007), *Teaching R.E. 7–11*, 2nd Edn. London: Falmer.

Channel 4 Learning, *Water, Moon, Candle, Tree and Sword*, DVD.

Copley, T. (2002), *Religious Education 7–11*. London: Routledge.

Erricker, C. and Erricker, J. (2000), *Reconstructing Religious, Spiritual and Moral Education*. London: RoutledgeFalmer.

Hay, D. with Nye, R. (1998), *The Spirit of the Child*. London: Fount.

Jackson, R. (1997), *Religious Education: an Interpretive Approach*. London: Hodder and Stoughton.

Jackson, R. (2004), *Rethinking Religious Education and Plurality*. London: RoutledgeFalmer.

Nesbitt, E. (2004), *Intercultural Education: Ethnographic and Religious Approaches.* Brighton: Sussex Academic.

Watson, B. (2007), *The Effective Teaching of Religious Education,* 2nd Edn. London: Pearson Longman.

Useful websites

www.bbc.co.uk
www.qca.org.uk
re-exs.ucsm.ac.uk
www.re-net.ac.uk
www.reonline.org.uk

14 Religious Education: Beyond the Curriculum

Elaine McCreery

'There is not an animal that lives on the earth, nor a being that flies on its wings but forms part of communities like you.' Qur'an 6.38

Introduction

At the heart of RE is the spiritual in which encounter and response are experienced. This leads us to the emergence of relationships, the many connections between ourselves and the wider world. In this chapter the myriad of connections that RE generates are explored, helping us to recognize the links that bind person to person and RE to the education of the child. It explores how RE connects to wider learning, to other people and to the global society into which children are taking their first steps.

Beyond the school

There are many opportunities for out-of-school learning in RE, both for organized trips and for independent work. Organized trips can include visiting places of worship, museums and important religious sites (see the example of visiting a place of worship below). Such visits give children the opportunity to have first-hand experience of religious phenomena plus the chance to talk with people of different faiths or people with an in-depth understanding of a tradition or place. As such they can offer an authentic picture of a particular tradition, which minimizes stereotyping and brings the tradition to life. They also offer teachers the opportunity to extend their own subject knowledge, ask questions, and clarify any misunderstandings.

Children can be set independent study tasks for out-of-school work. They can be asked to gather information about a tradition, from the internet, from newspapers, from conversations with adults. They could be asked to look out for evidence of religion as they walk round their neighbourhood. They can also investigate their own religious heritage from family mementoes such as photographs.

Case study: Babies

Mrs Johnson's class of seven-year-olds was doing a project on 'When we were babies'. The RE element of the unit was to do with identity and belonging. As part of the topic, the children were set homework which required them to ask their parents if they could take into school photographs of themselves as babies and/or any of their baby artefacts, such as toys, soothers or clothes. They were also asked to bring in objects or photos of any welcoming or naming ceremonies that they had had, for example, baptism certificates, christening shawls, family photographs, parties.

Homework later in the topic asked the children to talk to their parents about their names. Did their family name come from a particular place? Did it have any meaning? How was their given name chosen – were they named after a relative, a religious person, or because the name meant something?

Back in the classroom the children shared the information they had found. During whole-class discussion they were invited to explain something about their names. The class teacher then made a display called 'My name is special because…' and the children designed a name card with an explanation of their name. Elizabeth wrote, 'My name is special because it is my gran's name. I love my gran'. Sita wrote, 'My name is special because it is the name of the goddess. She is married to Rama and was kidnapped by Ravana'. Kieran wrote, 'My second name "O'Connor" is special because it is Irish and that's where my dad is from'.

Studying the local area

One of the aims of RE is to demonstrate to children that religion is not something that happened a long time ago – back in biblical times – or something that happens in foreign lands, but is a significant part of modern-day life in their own country. An effective way to demonstrate this is to use the local area as a resource for exploring the role religion plays in the life of the community. Focus could be made on one particular tradition or on several, depending on the resources in the local area and the aims of the unit of work. A trail around the area can reveal its historical and geographical development, which may include the impact that different communities have had over the years.

Evidence of religion in a local area
A walk around the local area may reveal some of the following features:

Buildings – these most obviously include places of worship, but it may be that over the years buildings have changed in their use. Many old churches are now used as places of worship for non-Christian groups. Some communities that are newer to Britain may convert old buildings into places of worship. The location of such buildings can be revealing of their importance to the community, for example a church at the centre of a village or on a hill.

Museums – local museums will trace the history of the area, noting the arrival and impact of different groups. Some areas have specialist museums dedicated to the history of a particular group, for example Jewish museums.

Shops – Many shops cater for particular religious groups, for example Christian bookshops. Others provide for such things as food laws and requirements, such as kosher and halal, or for clothing requirements. Many large supermarkets also have special sections which offer foods for different religious groups.

Place names – Many street and place names reflect significant events or people and can reveal religious connections that can be explored, for example St John's Street.

Schools – Some areas have faith schools, usually Christian and Jewish, but increasingly from other religious groups. Their faith school status is often indicated by their name, for example St Bernard's RC Primary School.

Organizations and facilities – Some religious groups provide social support and events for their communities for different age groups, such as Brownies and Guides for children, day centres or retirement homes for the elderly.

Charitable organizations – In busy shopping areas it is common to see people fund-raising for charity and many of these are religious in origin, for example Christian Aid. Posters and billboards may also advertise the work of these groups.

Decorations – At festival times, many streets may be decorated with lights and artefacts.

Memorials – these include war memorials, but there may also be plaques commemorating important people whose religious commitments underpinned their work for the community.

> ## Case study
>
> Matthew Street School is near a large supermarket that caters for the small Jewish community who live in the area. In Mr Dodds' class the children are eight years old. As part of their RE topic, the children were looking at the different religious communities who live in the area. The children had had some lessons exploring the lifestyle of a Jewish family. They knew that many Jewish people follow certain guidelines about the food they eat. One of the children had remarked that as there were no Jewish shops in the area, how could they buy kosher food? So Mr Dodds planned a visit to the local supermarket, to see if Jewish families could buy their food there.
>
> Before the visit, the children were reminded about some of the Jewish food laws so that they had an idea of what to look out for. Mr Dodds also drew their attention to the fact that it is not only Jewish people who have to be careful about what they eat. The children made a list of other people who might have to choose their food carefully and this included vegetarians, people with food allergies and Muslim people.
>
> During the visit the children used paper on clipboards to make notes on what they found. They noticed that there was a whole section of the shelves, fridges and freezer sections that had food labelled 'Kosher'. Mr Dodds bought some samples of these to examine back at school. The children also realized that there were many other foods that Jewish families could buy such as fruit and vegetables. They noticed other sections on the shelves displaying food made especially for the other groups they had talked about.
>
> Back at school, the children examined the packaging of the samples they had collected. Using what they had learned, they designed dinner menus for a Jewish family.

Working with faith groups

Many primary school teachers feel insecure about their subject knowledge in RE. Some are afraid of misrepresenting a religious tradition, or getting things wrong. Of course, teachers will need to update their knowledge and understanding as they approach each religion, but another valuable resource is local faith groups. Many places of worship are also community centres, involved in many aspects of people's lives. Such places often have an educational mission too and many are extremely willing to help others understand their faith.

Making contact with local faith groups need not be difficult, especially in schools that have children from different faith backgrounds, and parents can often be the first point of contact with a community. Some community centres have websites, and most will be listed in local phone books. Some even have an educational coordinator who organizes visits to schools or to the place of worship.

Local community groups can be involved in a range of work with the school. Primarily they offer an authentic view of the particular tradition and can offer subject knowledge. They could be involved in the teaching of particular topics, in the long-term planning for RE, and in dealing with any misunderstandings that individuals might have.

It is important that members of the faith group who get involved are clear about the role of RE in the school. They need to understand the legal requirements of RE, the nature of the syllabus that is used in school, and have an overview of the planned curriculum. This is essential to prevent any confusion about what the children should receive in terms of their RE. Also, be aware that if the person who speaks to the children has some standing in their community, then their response to them may be different than to other adults; for example, if the local imam comes to talk to the class in which there are children who attend his mosque.

Cross-curricular themes

When it comes to RE we have to be creative in relation to the activities we plan. In Chapter 13 the importance of engaging the children was recognized, and as part of this it is important to make use of a range of curriculum areas to explore religion. Some subjects seem to have obvious links with RE, such as English and history, but there are others that can be useful vehicles for exploring religious concepts, including cross-curricular aspects such as citizenship.

In any cross-curricular work it is important to keep in mind the learning objectives that are being addressed in order to avoid links which might be tentative at least and downright ridiculous at worst (for example, involving RE in a topic on 'transport' – donkeys? Noah's Ark?).

Planning needs to begin, as always, with the learning objectives, and the question which then needs to be asked is: how might the wider curriculum help us to explore these objectives? Of course this can be a two-way arrangement. For example, many literacy objectives can be addressed using RE as the source, as would be the case if examining different genres such as creation stories and parables.

In the example given in Figure 14.1, a unit of work is described that shows the contribution that each subject might make to the achievement of RE objectives. Notice too the potential of RE to contribute to the learning objectives of the other subjects.

Aspects for study	Teaching point	Curriculum links
History of the building	To explore the history of the community	History – buildings as primary evidence
Geography of the building	To show that it needs to be accessible to the community	Geography – movement of people
Design of the building	To show both the practical and spiritual features	Design Technology – fitness for purpose
Layout inside the building	To show the nature of worship there	RE – what is worship?
Key features	To explore what these reveal about beliefs	RE – the nature of belief and how it affects people's lives
Use of Music	To explore the nature of worship	Music – religious music, music from other traditions
Decoration	To understands some of the religious teachings	English – story Art – religious artistic expression
Furniture	To consider people's role during worship	Design Technology – considering needs
Other rooms/buildings	To explore its wider use by the community	Citizenship – local responsibility
Services/worship	To understand response to God	RE – the nature of belief and how it affects people's lives English – discussion, speaking and listening
Other uses of the building	To understand its role at key points in the year and in people's lives	RE – the nature of commitment
Noticeboards	To demonstrate the wider work of the community	Citizenship/sustainability – global responsibility

Figure 14.1 Studying a place of worship

There are several cross-curricular aspects that have close links with RE and which can be usefully brought together with it for teaching. These include: citizenship and sustainability; spiritual, moral, social and cultural education (SMSC); and personal, social and health education (PSHE). All relate to the recognition that children develop in many ways and that we as teachers have responsibility for this. There are many points of overlap among the different aspects and we need not be worried about exactly which one we are addressing (i.e. is it social or moral?). The important thing is that we recognize that all the work we do has an impact on children's general development and we must be aware of the messages we are conveying. Our values and concerns will have a direct effect on the topics we choose, the resources we use and the ways in which we present them to children.

In the example in Figure 14.2, a unit of work is described that brings RE together with aspects of citizenship, moral and spiritual development and sustainability. The topic relates to work that a class of 11-year-olds might do as they explore the Jewish and Christian stories of creation, but it extends the thinking to consider the implications of the stories for humankind today.

All the major world religions have something to say about humankind's responsibility towards the natural world. The world is seen as God's creation which therefore has to be treated with respect. In some traditions, humans are seen as 'caretakers' of the natural world. Through the topic the children are encouraged to recognize their own responsibilities towards the natural world, and realize that they do have the power to change things.

A central feature of the topic is the creation of a wildlife garden in the school grounds. Research can be undertaken to find out what kind of environments are good places for plant life, insects, animals and birds. Over the weeks the children can work on the wildlife garden, which not only contributes to their own development, but also becomes a permanent feature of school life and a reminder of their responsibilities.

The key aims of the topic are:

1. To consider our responsibility for caring for the world.
2. To put responsibility into action through the creation of a wildlife area in the school grounds.
3. To consider what world religions teach about our responsibilities.

Week	Activity
1	a) Nature walk. Focus on variety of species. Discuss feelings/responses to nature. Begin to discuss the origins of the world – views and beliefs.
	b) Survey the area to be used. Measure and consider practical implications.
2	a) Discuss environmental issues – what do we know? Find out more.
	b) Design area indicating specific features. Identify animal-friendly plants.
3	a) Discuss responsibility – what does it mean? What/who are we responsible for?
	b) Dig over area and weed. Plot and mark with sand where features are to be.
4	a) Creation stories from Judaeo-Christian traditions – implications for people.
	b) Dig pond and line. Lay other non-plant features e.g. logs, stones etc.
5	a) Examination of teachings from an Eastern tradition e.g. Hinduism/Buddhism.
	b) Make paths/walkways. Begin planting.
6	a) Evaluation of work. Sharing work and garden project with the rest of the school community.
	b) Complete planting. Hang bird/insect boxes.

Figure 14.2 Week/activity table

Source material for cross-curricular work from world religions

'Our ancestors viewed the Earth as rich, bountiful and sustainable. We know that this is the case, but only if we take care of it.' Dalai Lama of Tibet, Buddhism

'The dignity of nature as creation needs to be bound up with our responsibility for the preservation of life.' World Council of Churches, Christianity

'If there is but one tree of flowers and fruit within a village, that place is worthy of respect.' Mahabharata, Hinduism

'It is our God-given responsibility as stewards and partners in the on-going work of creation, to take action to alleviate environmental degradation and the pain and suffering it causes.' Consultation on Environment and Jewish Life 1992

'The Earth is green and beautiful, and Allah has appointed you his stewards over it. The whole Earth has been created a place of worship, pure and clean. Whoever plants a tree and diligently looks after it until it matures and bears fruit is rewarded.' Hadith, Islam

'For the sake of posterity, those countless generations of unborn children to come, let us save this Earth.' Guru Nanak, Sikhism

Issues in RE

Some teachers are wary of RE. They are aware that it is a highly personal and often sensitive subject. Some may be concerned that they would not know how to deal with situations should they arise in the classroom or wider school context. Clearly, secure subject knowledge can help to alleviate such anxieties, but it is also worth taking some time to consider how you would respond to certain situations. In this way you may prepare yourself should any situation arise. In the section that follows, questions are raised about potential situations and you are encouraged to think about how you might respond. It may also be worth discussing the situations with colleagues, maybe using role-play, to explore how such situations might develop and be resolved.

Handling beliefs

Everyone who enters a classroom, whether adult or child, brings with them their own set of beliefs and values. Part of the role of RE is to help children articulate these, share them with others, and learn how to live with others' values. As children get older, they are more likely to be aware of their own beliefs and those of their parents. Sometimes these beliefs will not be shared either by other children or the teacher. So how do we respond to differences of belief?

A fundamental starting point for RE is the establishment of an atmosphere of trust and respect in which children feel safe to express their opinions and beliefs. Clear rules for discussion need to be agreed, and guidance given as to how to listen carefully to someone else and respond to their point.

Children also need to be taught to handle difference. They need to be prepared for encountering difference without being threatened by it. Activities which help with this are ones which get children talking about the differences in their own preferences, for example films, football teams, hobbies, food. Discuss how far it matters that they prefer different things and how we respond if someone disagrees with us or us with them.

An issue that some teachers worry about is what to do about their own beliefs. Some questions teachers have asked or been asked include:

1. 'What if I don't believe in the material I am teaching about?'
2. 'Mrs Jones, how could God create the world in only six days? – it's impossible!'
3. 'What do you believe, Miss?'
4. 'John says that God doesn't exist – he's wrong, isn't he?'

Many teachers are concerned that they may unduly influence children, or may challenge what they are being taught at home, particularly if they are teaching very young children.

Let us take each of these in turn:

Managing our own beliefs

Often RE will involve us in teaching material that we do not believe, but this need not be a problem. Keep in mind that this is an educational activity; you are helping children make sense of the religious experience of humankind. You do not need to believe (in the religiously committed sense) in order to teach it. A comparison might be, for example, Communism. This is a distinctive philosophy that you can know and understand about, without believing it. What matters of course is whether your unbelief emerges so that you present material sceptically. This would be an issue, as you would be undermining a key aim of RE, which is about promoting respect for people's views that are different from your own. If you feel that there is a danger that this would be the case, then it is probably better if you do not teach RE.

Responding to 'ultimate' questions

Often, children will ask religious and spiritual questions which can only be answered from a faith perspective. The key to handling any of these kinds of questions is to recognize them as an educational opportunity. Avoid dismissing the child or changing the subject – this may only suggest to the child that the question is inappropriate or unimportant. First of all, when a child asks a deep or searching question, we must praise them for raising it – it demonstrates that they are thinking! You can reassure them that they are asking a question that humans have been thinking about for thousands of years!

Secondly, it can be useful to find out what made them ask that question now, to contextualize the question. You then need to consider whether you can deal with the question there and then, or need some time to think about it. An immediate answer will involve you explaining that such questions have to be answered from a religious perspective – Muslims may believe one thing, Christians another, an atheist something else. Allowing the child to present their own view and/or that of their parents is also valuable.

If you think it is something the wider class might benefit from engaging with, set aside a time when it can be discussed as a class. Invite the child to share their question and encourage the others to share theirs. Remind all of them that all thoughtful answers are valid, and also remind them that sometimes there are just no easy answers to the biggest questions humans face.

Revealing our own beliefs

Children are often very curious about their teacher (usually beginning with a fascination about your first name). This may involve wanting to know your view on religious matters. At some point we have to make clear to children that our private lives are just that! However, if we are involved in encouraging children to express their views and reveal their thoughts, it seems only fair that we are prepared to do the same. For some teachers this is a fairly straightforward event – they may be committed to a particular tradition and respond accordingly, 'I am a practising Muslim and I believe that…' Putting beliefs within a faith context is useful because it lets the children know where it belongs. For others, it may be that there is no direct answer – 'I really don't know if there is…' Ultimately, it is your choice, but consider that there is no evidence to suggest that a primary-aged child ever changed religion to that of their class teacher.

Managing children's beliefs

The aims of RE include giving children the opportunity to develop their own beliefs and so our RE work needs to provide space for them to do this in relation to the topics we

present them with. Some children will be growing up in religiously observant families; others may know very little about religion. Some children may have already begun to ponder the 'ultimate' questions, while others may never have given them a thought. When children express their views and beliefs we must treat them with respect and encourage other children to do the same. There will be times, however, when children are challenged by each other's views and teachers need to prepare themselves for this. Work that prepares children for handling difference and developing discussion skills is key here. If, however, the child wants you to be referee, avoid it. Locate their views firmly within the faith or secular traditions from which they come, and remind the child that such things are up to each individual to decide.

Pause for thought

In all of these situations, the role and response of the teacher is crucial. When we begin to teach RE, therefore, we must ask ourselves a range of questions. Take some time to think of your own responses to these questions:

1. How do I establish an atmosphere of trust and respect in my classroom?
2. How do I ensure that all children feel safe to express their views?
3. How far am I prepared to share my own beliefs with the children?
4. Are there some aspects that I choose not to discuss?
5. Am I clear about my views on particular subjects?

Handling controversial issues

Another aspect of concern centres around the controversial nature of religion. Many people see religion solely in terms of the conflict it appears to generate, or the intolerance it seems to show towards certain people or their way of life. Some believe religion to be the 'cause' of war or genocide, or at odds with western liberal values to do with sexuality and gender. Furthermore, religion deals with all kinds of sensitive issues such as death and suffering and teachers are unsure of how to deal with these when working with young children.

Death is probably one of the last 'taboos' in western society. While the media is happy to present all aspects of human experience – the pleasant and the more challenging – death remains largely undiscussed and adults are concerned about how children encounter it. In contrast, anyone who has lived or worked closely with children knows that they have a fascination for death and are more than happy to talk about it and include it in their games. Any study of religion must include reference to death; after all, the major world religions usually have a lot to say on the subject. There are two things to consider here. One is how we deal with death as it arises in the lives of the children; and the second is how we deal with it in RE. In the former, the teacher may have no control over when issues about death might arise and so needs to be prepared for events emerging out of the blue. In the latter, the teacher is able to plan carefully how to deal with aspects of death as they arise in the children's study of world religions. Clearly there are overlaps between the two, and the suggestions that follow may be of use in either context. The resources section at the end of this chapter directs the reader to more detailed information than is possible here.

In any work related to death, the atmosphere for discussion in the classroom has to be supportive (as discussed above). Any planned work must take into account what is happening in children's lives, recognizing that many of the children in the class may already have experienced bereavement. School offers a safe context in which to discuss death, but if there are recently bereaved children in the class, parental/carer advice is recommended.

Death can be explored with very young children through the notion of 'small deaths', where they look at the life cycle of flowers and small creatures. Children's story books offer an invaluable source for discussing death with books such as *Badger's Parting Gifts* (Susan Varley), *Granpa* (John Burningham) and *Charlotte's Web* (E. B. White). There are also books written specifically for teaching purposes such as *Waterbugs and Dragonflies* by Doris Stickney. Such stories would be useful for work on the Christian festival of Easter, for example, helping children to understand the death of Jesus in Christian tradition.

For older children the study of the death and funeral rituals of world religions will give them an insight into what different people believe happens after death. Any such study must include time for discussion of the beliefs that underpin the traditions plus the opportunity for children to express their responses to such beliefs and their own.

In the current climate, many children will be aware of the wars that are being fought around the world. They may also be able to identify particular groups who are involved, many of which may well be religious in affiliation. Once again, it is important that teachers are willing to talk to children about the terrible things that may be going on in the name of religion. Being able to listen to children's thoughts and anxieties, being vigilant about racism and offering alternative views are part of the teacher's responsibilities. In terms of RE, it is important to demonstrate to children that all the major world religions place emphasis on peace and non-violence, while recognizing that all religions at one time or other have been used to justify inhuman acts. It is also useful for children to recognize that there are some issues that adults cannot find solutions to, and that seeing events from their own perspective can make them insensitive to others' points of view and experiences. See the resources list at the end of the chapter for further reading and help on dealing with war with children.

Handling the views of other adults

Children are not the only people who may present us with a variety of viewpoints or challenge our position. We must also consider how we respond to other adults, including our colleagues and the children's parents.

Dealing with colleagues

Even if you are happy about teaching RE, recognize its value for children and enjoy the prospect of developing your RE teaching skills, you may occasionally come across colleagues who may be hostile to the subject. In England and Wales, teachers have a legal right to withdraw from the teaching of RE, but there are some colleagues who may not exercise this right, preferring instead to ignore the subject or approach it with little enthusiasm. You may be fortunate enough to work in a school where RE has a strong presence and where the head teacher and subject-leader are supportive. But you could also find yourself having to defend the work you do in your classroom. Once again, taking time to think of how you might react to such a situation can be useful.

Pause for thought

What would you say to a colleague who said:

'I'm not religious so I don't teach RE.'
'There's too much else to teach, I haven't got the time.'
'Children need to understand their own religion before they can look at other people's.'
'Religion only causes conflict; I don't want to inflict that on children.'
'Religion is something that parents are responsible for – not schools.'
'As a Christian I really feel I couldn't teach something I don't believe in.'
'All the children in our school are Christian, why bother teaching them about anything else?'

Dealing with parents

Some parents can also be uncomfortable about RE and many misunderstand its purpose in school. Some may be uneasy about schools dealing with religion, some may feel it should be their role solely, and others may be concerned about their children learning about different faiths. In England and Wales, parents have a legal right to withdraw their children from RE. However, some may be reluctant to do this, feeling that it may segregate their child.

Your school should make its approach to RE clear through its prospectus and policies and parents should be encouraged to refer to these for information. It is in the school's interest to involve parents in the development of such policies so that their input can be gained and shared with other parents. Class teachers can make parents aware of the topics their children will study in RE, either through letters home or wall displays of the work for the term ahead. Parents can also be involved in RE in many ways. They can accompany children on visits to places of worship, or be invited in to listen to a speaker. They can be asked to lend religious artefacts to school or invited in to talk about their own faith, or prepare foods typical of their tradition.

However, there may be parents who approach you with concerns about RE. You need to decide primarily whether this is an issue that you can resolve or whether you need to refer the parent to the head teacher.

Pause for thought

Take some time to consider how you would respond to a parent who said:

'I don't want my child learning songs from other religions.'
'I will be keeping my child off school tomorrow – he's not taking part in that Hindu thing.'
'I only want my child to learn about Christianity.'
'My child doesn't know the Lord's prayer – why don't you teach them it?'
'I'm worried about what the vicar is going to talk about in school next week.'
'What's going to happen when they visit the synagogue next week?'
'Why should my child celebrate Eid, she's not a Muslim?'
'I think it's my job to teach my child about religion, not school's.'

Religious Education in Faith Community Schools

The term Faith Community School is a designation that reflects something of the nature of the English dual education system. English state education has been a dual system of secular state schools and state schools of a religious foundation since the beginnings of a state system. The latter were often erroneously called church schools. Jewish, as well as Christian, schools have been integral to the English state education system since its inception in the mid-nineteenth century. In this present century Muslim and Sikh schools have followed Christian and Jewish schools into the state system. It is also incorrect to use the term Faith School as a designation for these schools as they have no monopoly of faith in any sense of that term. Faith Community more accurately reflects that range of religious groups that have been responsible for the foundation of this growing number of schools.

In a similar vein, the term religious education needs elucidation. In Faith Community schools religious education has two points of reference. Firstly, it refers to the curriculum subject that is a compulsory element of the curriculum of all English state schools which, in combination with the National Curriculum, forms the Basic Curriculum entitlement for all children. Additionally, religious education refers to the whole educational experience and life of the school and is closely associated with the school's ethos.

The curriculum subject RE functions at several levels within the Faith Community school context and these functions are often in tension. The tensions lie between the foundation aspirations of the faith communities and the search for a relevant postmodern twenty-first-century RE curriculum that will meet the complex demands of a twenty-first-century global community. The founding faith community frequently aspires to nurture religious faith as a primary objective of RE and this will shape both the content and delivery of the subject. This then places the truth claims of this faith community in tension with other truth claims encountered in a study of world religions. Some resolution of this particular tension may be addressed by RE teachers and school managers in three ways. Firstly, through an explicit recognition by all involved that such a tension exists and a decision to address this within school policy and practice. Secondly, an engagement in dialogue as a methodology, in which the first-person voice of the founding faith community speaks and listens to the first-person voice of other faith communities. Thirdly, an understanding that the process of dialogue recognizes the integrity of self and 'other' while accepting that change, but not compromise, may follow.

A second area of tension in curriculum RE in the faith community school is found in the area of the personal faith development of each child. While the faith community may wish to develop a pedagogy of nurture, religious education is education and not catechesis or indoctrination. Within all three Abrahamic traditions (Judaism, Christianity and Islam), for example, faith is a gift from God and not a deposit at the behest of the teacher or any faith leader. Similarly, a respect for religious freedom and individual human rights implies an invitation to, not an imposition of, faith practice. Since 1944, RE has been a compulsory subject in all English state schools, including state faith community schools, although the trustees of these schools may select the RE curriculum. In this latter context sensitivity is needed to offer RE that for some may be received at the level of faith nourishment and for others as compulsory RE within compulsory schooling. Even the youngest members of any faith community school need to feel invited to participate in faith activities if they are to appreciate the liberating experiences of belief.

When faith communities claim religious education takes place throughout the life of the school they understand this as an explicit whole-school undertaking. In this sense, the daily life of staff and pupils is one lived within a community in which faith, belief in God and respect for religious ritual and symbol is accepted and encouraged. In a secular society where faith and religion are tolerated as a private activity which should be kept out of the public domain, the state school is secular, and religion is limited to the religious education lesson. Parents who choose a faith community school for their children, be that Muslim, Sikh, Anglican, Jewish or Catholic, do so because they wish their children to be part of a school community in which faith and religion are not just respected, but lived and encouraged beyond the RE lesson. The tension here lies in concerns around segregation and ghettoization. Mono-faith schools can divide communities on faith grounds which, some would claim, make for a divided society in which misunderstanding, suspicion and mistrust may breed unchallenged. Faith community school leaders will point out that although mono-faith, faith community schools are often communities of social, economical and cultural diversity. They will point to the English Muslim state school where there are children from 24 different cultural backgrounds sharing the one faith or to the fact that, proportionally, there are more black African children in English Catholic state schools than in English secular state schools.

When a range of religious education curricula in English state faith community schools first met a largely mandatory National Curriculum in the latter period of the twentieth century a new dynamic began which involved young people from many walks of life: the nurturing of faith development was taking place at the same time as a generic development of English citizenship. Young English Anglican citizens, English Catholic citizens, English Jewish, Muslim and Sikh citizens were grappling with the nature of religious, civic and cultural identities and religious education was making its own formative contribution.

Reflecting on practice

An essential component in any RE work is evaluation. We need to know what kind of impact our RE teaching is having on the children. Assessment tasks may indicate the academic progress each child is making, but we also need to know the wider effect that our teaching is having. We need to reflect on the RE we have taught to identify how we might improve our provision. Evaluation of any taught unit of RE might include consideration of some of the following.

Aims

Has the unit:

- developed the children's understanding of what religion is about?
- enabled children to reflect on their own beliefs and values?
- developed positive attitudes towards the group being studied?
- developed the children's appreciation of diversity?
- developed the children's respect for the world they inhabit?

Activities

Did the unit include activities which:

- drew on children's prior knowledge and experience?
- gave children a sense of security?
- allowed children to express and exchange their views?
- provided for children's different learning needs?
- reflected the different religious, cultural, linguistic and racial backgrounds of the children?
- made links between home and school?
- allowed for a variety of response and engagement?
- presented an authentic picture of the tradition, avoiding stereotyping?

Resources

Were the resources:

- of good quality?
- authentic representations?
- treated with respect?
- effective?

Did the resources:

- reflect diversity within the tradition?
- portray positive images of the tradition?
- avoid gender stereotypes?

Assessment

Did the assessment tasks:

- allow for a variety of response?
- respect the personal viewpoint of the children?
- recognize different learning needs?
- focus on RE aims and objectives rather than literacy ones?
- help to identify misunderstandings?
- help to plan future work?
- help to identify individuals' progress?

Conclusion

In this chapter we have considered the relationships and interconnections which underpin religious education. We have raised and explored some of the issues which the reflective teacher of RE will examine in order to facilitate children's learning and have celebrated the role of RE in developing citizens of a global society. The significance and complexity of the notions highlighted served to emphasize the original premise: that at the heart of religious education is the spiritual.

References

Burningham, J. (2003), *Granpa*. London: Random House.

Stickney, D. (2004), *Waterbugs and Dragonflies – Explaining Death to Young Children*. London: Continuum.

Varley, S. (1994), *Badger's Parting Gifts*. London: Collins Children's Books.

White, E. B. (2007), *Charlotte's Web*. London: Penguin Books.

Resources

Books

Burns, S. and Lamont, G. (1993), *Values and Visions. A Handbook of Spiritual Development for Global Awareness*. London: Hodder and Stoughton.

Clough, N. and Holden, C. (2002), *Education for Citizenship: Ideas into action*. London: RoutledgeFalmer.

Hoodless, P. *et al.* (2004), *Teaching Humanities in the Primary School*. Exeter: Learning Matters.

Mallon, B. (1998), *Helping Children to Manage Loss. Positive Strategies for Renewal and Growth*. London: Jessica Kingsley Publishers.

Qualifications and Curriculum Authority (QCA) (2004), *The National Framework for Religious Education*. London: QCA.

Smith, S. (1990), *The Forgotten Mourners. Guidelines for working with bereaved children*. London: Jessica Kingsley Publishers.

Journals

British Journal of Religious Education

International Journal of Children's Spirituality

Journal of Beliefs and Values

Race Equality Teaching

Useful websites

www.ces.purdue.edu/terrorism/ – Myers-Walls, J. (2003), *When War is in the News*.

www.teacherworld.org.uk – National Union of Teachers, *War in Iraq – the impact on schools*.

www.crusebereavementcare.org.uk

www.childbereavement.org.uk

www.interfaith.org.uk

www.rethinkingschools.org/war

Recommended websites

Art and Design

www.educationalwebadventures.com/pintura/
A. Pintura Art Detective
ngfl.northumberland.gov.uk/art/infosheets/default.htm
Art Information Sheets
www.digitalpalette.org.uk/flash/digipal_intro.swf
Digital Palette
www.show.me.uk/
Show Me
www.ibiblio.org/wm/paint/auth/
Web museum artist Index

Design & Technology

ngfl.northumberland.gov.uk/dt/dtclip/index.htm
D&T Clip Art Library
www.dtonline.org/
D&T Online
web.data.org.uk/data/index.php
Design and Technology Association
ngfl.northumberland.gov.uk/dt/default.htm
Design and Technology Resources
www.childrensuniversity.manchester.ac.uk/interactives/artanddesign/talkingtextiles/
Talking Textiles

History

www.nationalarchives.gov.uk/
National Archives

www.channel4learning.net/sites/essentials/history/index.shtml
History Essentials

www.bbc.co.uk/history/forkids/
History for Kids

carlos.emory.edu/ODYSSEY/MidElem_Home.html
Odyssey Online

www.pastexplorers.org.uk/
Past Explorers

MFL

www.bbc.co.uk/schools/primaryfrench/index_flash.shtml
BBC Primary French Language Lab

www.ltscotland.org.uk/mfle/c4modernlanguages/
Chez Mimi and Hennings Haus

www.studyspanish.com/travel/
Learn Spanish

www.primaryfrench.co.uk/
Fun French

www.asterix.tm.fr/
Asterix

Music

www.artsalive.ca/en/mus/index.asp
ArtsAlive Music

www.creatingmusic.com/
Creating Music

ngfl.northumberland.gov.uk/music/index2.htm
The Music House (free software)

www.bbc.co.uk/northernireland/schools/4_11/music/mm/index.shtml
Musical Mysteries

www.playmusic.org/stage.html
PlayMusic Orchestra

PE

www.primaryresources.co.uk/pe/pe.htm
PE Resources

www.teachingideas.co.uk/pe/contents.htm
PE Teaching Ideas

www.esaa.net/
English School Athletics Association

www.olympic.org/uk/index_uk.asp
International Olympic Committee

www.bam.gov/
Body and Mind

RE

http://betterre.reonline.org.uk/index.php
Better RE

http://mythicjourneys.org/bigmyth/
Big Myth (Creation Stories)

http://atschool.eduweb.co.uk/carolrb/
The Rainbow Family (World Religions)

www.bbc.co.uk/schools/religion/
Religious Festivals

www.educhurch.org.uk/index.html
Educhurch

Index

itinuum

Related Titles

ISBN	TITLE	AUTHOR
978-08264-8839-8	Primary Curriculum: Teaching the Core Subjects	Boys, Rosemary and Spink, Elaine
978-08264-9273-9	Observing Children and Young People 4th Edition	Sharman, Carole; Cross, Wendy and Vennis, Diana
978-08264-8344-7	Teaching 3-8 3rd Edition	O'Hara, Mark
978-08264-9039-1	Primary ICT and the Foundation Subjects	Williams, John and Easingwood, Nick
978-08264-8760-5	Teaching Physical Education in the Primary School	Pickup, Ian and Lawry, Price
978-08264-5110-1	Teaching Art and Design 3-11	Cox, Sue and Watts, Robert
978-08264-7706-4	Teaching Foreign Languages in the Primary School	Kirsch, Claudine

ORDER NOW!
From your preferred bookseller

Or contact us at:
Tel +44 (0)1202 665 432
Email orders@orcabookservices.co.uk

www.continuumbooks.com